Building Justice in Post-Transition Europe?

After the collapse of the Berlin Wall in 1989 and the disintegration of the Soviet Union, scholars focused on the problems of legal transitions within the newly emerging democracies. Two decades on, these states are in 'post-transition' conditions, having undergone and continuing to experience political, economic and constitutional upheavals to varying degrees. This book provides an interdisciplinary perspective on this largely unexamined topic.

Part I of the book sets the scene with a socio-historical overview and a theoretical chapter, both of which contextualise the book within current debates and provide the theoretical direction of the book as a whole. The later chapters set out contrasting perspectives and consist of themed essays on individual legal systems, investigating these through approaches ranging from socio-legal study to political economy. The book aims to refine important directions for the comparative conceptual study of criminal law policy and processes of criminalisation in emerging democratic states. The result is a significant contribution to the understanding of this subject in the fields of criminology, law, philosophy and political science.

The book will appeal to academics, policy-makers and practitioners who are attempting to grapple with the area of 'transitions' in the fields of criminology, law, philosophy and political science. As a distinctively interdisciplinary text, it brings together analysis of both the social processes of creating (and abandoning) criminal law and a philosophical reflection. The book provides a comprehensive and critical analysis that points to future directions in criminalisation in the emerging democratic states of Eastern Europe.

Kay Goodall is a Senior Lecturer in Law in the School of Law at the University of Stirling, Scotland. Her research interests lie in conceptualising racism, religion and sectarianism in domestic and transnational criminal law.

Margaret Malloch is a Senior Research Fellow in the Scottish Centre for Crime and Justice Research at the University of Stirling, Scotland. Her research interests lie in justice and diversity; and crime and social justice.

Bill Munro is a Lecturer in Criminology in the School of Applied Social Science at the University of Stirling, Scotland. His research interests lie in critical theory; deviancy, social control and risk; justice in transition and alternatives to custody.

Routledge Frontiers of Criminal Justice

1. Sex Offenders: Punish, Help, Change or Control?
Theory, policy and practice explored
Edited by Jo Brayford, Francis Cowe and John Deering

2. Building Justice in Post-Transition Europe?
Processes of criminalisation within Central and Eastern European societies
Edited by Kay Goodall, Margaret Malloch and Bill Munro

Building Justice in Post-Transition Europe?

Processes of criminalisation within Central and Eastern European societies

Edited by
Kay Goodall, Margaret Malloch and Bill Munro

Routledge
Taylor & Francis Group
LONDON AND NEW YORK

First published 2013
by Routledge
2 Park Square, Milton Park, Abingdon, Oxon, OX14 4RN

Simultaneously published in the USA and Canada
by Routledge
711 Third Avenue, New York, NY 10017

Routledge is an imprint of the Taylor & Francis Group, an informa business

First issued in paperback 2014

British Library Cataloguing in Publication Data
A catalogue record for this book is available from the British Library

Library of Congress Cataloging-in-Publication Data
Building justice in post-transition Europe : processes of criminalisation within Central and Eastern European societies / [edited by] Kay Goodall, Margaret Malloch and Bill Munro.
p. cm. -- (Routledge frontiers of criminal justice ; 2)
Includes bibliographical references.
1. Crime--Europe. 2. Criminal justice, Administration of--Europe. 3. Criminal law--Europe. 4. Law enforcement--Europe. 5. Post-communism--Europe. I. Goodall, Kay Eileen. II. Malloch, Margaret S. III. Munro, Bill (William G.)
HV6938.5.B85 2012
364.943--dc23
2012003040

ISBN: 978-0-415-69713-2 (hbk)
ISBN: 978-0-415-62240-0 (pbk)
ISBN: 978-0-203-10969-4 (ebk)

Typeset in Times New Roman
by Taylor & Francis Books

Contents

Tables

Acknowledgements

This book emerged from a symposium that was held at the University of Stirling in 2009. We would like to thank the following people for their contribution: Yulia Chistyakova who co-organised the event and Graeme Hampton who provided administrative support. Thanks to all the members of the University Crime and Justice Cluster, in particular Antony Duff, Gill McIvor and Niall Hamilton-Smith. We would like to acknowledge the input of all the symposium participants who made the event so engaging and productive. We are very grateful to the University of Stirling for funding the symposium and to Ian Simpson and Daniela Bolle in particular for their encouragement and support.

In the transition from symposium to book, we would also like to acknowledge the support of Thomas Sutton at Routledge and the three anonymous reviewers who assisted us in sharpening our focus.

This book has been the work of a team. Furthermore, it has been a process in which each of our authors has not only contributed excellent chapters, for which we are very grateful, but has also generously given their time throughout, with dedication and enthusiasm. Thank you to everyone.

The editors

Notes on contributors

Yulia Chistyakova is a Teaching Fellow in Criminology in the School of Applied Social Sciences at Durham University, England. Her research interests are crime and police reform in post-Soviet societies.

Kay Goodall is a Senior Lecturer in Law in the School of Law at the University of Stirling, Scotland. Her research interests lie in conceptualising racism, religion and sectarianism in domestic and transnational criminal law.

Arunas Juska is an Associate Professor of Sociology at East Carolina University, USA. He specialises in and writes extensively on the Baltic region, with special focus on rural development as well as policing in Lithuania.

Margaret Malloch is a Senior Research Fellow in the Scottish Centre for Crime and Justice Research at the University of Stirling, Scotland. Her research interests lie in justice and diversity; and crime and social justice.

Bill Munro is a Lecturer in Criminology in the School of Applied Social Science at the University of Stirling, Scotland. His research interests lie in critical theory; deviancy, social control and risk; justice in transition and alternatives to custody.

Ben Noble is a DPhil Candidate in Politics in the Department of Politics and International Relations, and Graeme Gates Scholar, New College, University of Oxford, England. He is also Visiting Scholar at the Institute of Law and Public Policy, Moscow, Russia, and recipient of an Alfa Fellowship and a Leverhulme Trust Study Abroad Studentship. His research interests lie in post-Soviet legislative politics, theories of institutional change and the political dynamics of criminal code reform.

Kimmo Nuotio is a Professor of Criminal Law at the University of Helsinki, Finland. He is also vice-director of the Centre of Excellence Foundations of European Law and Polity Research funded by the Finnish Academy as well as the Dean of the Faculty of Law. His research interests lie in the theoretical foundations of penal liability, modernisation of criminal law, the risk society and the welfare state and Nordic, European and international criminal law

Nina Peršak is a Professor of Criminology and Sociology of Law in the Department of Penal Law and Criminology, Faculty of Law, University of Ghent, Belgium, and a member of the IRCP Institute. Her research interests lie in the areas of criminology, criminal law, legal philosophy, victimology and social psychology.

Annette Robertson is a Senior Lecturer in Criminology in the School of Law and Social Sciences, Glasgow Caledonian University, Scotland. Her research interests lie in post-Soviet policing in Russia.

Peter H. Solomon, Jr is Professor of Political Science, Law and Criminology, and Member of the Centre for European, Russian and Eurasian Studies, at the University of Toronto, Canada. His research interests include reform of criminal law and justice in post-communist states, including Russia and Ukraine, and legal transition in comparative perspective.

Charles Woolfson is Professor of Labour Studies at Linköping University, Sweden. His research interests lie in industrial relations, the working environment and the post-communist new member states.

Preface

This book emerged from a symposium held in 2009 at the University of Stirling. The focus of that symposium was to provide a forum to take further the existing research on justice in transition and processes of criminalisation. It had several objectives. It was designed to encourage international collaboration. It sought to share ideas and experiences in a post-Soviet socio-political territory where the institutional structures of the emerging states are relatively new and where little has been written or studied around these legal transitions. It furthermore provided an opportunity to engage with international work that has been developing at the levels of theory, policy and practice. The outcome we aimed for was to make a significant contribution to knowledge across the fields of criminology, law, philosophy, political science and Eastern European and post-Soviet studies.

The book expands on the debate initiated at that event. In particular, it examines the shift to post-transitions in the former Soviet and satellite states and the consequences this has had in terms of processes of criminalisation within states generally, and criminal justice systems specifically. Some chapters here are revised papers from the symposium; others are wholly new.

Sometimes, edited collections suffer from the disparate orientations of authors who have not met and debated as a group: we have aimed in this project to overcome that. The project does not just synthesise what our authors have contributed; our aim was to effect a syncretic debate, drawing in new researchers with contrasting outlooks. It is our hope that we have provided a stronger and more comprehensive forum for examining and analysing the key issues in this area.

What emerges is that the crucial role of criminalisation is not a new feature of transition or of these post-Soviet states. It was, for instance, central in maintaining the ideological grip of communism through the regulation of dissent by the policing of 'political' crimes. Modern states, in the post-Soviet states as in the old 'West', cling to criminal law and policy as matters for domestic governance and sovereignty, only with great reluctance to be relinquished to others. Yet decriminalisation, less often considered in the post-Soviet context, was not necessarily pressed on these states from outside (as we see, for instance, in Ben Noble's chapter on legal concepts governing same-sex relationships). Emerging conceptions of criminalisation and decriminalisation are not only the results of changing concepts of justice during transition and post-transition: they change social understandings of justice itself.

Building Justice in Post-Transition Europe? examines the pursuit of democratisation, shifts towards economic change and the impact this has on criminal law, resulting in new forms of both regulation and mechanisms of decriminalisation that emerge alongside moves towards political and economic change. Changes in the law and their application are often related to the extent of real democratisation in a state (notably the shift of power from the state). However, transitional shifts to new forms of economic organisation can result in other challenges to the development and operation of the law, influenced as it is (in both form and application) by domestic and global organisations, and particularly by economic precedents.

Our work develops a multi-disciplinary, transnational contribution to the understanding of this subject, which we hope will be an original forum for international collaboration around legal transition and processes of criminalisation. The debate is much needed at a time of (often poorly understood) rapid and distinctive developments in the post-Soviet and the new European Union states. As Kimmo Nuotio's chapter on Finland demonstrates, however, not all that seems distinctive is to be found on one side of the 'old' and 'new' European divide. The book develops scholarly and academic work on legal transitions and attunes this to emphasise processes of criminalisation that are omitted from existing transitional studies, yet are of fundamental importance to the experiences of both citizens and states.

Part I

A socio-historical overview

1 Social and legal transitions and criminalisation

Kay Goodall, Margaret Malloch and Bill Munro

One of the purposes of multi-disciplinary study has been to broaden understandings of the relationships between the accepted concepts within a particular discipline by aligning them with a broader disciplinary constellation (Klein 1996). However, the works that make up any intellectual discipline exist within inherited institutional traditions and are apprehended only through the accumulated layers of previous interpretations and methodological habits developed by these traditions (Said 1995). A key problem, therefore, raised by the inevitable crossing of disciplinary boundaries is the question of disciplinary integrity; in other words, the problem of weakening the theoretical rigour of a particular discipline and its historical context by aligning it in part with different disciplinary approaches and frameworks.[1] Therefore, to map multi-disciplinary boundaries is a difficult task complicated by what Klein (1996: 4) refers to as a 'jungle of phenomena'. Multi-disciplinary activities encompass a 'complex and contradictory set of practices located along shifting coordinates' and touch on questions of epistemology, history, divisions of geographical space and cultural politics. Damaška (1986) highlights this complexity when grappling with the scale and diversity of institutions and processes through which justice is administered in modern states. It is not always possible to meet such a range of institutions and processes of administration in terms of a common vocabulary, and our initial points of reference are often inadequate to our task. If superficial similarities in the forms of justice often mask profound differences in institutional settings when comparing Western systems,[2] then matters become more complex when the administration of justice in the former Soviet Union and its East and Central European spheres of influence is considered. Whether the divisions and contradictions of history, culture and place can be made intelligible is a theoretical as well as an empirical problem, and it is doubtful whether a single framework can be developed for us to fully trace the diversity of European transitions. As Offe (1996) notes, many fundamental concepts used to interpret complex social phenomena such as political and economic transition have a dual political status, one analytic and the other normative. It is important, therefore, in a collection such as this to balance the relationship of the historical to the structural as well as attempting to resolve the antagonism between the empirical and the normative. This chapter considers just some of the theoretical and socio-historical contexts that may work towards such a framework for understanding the concepts of justice, their role in transition and criminalisation in East Central European states.[3]

An important area of transition research, which has been well theorised elsewhere and is not dealt with in this volume, other than in the discussion in Peršak's chapter, is that of *transitional justice*, which is concerned with how new regimes deal with the crimes and human rights violations of the old. How new regimes carry out this complex and conflicting process is essential for the development of legal and political cultures and for identity formation in post-communist society (Stan 2008; Skapska 2010). As Roht-Arriaza and Mariezcurrena (2006: 2) have outlined, the contemporary landscape of transitional justice is situated firmly within the legal context of human rights centred on principles of truth and justice. This work, focusing on 'prosecutions and criminal investigations, truth commissions, vetting or cleansing of security forces, and … formal reparations programs', has moved beyond Eastern Europe with a geographical range including Ireland, South Africa, Sierra Leone, Peru, Columbia, East Timor, Rwanda, Iraq and Afghanistan (McEvoy and McGregor 2008). Our focus here is on 'post-transition', explained below.

Societies in transition

Following the collapse of the Berlin Wall in 1989, transition literature focused on legal transitions in the former Soviet satellites of East Central Europe (Přibáň and Young 1999; Přibáň et al 2003).[4] The aim of such work was to examine how liberal democratic institutions and systems of justice were developing and how they were adapting to post-communist conditions. Twenty years on, the complexities of transitions have been widely reflected upon in the academic literature, and much of the focus now is on the contexts and semantics of what has been termed 'post-transition' conditions (Febbrajo and Sadurski 2010) and the constitutional developments and limitations regarding the new democratic states and European Union (EU) integration (Přibáň 2009a, 2009b, 2010). Echoing Damaška's (1986) concerns, outlined above, relating to the diversity of arrangements and institutions through which justice is administered; when examining processes of criminalisation, there exist severe limitations in adopting a strictly legal definition that ignores the contradictions between the new procedural and institutional practices, the cultural life of a country and the emergence of new property relations.[5] These contradictions not only operate at different legal levels, both supranational and intergovernmental, but also across geographical space, and in turn highlight different levels of transition: democratic, market and, on the level that criminal law is most concerned with, social integration (see Offe 1997).[6] It is to this relationship between geography, politics and social integration that we now turn.

Geography, politics and government

Damaška (1986) attempted to unify two perspectives in order to construct a framework for the comparison of legal administrations in modern states. The first focused on the legal process's relation to politics, in other words, to the structure of state authority; the second related to the role, or function, of government.[7] The understanding of transitional regimes can only be achieved when viewed in relation to both the domestic political struggles in which the actions and opinions of national states are shaped and the external political authority exerted by hegemonic states and transnational organisations. It is impossible to explain the development of criminal laws and policing practices without reference to how this double set of influences operates across territorial space (see Andreas and Nadelmann 2006).

Modern epistemology has inherited the notion of space as a passive locus of social relations. The persistence of such a notion, Lefebvre (1991) argues, is due to a double illusion: the illusion of transparency – space as intelligible; and the realistic illusion – the illusion of natural simplicity. In countering these illusions, Lefebvre (1991) argues that space has an active operational role as knowledge and action within a particular mode of production. Space is therefore a social and political product engendered by the state. It serves in the establishment of a 'system' in which political authority, governmental function and cultural identity come together. Although geographical space is often perceived as a passive locus of social relations, geo-political[8] concepts usually carry their origins with them (Anderson 2009).

Neither 'Eastern Europe' nor 'Western Europe' exists as a unified or monolithic entity. As Bideleux and Jeffries (2007) argue, many of those who occupy 'the lands between' Germany, Italy and the former Tsarist and Soviet empires object to the Western habit of referring to their region(s) as Eastern Europe. The territories represented by both terms only became formally distinct economically and politically in the Yalta and Potsdam agreements of 1945. After World War II, the system of sovereign nation-states was established formally but, from a global perspective, very few countries actually achieved real independence and autonomy. The now common upper-case 'East' and 'West' distinctions therefore do not represent the geographical halves of Europe but spheres of political influence. 'Western Europe' did not achieve institutional expression until the establishment of the Council of Europe in 1949 (Bideleux and Jeffries 2007).

Under the Comecon[9] and Warsaw Pact systems, Eastern European countries were not completely sovereign and were limited by Soviet control. During the Cold War, Western politicians often referred to this 'incomplete sovereignty' as the Brezhnev Doctrine, a term that in turn did much to hide the interdependence of the Western European allies. As Hui (2011) argues, both camps in the Cold War were systems of allied nations, and policy changes in the hegemonic countries on each side profoundly affected the other states within their sphere of influence. However, it was not only countries within the two blocs that bowed to influence from their dominant hegemons. Gowan (1990) writes that there existed an unstated premise that, with regard to East–West relations, the 'West' had very little to do with East Central Europe. In reality, the 'West' had a complex and highly structured political, historical and economic relationship with East Central Europe before 1989.[10] Before 1989, economic relations between the Comecon states and the world capitalist market were governed by political institutions in the West. Key among the governments of the Organisation for Economic Co-operation and Development (OECD) countries were the United States and West Germany. In relation to criminal law, Eastern bloc states had developed their own multilateral law enforcement agreements during the Cold War and were parties to many of the international law enforcement conventions. Although law enforcement relations between Western Europe and the Eastern bloc had been infrequent and often hostile up to the 1980s, regular relations did exist between policing agencies in Austria and their colleagues in a number of Soviet bloc states (Andreas and Nadelmann 2006).[11] By 1990, most East Central European countries had applied for membership of Interpol and were seeking closer relationships with Western law enforcement agencies. Regardless of this, little is written in the transition literature about what legal and economic structures were in place in East Central Europe before 1989 and the relationship of these structures to 'Western' influence. We will return to this later in this chapter when we discuss the social and economic nature of democratic transitions.

Geographical space as an active locus of cultural identity can be traced in the use of the term 'Central' Europe to distinguish the Visegrád[12] countries from the rest of Eastern Europe. The cultural association of *Mitteleuropa* to distinguish the Visegrád countries from the rest of Eastern Europe is tied to the tensions created by West–East spheres of influence. Kundera (1984, 2007) argues that 'Geographic Europe' (an area encompassing a geographic space from the Atlantic to the Ural Mountains) had always been divided between two separately evolving halves, the first of which was bound to ancient Rome and the Catholic Church, and the second based in Byzantium and the Orthodox Church. The border between these two Europes shifted several hundred kilometres to the west after 1945 and, consequently, several nations that had previously considered themselves to be Western were now part of the East. Kundera's argument is that, because of this historical anomaly, three cultural/geographic formations developed after the war: Western Europe, Eastern Europe and, for Kundera the most problematical, *Mitteleuropa*, a Europe situated in the centre – one that was culturally in the West but politically in the East.

> What does Europe mean to a Hungarian, a Czech, a Pole? For a thousand years their nations have belonged to the part of Europe rooted in Roman Christianity. They have participated in every period of its history. For them, the word 'Europe' does not represent a phenomenon of geography but a spiritual notion synonymous with the word 'West'. The

> moment Hungary is no longer European – that is, no longer Western – it is driven from its own destiny, beyond its own history: it loses the essence of its identity.
>
> Kundera (1984: 33)

The notion of *Mitteleuropa* therefore carries with it an ideological and political burden that is difficult to justify on geographical grounds alone. Bideleux and Jeffries (2007) argue that, in glossing over cultural, political and historical divergences between Western and Central Europe and by claiming that Central Europe has long been innately Western in spirit, authors such as Kundera encouraged their fellow citizens to underestimate the scale of the economic and social adjustments that would have to be made if they were to become part of the West.

The East–West political and economic engendering of space in relation to processes of criminalisation can be found in EU harmonisation where law enforcement funding, through such programmes as Phare (Poland and Hungary Assistance for Economic Restructuring), became an important mechanism for EU aid. The stimulus behind this was the EU desire to make East Central Europe a law enforcement buffer zone that would deter unauthorised entries and activities as well as exclude asylum seekers, migrant smugglers and other 'undesirable' entrants. For East Central European accession states, admission into the EU required three simultaneous moves: a strengthening of their own law enforcement capabilities; increased cooperation with EU law enforcement; and tightening border controls with non-EU neighbours. Thus, EU enlargement was directly linked to 'Western' definitions of the crime problem and strategies for policing (Andreas and Nadelmann 2006), definitions which in their turn reproduced the cultural assumptions that underpinned the negative tensions of East–West identities. As Anderson (2009) and Febbrajo and Sadurski (2010) have pointed out with regard to the new states, EU 'conditionality' reflected a considerable amount of double standards and hypocrisy, particularly those conditions relating to minority rights and the criteria for economic convergence (see also Grabbe 1999). As Febbrajo and Sadurski (2010: 1) note: 'CEE applicants were tested, among other things, on their knowledge of minority rights, while no authoritative instruments relating to this matter had been endorsed or implemented by the "old" member states at the time.' Anderson (2009: 44) highlights a similar lack of equity between 'new' and 'old' member states in relation to economic convergence. 'If the effort of adhering to the convergence criteria for monetary union is already straining prosperous Western societies to breaking point, can impoverished Eastern ones be expected to sustain them? No previous candidates, however initially disadvantaged, had to scale such a macro-economic cliff'. Kuus (2004) argues that the dichotomy of Western Europe versus Eastern Europe frames EU and North Atlantic Treaty Organization (NATO) enlargement and is in turn underpinned by a broadly orientalist discourse that assumes essential differences between Western and Eastern Europe in terms of an essential Europeanness – with Eastern European otherness being defined as lacking this essential feature.

The lack of equity between 'new' and 'old' member states in relation to economic convergence, minority group rights and the problematic relationship to criminalisation and the construction of an Eastern 'other' is particularly evident when a gendered analysis is applied, revealing the intersections of gender, class and ethnic group. A number of analysts (Heinen 1992; Janova and Sineau 1992; Mayhall 1993; Watson 1993; Waylen 1994) have argued that there needs to be an examination of the impact of 'democratisation' on gender relations, a situation often overlooked as a result of the limited influence of women's movements in Eastern European transitions.[13] This has significance for an examination of processes of criminalisation, particularly in view of the impact of economic liberalisation and the altered role of the state as it affects welfare arrangements, childcare provisions and employment structures (Razavi 2001). Indeed, as Waylen (1994) argues, both the increase in the sex industry and evidence of rising rates of rape and violence against women in many parts of East Central Europe and should give considerable cause for reflection on the gendered impact of change.

Increasing evidence of the forcible movement of people for the purpose of exploitation ('trafficking'), where the victims are predominantly women and young girls trafficked for sexual exploitation into and from Europe, highlights the increasing population flows facilitated by processes of globalisation, but is also indicative of the incorporation of economic and political transitions into the global capitalist system (see Segrave et al. 2009). Anderson (1992: 8) notes that social unrest may 'push' many to flee from political repression, but notes the 'pull' of the market as it affects the majority; an institution that he describes as 'the most deeply subversive institution that we know'. As Razavi (2001) notes, processes of democratisation are not automatically 'gender-equitable'; indeed, Mayhall (1993: 91) argues that 'the processes of democratization and nationalism are gendered and that the patriarchal socialist order of nation-states has merely shifted to a different type of hierarchy which is glossed over as "democratisation"' (see also Watson 1993). This also has resonance for minority ethnic groups in societies that are undergoing, or have undergone, transition (Žižek 1990; Offe 1997). Indeed, the priority given to rebuilding economic and state systems can detract attention from the transition process and to what it aspires, in relation to the rights of citizens and in terms of the regulation of, and protection of, these rights (see Woolfson 2006). Thus, not only do political and governmental priorities structure criminal law, economic conditions lie at the source of the criminal law and the construction of the legal subject.

Transitions to democracy

Shifts from authoritarianism to liberal democracies have not always been smooth and without challenge. In the context of Central and Eastern Europe, a number of issues remain key: for example, democratisation is not the same everywhere. In some countries, there is little evidence of 'electoral democracy'. In others, the opportunity for populist participation is limited, and the demise of welfare provision is juxtaposed with inadequate protections for individual rights. The changes that occur are often symbolic rather than actual, as some of these chapters testify. Similarly, the impact of change can have differential effects on social groups (as Munro's and Juska and Woolfson's chapters illustrate). The development of judicial institutions also affects the potential for 'democratic resilience and consolidation' (Magalhaes 1999; Solomon 2008b). Damaška's (1986) framework for the comparison of legal administrations in modern states focused on the legal process's relation to politics, and we saw above the role of politics in determining not only the policies relating to criminal law in the accession states, but also, more fundamentally, to the definition of crime as well. Damaška's (1986) second perspective was to look at the function and role of government. This second perspective, however, is more difficult in relation to transitional regimes. Hence, before being able to define how the role of government in the administration of justice is conceived in transitional society, we must first turn to the nature of the societies at either end of the transition process.

Arato (2000) argues that everything in politics is transitional and, in order to distinguish transition to democracy, or from authoritarian rule, from the general patterns of change in political systems, we should be clear in focusing on the transition of *regime*. Rather then than focusing only on the question 'transition to what?', Wolf (1986) suggests the question 'transition out of what?' As with the unstated premise mentioned earlier that the 'West' had very little to do with East Central Europe before 1989, so there has existed a silence in much of the transition literature as to the political and economic nature of the Soviet Union and its East and Central European sphere of influence before the collapse of communism. This is surprising given the debates on that question since the victory of the October Revolution in 1917. The initial theoretical understanding of the revolution as an incomplete revolution (see Trotsky 1969) was changed with the beginning of the New Economic Policy (NEP) and the adoption of the theory of socialism in one country. This official statement of the nature of Soviet society was challenged by three theoretical frameworks beginning with Trotsky's analysis of the Soviet bureaucracy: the 'transitional society' or 'degenerated workers' state' theory (Trotsky 1937; Mandel 1981, 1987); the theory of bureaucratic state capitalism (Cliff 1974; James 1986); and the theory of 'bureaucratic collectivism' (Burnham and Schactman, as discussed in Trotsky 1973). At the heart of these debates were the nature of the USSR and its satellites and the role of socialist planning and the law of value. Three questions that such a range of theories might raise are: what is the nature of the transition within each of the countries (i.e. communist to capitalist, planned economy to capitalist, or state capitalist to capitalist)? Second, do the transitions move towards the creation of new regimes, or are they moving towards the restoration of older regimes?

Third, does the nature of the political and economic structure of the Soviet Union and its East and Central European sphere of influence make problematic comparisons with other regimes that have undergone, or are undergoing, transition? The first two questions are outwith the scope of this introduction; they are considered in the chapters that follow. In answering the third, there are four possible interpretative lines based on historical and contemporary analogies: transitions in North Europe from liberal oligarchy to mass democracy; transitions from authoritarian rule in Southern Europe and Latin America (Portugal, Spain, Chile); the Chinese model of transition; and lastly the Arab uprisings of 2011.

Arato (2000) argues that, although political change in the context of legal continuity and negotiated settlement makes the North European transition to democracy an attractive analogy, the comparison between declining bourgeois parties and state parties facing collapse of the party-state cannot be sustained. The democratisation of inclusive hegemonies (i.e. populist dictatorships) is a different and much more difficult matter than was the introduction of mass democracy under competitive (i.e. liberal) oligarchies. Likewise, Southern European and Latin American regime change, although attractive in terms of variability of paths, did not involve a change in the fundamental economic model. The general crisis of the communist regimes that broke out in 1989 began in China and was part of the larger global collapse of the planned economy. However, although the crisis in China occurred in the context of an economic crisis, it appeared to be political in form. According to Hui (2011), when the period of reform and opening up began, China already had a self-reliant national economic system. China's reform was active and self-directed, and was different from the internal collapse that triggered the revolutions of Eastern Europe.

There are a number of similarities between the Arab uprisings of 2011 and the fall of the regimes in the Soviet bloc 1989–91 (as well as more appropriately the European revolutions of 1848–49: see Marx 1973a). First, each of the uprisings has indigenous roots in their local society; second, although each of these uprisings was historically specific in its time and place, the similarity to democratic transitions lies in the domino effect of the political upheavals, each detonating the other, across a specific geographical area. A third similarity between the two has been the longevity and intensity of the Arab tyrannies (Anderson 2011).

However, two important differences prevent comparison with the Arab uprisings. First, like the Southern European model, successful political change will not involve a fundamental change in the economic base, and second, most of these tyrannies were up to now allies of the West as well as having been aided and supported by Western governments. They are therefore part of a shift within a Western sphere of influence rather than an opening up to new markets and territorial alliances.

Throughout this chapter, we have focused on the relationship of politics and the role of government to legal administrations and the processes of criminalisation in modern states. However, what the previous discussion on comparisons between regimes points to is the limitations of these approaches when relating new procedural and institutional practices, social integration and the emergence of new property relations. Damaška (1986) explicitly rules out any attempt to relate the administration of justice to the socio-economic organisation of society. Although admitting that there are many aspects of the legal process that can profitably be studied from a socio-economic perspective, he rejects such an approach as proving too difficult when relating those processes to economic variables.

One difficulty was emphasised by Marx (1973b) when writing on the relationship of Roman private law to modern production, in which he argued that relations of production develop unevenly as legal relations. However, these difficulties in themselves should not turn us away from theoretically acknowledging the importance of socio-economic considerations to the foundation of legal systems. Within modern legal systems, there exist a number of decisive factors that legitimate obligation to the law within a particular society, but also specify who has the *power* to alter the law. These rules of *recognition* (see Hegel 1967) rely on habit, or passive acceptance, and are therefore blind to broader social and political influences on legal decision making. Such rules are accepted without argument and are internalised by those who are subject to a particular legal system.[14] Earlier, we saw the role of Western political objectives determining the very substance of transitions in relation to the criminal law. We also saw the importance of financial aid to encourage East Central European governments to cooperate in Western-defined security strategies. Emphasising the key US role in developing local capacity to meet EU requirements, a senior Macedonian law enforcement official commented 'the road to Brussels goes through Washington' (cited in Andreas and Nadelmann 2006: 185). To ignore the economic imperatives behind EU and US interests in the implementation of state agreements on criminalisation and defining what kind of activities can be criminalised would be to evade a key determinant at the heart of the problem. Not only can we not separate the political and the governmental from legal considerations, but economic considerations also lie at the core of the criminal law and the construction of the legal subject (Norrie 1998, 2011).

Criminalisation and social integration

Norrie (2011) argues that the taken-for-granted formal freedom at the core of the criminal law is the historical product of a market society based on the exchange of commodities. His argument, closely following Hegel, outlines how property constitutes legal subjectivity. The abstract, formal and legal subjectivity of Kantian right exists in contradiction to the motives or inclinations of moral actors. Each private owner exists abstractly, for themselves and outside the community (see Rose 1981). The 'formal freedom adequate to the market and instantiated in the legal subject existed in contradiction with and within a world that denied agents the context in which to translate their formal freedom into a realm of "real freedom" or "free community"' (Norrie 2011: 138–39). This notion of 'real freedom' or 'free community' was developed in Hegel's notion of *Sittlichkeit* (ethical life). The notion of *Sittlichkeit* contains the thesis that, in social reality, there already exist spheres of action in which moral norms, interest and values have been fixed in the form of institutionalised interaction (Honneth 2000). The argument, in relation to criminal law, is that historical, political and economic considerations structure the abstract nature of legal form.

> Modern law expresses a notion of human freedom that is abstract, universal, and formalistic, and in its abstraction and universality, one that is important but also importantly limited. It is important because it articulates a general sense of individual political freedom, one that is associated with a basic idea of agential freedom. It is importantly limited because it operates by way of a formalisation of ethical categories that excludes substantive moral concerns that pertain in different social contexts.
>
> Norrie (2011: 139)

Newly emerging policies on crime control influenced by the shifts in social structures brought about by legal transitions may also reconfigure the field of crime control in ways contrary to those intended and replicate the collective experience of crime and insecurity prevalent in Western jurisdictions (see Garland 2001). This has led to claims of a crisis of criminalisation in liberal democracies, or 'overcriminalisation' (Husak 2008). Newly emerging policies on crime control depend not only on the institutional settings on which forms of justice are grounded in order to succeed, but also on the existence of widespread social routines and cultural sensibilities (Garland 2001). Attention to this process is emerging, for example in Lithuania (Dobryninas and Sakalauskas 2011) and Estonia (Saar 2004). Criminalisation remains an important technique in depoliticising political processes, now being harnessed to new aims such as the individualisation of social problems in neo-liberal economies. It is also a key source of inter-state struggles for power.

Structure of the book

The key issues set out in *Building Justice in Post-Transition Europe?* constitute the development of a critical analysis that examines how states in transition have attempted to make and implement legal reforms, the motivation behind change and the extent to which 'justice' played a part. Our focus is on the 'new democracies', considered also in the contexts of the more established democracies of Finland and Slovenia. The significant changes that took place in Russia and the Ukraine and East Central Europe resulted in new economic and social systems as well as political systems. Accordingly, changes in law cannot be seen in isolation from the process of economic liberalisation.

By examining the modernisation of criminal law and regulatory strategies (of criminalisation and decriminalisation), local, national and global influences will be considered. The impact of these influences in the creation and enactment of criminal codes will be examined and the wider international context considered as it impacts on how these codes are implemented and enforced. The emergence of new forms of 'law and order' will be considered and critiqued.

Bill Munro's contribution in Part I contextualises the book within current debates and sets the theoretical direction for the book as a whole. Munro's account draws on civil society as a key arena for social integration in East Central European society. Civil society as a civil sphere can be constructed as a world of values and institutions that generate the capacity for social criticism and democratic integration. However, the governing aims of many of the leading international institutions to swiftly create a capitalist class with strong entrepreneurial instincts has in many places allowed the civil sphere to be dominated by a 'violent entrepreneurship' (see Volkov 2002; Varese 2001). This aspect of Western policy has often been overlooked in debates on criminalisation within Eastern Europe where the focus has been on a general rule-of-law discourse and on the levels of conventional criminality in the East. The chapter develops an alternative conception of civil society and argues that the civil sphere can be as repressive as it is liberating, enabling not only social integration but violent exclusion.

Part II focuses on criminalisation and (as we observed earlier), a development less often considered, decriminalisation, both in traditional arenas of criminal law and in state-level, corporate and organised criminal activity. Nina Peršak considers the political forces behind trends in criminalisation in Slovenia and reflects on the importance, role and symbolism of the criminal law, which enjoys high public trust there in comparison with the low social trust – or distrust – held in the Slovenian judiciary. Obvious sources of influence on the changing Slovenian criminal legal system are the need to instantiate a new national compact breaking with the communist past and the drive through, first, the process of accession and, then, membership of the EU to associate with the European 'Other', particularly in the process of re-engagement with the Slovene criminal code with its historical origins in Germanic law. However, other political factors were also prominent, and some more recent changes in the criminal law can be explained as a symptom of a punitive (populist, yet not always popular) turn. Considering examples of criminalisation, she argues that what is needed is a principled (normative) approach to criminalisation, a set of substantive (rather than formal) principles as legitimate grounds for criminalisation. Rejecting the over-used and weakened principle of legality, she suggests something akin to the Anglo-American 'harm principle'. She concludes, however, by emphasising the distinctive, sometimes unique, experience of Slovenia and hence its value in demonstrating the need for a situational and historical understanding of criminal transitions.

Arunas Juska and Charles Woolfson analyse a very different experience, the policing of political dissent in Lithuania. Lithuania, they fear, is becoming a state that is no longer viable. They begin by showing how, in some observers' views, emigration has become so severe as to amount to evacuation. Developing two key meta-narratives to describe what is happening, they emphasise that the travails of Lithuania are not simply a result of recession. Not only its emigrants, but a significant proportion of its population, are rejecting their own society. What analysts have seen as Lithuania's crises are in fact symptoms of deep changes in the prevailing interpretations of the social compact between the state and society, and between individuals and the wider polity. Through a socio-historical analysis, Juska and Woolfson lay out the move from a relatively optimistic ethno-national political paradigm to a new discourse of 'social disenfranchisement'. Starting from the *de facto* absence of criminalisation of entrepreneurial practices during the period of privatisation of state property in the early 1990s, through the political crisis of 2003 when President Rolandas Paksas was impeached for his ties to Russian criminal elements, to the consequences of the onset of deep economic recession in 2008, a terrible transformation has taken place. As austerity measures have grown and the increasing authoritarianism of the Lithuanian state has been expressed in the militarisation of policing and the restriction and criminalisation of political protest, a popular perception of the oppressive nature of the state has grown alongside. The ideologies can be understood as two meta-narratives of the relationship between state and society: the first, a socially optimistic ethno-nationalism coming to be replaced by the second, a disillusioned discourse of social disenfranchisement in which the state is seen as imposing a near-feudal 'social serfdom'. Juska and Woolfson conclude that, among the terrible harms caused, among other things, by a 'failed post-Soviet experiment in neo-liberal free market reconstruction … the most profound cost is levied in the regressive loss of a social dimension to human existence'.

Kimmo Nuotio's study of ideological turns in the reform of the criminal law offers a contrasting perspective to political approaches. His discussion is refracted through a socio-historical insight into criminal law reform in Finland in the period 1972–76. Much has been said about socialist conceptions of crime and how they differed significantly from the Western liberal traditions, focusing more on the individual than the state and the society. Nuotio presents an 'intermediate position': the twentieth-century history of criminalisations in the Finnish penal code. The important lesson is that, in a liberal Western state, the shifts were also sharp. A major initiative in the 1970s to develop principles of criminal law led to a dominant sociological and social policy perspective, and it coloured many issues of how to understand and conceptualise an offence in legal terms. That story and its successes and failures, as Nuotio demonstrates through an engaging metaphor of the building of a great cathedral, is part of the more general story of modernising criminal law – yet also a reform project of a magnitude not now to be found in late modern society.

Peter Solomon also considers changing criminal law in a changing state, examining the shifts that took place during the transition to the current Russian Federation. Providing a contrast and counterpart to the unique

Slovenian and Finnish stories, he draws out theoretical directions for a study of transition experiences that seeks comparative analyses, not to establish a uniform answer, but for the possibility of tendencies and commonalities. Nonetheless, the chapter emphasises the importance of looking beyond the important focus on political regime or economic system to other sources of changes in criminal law, some perennial and some new and less predictable, some fluctuating among new directions, reversals and balances. He singles out important developments in Russian criminal law and policy, including, among other things, the decline of hooliganism as a charge; uncertainty and instability around the borders of lesser criminal offences (including the fastest growing charges: theft and possession of drugs); crimes responding to new challenges (such as crimes against the administration of justice, infecting a person with AIDS and human trafficking); additions in response to global pressures (trafficking, organised crime); and the replacement of economic crimes with new offences relating to taxes and business operations. Unlike the Finnish project, there was never a grand design; rather, it came in great waves, from 'spontaneous and disorganised work'. Not all developments were punitive: an important battle continues, for instance, over decriminalisation and the downgrading of punishments for business offences. Challenging accepted wisdoms, he argues that many of these changes relate only indirectly, if at all, to changes in political regime. The resolution of conflicts between individual lawmakers, the reform proposals of experts and the counterclaims from law enforcement officials play a greater role.

Ben Noble's chapter concentrates on the undertheorised concept of decriminalisation. His arguments are illustrated by a historical study of the decriminalisation of sex between men. Between 1991 and 2003, most states of the former Soviet Union decriminalised this form of sexual congress. The process of legal reform was remarkably uncontested. This ease is most often attributed to pressure from the Council of Europe in the form of membership conditionality; indeed, he observes that Western influence is regularly invoked to explain progressive legal change in former Soviet states. His study demonstrates, however, that such an explanation is insufficient; indeed, in this case, inaccurate. Analyses of this kind must distinguish between policy convergence and policy interdependence. Through a comparative political analysis of legal change, and using methods of process-tracing techniques, he isolates other causes of decriminalisation, including domestic reform politics in four of the states and the wider international influence in some Central Asian states, itself in turn largely influenced by Russian legal reforms. Placing post-Soviet reform into a longer historical narrative, he argues persuasively, is vital. He concludes that the appealing and simple story of the Western liberalising influence denies us the opportunity to appreciate the complexities and possibilities of progressive change. No such study would be complete without insight into the social world of the law. In a striking example, he points out that, in Kyrgyzstan, many members of society – including gay men themselves – do not know that sex between men is lawful.

Part III takes us to the roles of policing and justice in transition. Yulia Chistyakova investigates police abuse of power in contemporary Ukraine. Examining studies suggesting that it is difficult to identify the changes in formal rules that lead to desirable changes in police behaviour, she asks whether the apparent answer of criminalisation is really the solution. The legal rights and duties need to be understood, she maintains, in the light of post-Soviet reforms that attempted (with little success) to prioritise human rights in police work and place constraints upon the use of power by the police. Ukraine aspired to a liberalising model of criminal law, pursued as the past abuses permitted by authoritarian policing were brought into the spotlight. Nonetheless, deepening social divisions and inequalities, and the escalation of conflict and lethal violence, encouraged democracy to be driven off political agendas, replaced by a return to repressive methods of policing and crime control. She observes how the impetus for reform also it seems faced the challenge of the lack of public trust in 'compromised' justice institutions inherited from autocratic regimes – an interesting contrast to the deep trust in criminal law (if not in the judiciary) Nina Peršak identifies in Slovenia.

Her study is set against a backdrop of empirical evidence, human rights perspectives and international legislation on ill-treatment and torture. This last has not prevented a growth in the use of torture – indeed so much so that it appears to have become systemic. Crucial here are the limitations of adopted measures and the barriers to reform rooted in existing practices and institutions of policing. The deeply corrupting influence of police performance indicators based on clearing up crime reports, which encourage brutal methods of investigation, is laid out in disturbing descriptions in this chapter. These human rights abuses are concealed by lack of transparency and state-level denial – and sometimes supported by public attitudes which regard such behaviours as the only means of combating crime. 'Violent entrepreneurship' enters the mix: police officers use torture and coercion not only in the fulfilment of their professional duties, but also as a method of extortion, encouraged by very low pay. Those who suffer most are socially disadvantaged groups subject to what amounts to 'structural violence'. She predicts that, unless effective political accountability mechanisms are in place, criminalisation of torture and abuse of power will have limited capacity to effect change. Nonetheless, she observes, the symbolic and moral significance of criminalising abuse of power needs to be taken into account. The chapter dramatically illustrates the complexity of regulating police use and misuse of power.

Annette Robertson also analyses the reform of the police (the militia), this time in the Russian Federation since it became an independent state in 1991. Ambitious reforms were envisaged for the militia, which proposed – on paper at least – the development of democratic policing structures and organisations in which the priority would be to serve the public. However, she argues, the rule-of-law project was hindered by inertia, a lack of political will and an apparent tendency to retreat to past practices and ideologies. What resulted was an inconsistent implementation of reforms – and some of the more positive developments have since been eroded by a retreat to past practices and ideologies, alongside the growth of militia abuse of power, both on and off duty. Robertson sets these problems in a study of empirical evidence and a political analysis of governance to throw light on intrinsic and extrinsic obstacles related to the militia's problematic role in building justice in Russia. Her focus is on the latest wave of reform that resulted in the coming into force of the new 'Law on the Police' in March 2011, and the key problems that still present immense obstacles. She considers, among other things, the lack of independent oversight, endemic corruption and what appears to be an increasing politicisation of the militia. In transition states such as Ukraine, the police, she argues, have a larger role to play beyond the standard functions of crime prevention and maintenance of social order: they are intrinsic to the promotion and maintenance of the new legal structures and processes. With misgivings, she looks ahead to the development of justice in Russia and suggests that, as transition continues, democratic principles risk being rolled back. Further criminalisation is not required, she concludes. What is needed is enforcement.

Our collection ends with a concluding analysis by the editors that looks forward to the next stage of research and debate. Each of the authors has opened up analyses that go beyond the domestic laws of the states they studied. This final chapter discusses the theoretical implications of these analyses. Considering where we might travel next, it suggests themes in this area that deserve further exploration.

Notes

1 For example, as Beetham (1991) argues in relation to the question of legitimacy, a central issue in this volume, philosophers and social scientists differ in their interpretations. What is legitimate for the philosopher is what is morally justifiable or rightful: the moral justifiability of power relations. Legitimacy for the social scientist is understood as *belief in legitimacy* by particular historical subjects in particular historical societies.

2 Damaška's (1986) metaphor of the two faces of justice originally referred to Western European and Anglo-American systems of justice.

3 It was Tomas Garrigue Masaryk, the founder and first president of Czechoslovakia, who coined the name 'East Central Europe' during World War I as a counter to the German use of the term *Mitteleuropa* (Bideleux and Jeffries 2007).

4 Febbrajo and Sadurski (2010: 1) argue that transitions involve both the importation of 'foreign legal models and institutions, and a re-emergence of the local legacies of the pre-communist past'.

5 See also Solomon (2008a) for an analysis of the role of Russian officials in the implementation of policies, and Ledeneva (2009) for a 're-examination of corruption in post-communist societies'.

6 Bideleux and Jeffries (2007) also offer a broader definition of transition and outline a 'triple transformation' undergone by East Central Europe and most of the Balkans in 1989: from communist dictatorship to pluralistic democracy; from centrally administered to market economies; and from Soviet hegemony to fully independent nation statehood.

7 Damaška (1986: 11) writes that 'where government is conceived as a manager, the administration of justice appears to be devoted to fulfilment of state programs and implementation of state policies. In contrast, where government merely maintains the social equilibrium, the administration of justice tends to be associated with conflict resolution'.

8 States have relied on criminal laws and law enforcement agents to control interactions between their domestic realms and foreign territories. See Kant's (1991) conceptualisation of the sphere of rightful relations among nations (*Voelkerrecht*) resulting from treaty obligations among states.

9 The *Council for Mutual Economic Assistance* was an Eastern European economic confederation led by the Soviet Union. Established in 1949, it was the mirror of the West's Council of Europe.

10 The foreign offices and finance ministries of these countries decided matters in a number of multilateral institutions with an apparently non-political role. The illusion was sustained by the fact that the intergovernmental negotiations within these institutions remained for the most part shrouded in secrecy while the public spokespersons for these bodies were not leaders of states, but international civil servants (Gowan 1990).

11 Romania and Hungary were admitted to Interpol in 1973 and 1981 respectively (Andreas and Nadelmann 2006).

12 The Visegrád countries are the Czech Republic, Hungary, Poland and Slovakia. Representatives of the four countries met originally in the Hungarian town of Visegrád in 1991 to further their interests in relationship to European integration. All four Visegrád countries became part of the European Union in 2004 (see Anderson 2009).

13 Women were active participants in dissident and opposition groups before and during transitions but, in general, they did not highlight gender-specific issues, according to Waylen (1994) and Razavi (2001: 221), who also notes that feminist activists often lacked 'class-based access to party forums'. However, Heinen (1992) provides an account of women's activism against challenges to abortion rights by the Catholic Church in Poland.

14 See also Hart (1997) on rules of recognition. Hart's position is very different from Hegel's argument on legal recognition, although they are similar on the point of their unconscious internalisation. Hart (1997) argues that rules of recognition are capable of being looked at from two points of view – from an *internal* and from an *external* point of view. Those *internal* to the system accept rules of recognition without reflection, i.e. such rules are therefore valid *unconsciously* (although this does not mean that subjects are unaware of them). Those who are *external* to the system will understand the rules as valid with reference to a particular system of meaning, i.e. they are consciously aware that the rules of recognition refer to a particular system.

Bibliography

Anderson, B. (1992) 'The New World Disorder', *New Left Review*, I/193: 3–13.

Anderson, P. (2009) *The New Old World*, London: Verso.

——(2011) 'On the Concatenation in the Arab World', *New Left Review*, 68: 5–15.

Andreas, P. and Nadelmann, E. (2006) *Policing the Globe: Criminalization and Crime Control in International Relations*, Oxford: Oxford University Press.

Arato, A. (2000) *Civil Society, Constitution and Legitimacy*, Oxford: Rowman & Littlefield.

Beetham, D. (1991) *The Legitimation of Power*, Hampshire: Palgrave MacMillan.

Bideleux, R. and Jeffries, I. (2007) *A History of Eastern Europe: Crisis and Change*, Abingdon: Routledge.

Cliff, T. (1974) *State Capitalism in Russia*, London: Pluto.
Damaška, M. (1986) *The Faces of Justice and State Authority*, New Haven, CT: Yale University Press.
Dobryninas, A. and Sakalauskas, G. (2011) 'Country Survey: Criminology, Crime and Criminal Justice in Lithuania', *European Journal of Criminology*, 8(5): 421–34.
Febbrajo, A and Sadurski, W. (2010) *Central and Eastern Europe after Transition*, Aldershot: Ashgate.
Garland, D. (2001) *The Culture of Control: Crime and Social Order in Contemporary Society*, Oxford: Oxford University Press.
Gowan, P. (1990) 'Western Economic Diplomacy and the New Eastern Europe', *New Left Review*, I/182: 63–82.
Grabbe (1999) 'A Partnership for Accession? The Implication of EU Conditionality for the Central and East European Applicants', Robert Schuman Centre Working Paper 12/99, San Domenico di Fiesole (FI): European University Institute.
Hart, H.L.A. (1997) *The Concept of Law* (2nd edn), Oxford: Oxford University Press.
Hegel, G.W.F. (1967) *The Philosophy of Right*, Oxford: Oxford University Press.
Heinen, J. (1992) 'Polish Democracy is a Masculine Democracy', *Women's Studies International Forum*, 15(1): 129–38.
Honneth, A. (2000) *Suffering from Indeterminacy: An Attempt at a Reactualisation of Hegel's Philosophy of Right*, Amsterdam: Van Gorcum.
Hui, W. (2011) *The End of the Revolution: China and the Limits of Modernity*, London: Verso.
Husak, D. (2008) *Overcriminalization: The Limits of the Criminal Law*, Oxford: Oxford University Press.
James, C.L.R (1986) *State Capitalism and World Revolution*, New York: Charles Kerr Publishers.
Janova, M. and Sineau, M. (1992) 'Women's Participation in Political Power in Europe', *Women's Studies International Forum*, 15(1): 115–28.
Kant, I. (1991) *Political Writings*, Cambridge: Cambridge University Press.
Klein, J. (1996) *Crossing Boundaries: Knowledge, Disciplinarities and Inter-disciplinarities*, Charlottesville, VA: University of Virginia Press.
Kundera, M. (1984) 'The Tragedy of Central Europe', *New York Review of Books*, April: 33–38.
——(2007) *The Curtain: Essays*, London: Faber.
Kuus, M. (2004) 'Europe's Eastern Expansion and the Reinscription of Otherness in East–Central Europe', *Progress in Human Geography*, 28(4): 472–89.
Ledeneva, A. (2009) 'Corruption in Postcommunist Societies', *Perspectives on European Politics and Society*, 10(1): 69–86.
Lee, M. (ed.) (2007) *Human Trafficking*, Cullompton: Willan Publishing.
Lefebvre, H. (1991) *The Production of Space*, Oxford: Blackwell.
Magalhaes, P. (1999) 'The Politics of Judicial Reform in Eastern Europe', *Comparative Politics*, 32(1): 43–62.
Mandel, E. (1981) 'The Laws of Motion of the Soviet Economy', *The Review of Radical Political Economics*, 13(1), Spring: 35–39.
——(1987) 'Bureaucracy and Commodity Production: The Theoretical Basis of a Marxist Interpretation of the USSR', *Quatrième Internationale*, April. Online. Available www.ernestmandel.org/en/works/txt/1987/bureaucracy_and_commodity_production.htm (accessed 20 December 2011).
Marx, K. (1973a) *Political Writings: The Revolutions of 1848*, London: Penguin.

——(1973b) *Grundrisse: Foundations of the Critique of Political Economy*, London: Penguin.
Mayhall, S. (1993) 'Gendered Nationalism and "New" Nation-States', *Fletcher Forum of World Affairs*, 91: 91–100.
McEvoy, K. and McGregor, L. (eds) (2008) *Transitional Justice from Below*, Oxford: Hart.
Mitsilegas, V. (2009) *EU Criminal Law*, Oxford: Hart.
Norrie, A. (1998) 'Simulacra of Morality'? Beyond the Ideal/Actual Antinomies of Criminal Justice', in A. Duff (ed.) *Philosophy and the Criminal Law: Principle and Critique*, Cambridge: Cambridge University Press.
——(2011) 'Legal Form and Moral Judgement: Euthanasia and Assisted Suicide', in R.A. Duff, L. Farmer, S.E. Marshall, M. Renzo and V. Tadros (eds) *The Structures of Criminal Law*, Oxford: Oxford University Press.
Offe, C. (1996) *Modernity and the State: East, West*, Cambridge, MA: MIT Press.
——(1997) *Varieties of Transition: The East European and East German Experience*, Cambridge, MA: MIT Press.
Přibáň, J. (2009a) 'The Juridification of European Identity, its Limitations and the Search of EU Democratic Politics', *Constellations*, 16(1): 44–58.
——(2009b) 'From "Which Rule of Law?" to "The Rule of Which Law?"', *Hague Journal on the Rule of Law*, 1: 337–58.
——(2010) 'Constituting the Heterarchy of European Constitutionalism in the EU's New Member States', in A. Febbrajo, and W. Sadurski (eds) *Central and Eastern Europe after Transition*, Aldershot: Ashgate.
Přibáň, J. and Young, J. (1999) *The Rule of Law in Central Europe: The Reconstruction of Legality, Constitutionalism and Civil Society in the Post-Communist Countries*, Aldershot: Ashgate.
Přibáň et al. (2003) *Systems of Justice in Transition: Central European Experiences since 1989*, Aldershot: Ashgate.
Razavi, S. (2001) 'Women in Contemporary Democratization', *International Journal of Politics, Culture and Society*, 15(1): 201–24.
Roht-Arriaza, N. and Mariezcurrena, J. (2006) *Transitional Justice in the Twenty-First Century: Beyond Truth versus Justice*, Cambridge: Cambridge University Press.
Rose, G. (1981) *Hegel Contra Sociology*, London: Athlone.
Saar, J. (2004) 'Crime, Control and Criminology in Post-Communist Estonia', *European Journal of Criminology*, 1(4): 505–31.
Said, E.W. (1995) *Beginnings: Intention and Method*, London: Granta Publications.
Segrave, M., Milivojevic, S. and Pickering, S. (2009) *Sex Trafficking: International Context and Response*, Cullompton: Willan Publishing.
Simpson, G. (2004) *Great Powers and Outlaw States: Unequal Sovereigns in the International Legal Order*, Cambridge: Cambridge University Press.
Skapska, G. (2010) 'Settling Accounts with the Past, the Conceptualization of Difference and the Dilemmas of the Law-Governed State', in A. Febbrajo, and W. Sadurski (eds) *Central and Eastern Europe after Transition*, Aldershot: Ashgate.
Solomon, P. (2008a) 'Law in Public Administration: How Russia Differs', *Journal of Communist Studies and Transition Politics*, 24(1): 115–35.
——(2008b) 'Realizing Judicial Independence and Accountability under the Russian Constitution of 1993', Paper prepared for *The Russian Constitution at 15, Comparative Assessments of Constitutional Implementation Project*.
Stan, L. (ed.) (2008) *Transitional Justice in Eastern Europe and the Former Soviet Union: Reckoning with the Communist Past*, London: Taylor and Francis.

Trotsky, L. (1937) *The Revolution Betrayed*, London: Faber and Faber.
——(1969) *In Defence of Marxism*, New York: Pathfinder.
——(1973) *Permanent Revolution*, New York: Pathfinder.
Varese, F. (2001) *The Russian Mafia: Private Protection in a New Market Economy*, Oxford: Oxford University Press.
Volkov, V. (2002) *Violent Entrepreneurs: The Use of Force in the Making of Russian Capitalism*, London: Cornell University Press.
Watson, P. (1993) 'The Rise of Masculinism in Eastern Europe', *New Left Review*, I/198: 71–82.
Waylen, G. (1994) 'Women and Democratization: Conceptualising Gender Relations in Transition Politics', *World Politics*, 46(3): 327–54.
Wolf, F.O. (1986) 'Eco-Socialist Transition on the Threshold of the 21st Century', *New Left Review*, I/158: 32–42.
Woolfson, C. (2006) 'The "Conventionalization" of Safety Crimes in the Post-Communist New Member States of the European Union', *Critical Criminology*, 14(4): 339–64.
Žižek, S. (1990) 'Eastern Europe's Republics of Gilead', *New Left Review*, I/183: 50–62.

2 *Antisittlichkeit*

Organised crime and the antinomies of civil society

Bill Munro

> All strands of the history of the conception of civil society … meet in Hegel's *Rechtsphilosophie*. He is the representative theorist of civil society because of the synthetic character of his work and … because he was the first and most successful in unfolding the concept as a theory of a highly differentiated and complex social order.
>
> Cohen and Arato (1992: 91)

Introduction

'Civil society' has been used as a transitional concept, a means of crossing the bridge from the Cold War era of 1950 to 1989 to the present (Nairn 1997). It is traditionally viewed as a key arena for social integration. Many theorists, such as Cohen and Arato (1992) and Alexander (2006), present civil society as a civil sphere, a world of values and institutions that generate the capacity for social criticism and democratic integration at the same time. However, the governing considerations of many of the leading international institutions to swiftly create a capitalist class with strong entrepreneurial instincts in post-communist societies had in many places allowed the civil sphere, such as it existed, to become dominated by interests counter to those traditionally associated with liberal theories of civil society. In many cases, entrepreneurial instincts were generated with considerable levels of accompanying violence (Varese 2001; Volkov 2002). This aspect of one of the consequences of Western policy has often been overlooked in debates on criminalisation within Eastern Europe where the focus has been on a general rule-of-law discourse and on the levels of conventional criminality.[1]

This chapter will examine the discrepancy between the formal aims of democratic and economic processes in transition and the social actuality in which they take place. The chapter focuses on Eastern European social transitions in order to contextualise this relationship between transitions to democracy and what Volkov (2002) terms 'violent entrepreneurialism'. It will present an historical account of civil society which shows the civil sphere to be as repressive as it is liberating (see Alexander 2006), and enabling not only social integration but violent exclusion. In this account, civil society is presented as exhibiting a darker dialectic that can undermine the public sphere by exposing it to deep-seated structural conflict. This conflict of interest, in turn, raises doubts about whether civil society is capable of generating institutions that can lay the foundations for social interaction and self-determination (see Hegel 1967; Avineri 1974; Harvey 1981; Honneth 2000; Arrighi 2007).

Modernisation theory: moving backwards into the future

Jameson (1972: v) writes that the 'history of thought is the history of its models'. These models tend to follow a predictable trajectory of crisis: where the new models emerge, a period of stability occurs followed by a return to crisis when the models are no longer able to provide answers to the questions of their time. As a new model becomes established, it serves as a medium through which a new view of the social world initially becomes accepted. It then becomes a standard explanation within its relevant discipline. Crisis comes when the model itself becomes inadequate in dealing with the problems it may itself have produced, thus calling into question the premises on which the model was originally constructed. Hui (2011) argues that we are living in an era in which the model of political change based on the classical nineteenth-century conception of revolution has come to an end. In its place entered a post-revolutionary conception of social change that relocated the culmination of the historical process from communism to liberal capitalism (Fukuyama 1993).

In 1989, the breakup of the Soviet Union and Eastern Europe was analysed through ubiquitously deployed tropes such as 'transition', 'modernisation' and 'development'; terms that dominated political and media discourse, yet at the same time concealed their contradictions (see Hui 2011). Such concepts, under the guise of universality, hid partial value judgements as well as an *inverted* teleology. Concepts used to interpret transition – 'democratisation', 'marketisation', 'civil society' – took on a dual political status, one analytic and the other normative (see Offe 1996). Analytic research on transitions concerned itself with general, descriptive and explanatory statements about the conditions and motive forces of transition (see Alexander 1995); normative thinking on transition was characterised by a number of ideal traits. Here, concepts established dimensions of evaluation in which ideas or social relations that were being replaced could be criticised as regressive, archaic or deficient, whereas those that underlined the changes towards which a society was moving were represented in turn as progressive, modern and necessary. 'Modern' therefore becomes defined with reference to the social organisation and culture of specifically Western societies, typified as individualistic, democratic, capitalist, scientific, secular and stable. The blurring of such concepts also increased their ideological force; as Bideleux and Jeffries (2007) note, modernisation theories over-optimistically perceived or treated democratisation as an inevitable concomitant of economic, educational and technological development. In this way, the teleological dimension of modernisation theory lay in the claim that progress follows a single course towards a market economy and political democracy. As Burawoy (1992) argues, modernisation theory's teleological view of the future failed to come to terms with the specificity of East Central Europe's experience and the significant obstacles to development. In earlier versions of the theory, it was in order for 'backward' countries to approach the condition of liberal capitalist democratic societies that modernisation theory presented as desirable. The concepts of 'modernisation' and 'Westernisation' were treated as equivalents. Alexander (1995: 13) writes that, because the basic unit of reference was one's own time totalised as 'Western' society, it must be characterised as a whole regardless of the social or political divisions in existence.

> For Western but especially American and American-educated intellectuals, modernization theory provided a telos for postwar society by making it 'historical.' It did so by providing postwar society with a temporal and spatial identity, an identity that could be formed only in a relation of difference with another, immediately preceding time and place.

The process of modernisation was uncritically accepted as progress, and the achievements of modernity, the achievements of the West, were set up as an example to follow blindly. The end of the age of revolution and the move to a gradualist model of change has meant that history no longer 'wins its claim to be an independent mode of understanding in its own right' (Jameson 1972: vi). The ideological function that post-revolutionary and modernisation theory serves is clear; the 'end of history is not the arrival of a perfect system, but the elimination of any better alternatives to this one' (Anderson 1992: 336).

This *inverted* teleology is characterised by Eagleton (2003) as a *Janus-faced* temporality in which an appeal to an earlier social order (the idealised form) is sought in order to move backwards into a future that has transcended the present altogether.[2] It is from this *Janus-faced* temporality that we interpret the 1989 revolutions.

In discussing the transition from authoritarian rule, Arato (2000) draws on Karl Marx's 1843 statement that 'it is not easy to interpret the revolutions of others' to highlight the problems of interpreting simultaneous political and economic change. Although, as he argues, there is a wide range of interpretations and each contains a certain measure of truth, they are all necessarily partial. Their single uniting feature is an implicit awareness of the *Janus-faced* nature of modernisation. Arato (2000) outlines four categories under which the 1989 revolutions were interpreted: conservative revolution, postmodern revolution, imitative revolution and liberal revolution.

Conservative revolution

The 'incomplete revolution' of 1989 is perceived to be the completion of the European civil war that began in 1917 with the Russian revolution. An incomplete revolution, a term adopted from Marx, is a revolution that preserves an existing class structure. This type of revolution is conservative in the sense that it stops at the 'threshold of the bourgeois and the nation, seeking … to preserve rather than to eliminate them' (Arato 2000: 5). In the context of *inverted* temporality of 1989, as a result of the elimination of the symbols and institutions of bourgeois democracy, 'incomplete revolution' has come to mean the restoration of the bourgeois and the nation rather than their preservation. The thesis of the conservative revolution points to very real restorationist tendencies present in all the relevant countries.

Postmodern revolution

The 1989 revolutions are postmodern in the sense that, unlike 'modern' revolutions, postmodern revolutions overthrow modern rather than pre-modern regimes' (Arato 2000). In this interpretation, postmodern revolutions are also restorationist. A return to modernist conditions before the communist revolutions usurped the authentic history of the countries undergoing transition. In this interpretation, 1956 in Hungary, 1968 in Czechoslovakia and 1981 in Poland represent the dates when the national histories of each country were interrupted. Although emphasising 'the raging passion to restore' (Arato 2000: 14), postmodern interpretations emphasise the end of the epoch of revolutions and 'the rejection of utopian narratives and the hubris of making history' (Arato 2000: 15).

Imitative revolution

An exception to the other categories listed is what Arato (2000) calls the 'imitative' or 'rectifying' revolution (Habermas 1990) interpretation. It is distinct from the other categories in that it is an interpretation based on a conception of an incomplete revolution that is closer to Marx's original definition, i.e. the revolutions are incomplete because bourgeois democracy by itself is not capable of completing them. This perspective is drawn from Habermas's (1985) earlier conceptualisation of modernity as an incomplete project. This perspective counters the restrictions and silencings of a merely technological account of progress and modernisation. In terms of the claims demanded and the forces of change, the 1989 revolutions are understood as revolutions in the modern sense. However, for Habermas (1990), the revolutions in East Central Europe lacked a future-oriented perspective beyond the extension of boundaries of the existing version of modernity.

> In Poland and Hungary, in Czechoslovakia, Romania and Bulgaria … the abolition of the people's republic has occurred under the sign of a return to old, national symbols, and, where this was possible, has understood itself to be the continuation of the political traditions and party organisations of the interwar years. Here—as revolutionary changes

> gather force and become revolutionary events—is also where one finds the clearest articulation of the desire to connect up constitutionally with the inheritance of the bourgeois revolutions, and socially and politically with the styles of commerce and life associated with developed capitalism, particularly that of the European Community.
>
> Habermas (1990: 4–5)

This return to the past breaks with the project of modernity originally formulated in the eighteenth century. It is not only the outward forms of bourgeois democracy and civil society that are unable to complete the revolution and compel solidarity and meaning; economic and technological development cannot do this either (see Bernstein 1989). Habermas's (1992) account differs from Marxist accounts in that he defends the bourgeois norms of civil society – personhood, reciprocity, justice and equality – as important and necessary to protect and nourish a public sphere and not merely as the ideological projections of an exploitive economy. However, he warns that these norms and ideals become ideological if the structural and communicative framework of civil society is absent.

Liberal revolution

The liberal revolution interpretation views constitutional politics as being dominated by a single choice between open and liberal societies and closed and illiberal societies. Open societies can only be maintained if supported by fundamental rights, legitimate government and a free market economy. In this interpretation, a strong civil society and democratic political culture is necessary to underpin an open society (Arato 2000). The liberal perspective views civil society as a civil sphere, 'a world of values and institutions that generate the capacity for social criticism and democratic integration at the same time' (Alexander 2006: 4).

Liberal revolution and the antinomies of civil society

Alexander (2006) argued that civil society could be conceived in three ideal ways. The first is linked to the Scottish Enlightenment where the essential feature of civil or 'civilised society' was understood as an institution outside the state but including the capitalist market, i.e. including economic society. The concept was first used by Adam Ferguson (1966) in his book *An Essay on the History of Civil Society* in 1767. Much ambiguity has always surrounded the concept and even in the eighteenth century there was a *Janus-faced* aspect to its development that reflected perhaps Ferguson's orientation towards the two faces of eighteenth-century Scottish society: the '*Gemeinschaft* of the clan, belonging to the past, the *Gesellschaft* of the "progressive" and commercial Lowlands' (Forbes 1966: xxxviii–xxxix). As Forbes (1966) writes, in Scotland, there was opposition between Highlands and Lowlands, and Ferguson was born practically on the dividing line itself. Ferguson saw the *Janus* nature of modern civilisation expressed in the paradox where the progress of commerce and manufacturing gives rise to personal liberty, security and the rule of law, but simultaneously produces what he saw as a mediocre society full of mundane citizens pursuing relatively worthless objects.

Although the concept of civil society was ambiguously defined by Ferguson (1966), Nairn (1997) argues that, in eighteenth-century Scotland, the notion of an extra-political society was relatively clear and a matter of daily experience. The reason for this was because it had been spelt out by the Treaty of Union.

> The new unified British regime was obliged by that very unusual constitutional deal to guarantee and maintain, necessarily at a distance, such a range of bodies 'for all time to come'. That is, the rights of Scottish sub-parliamentary or extra-political society, including its dispositions on property, local government, commercial and civil law, and so on. So it was relatively straightforward to perceive such an assortment of things both as having a common character, and as autonomous in the sense of not being state-dominated in a day to day sense. The common character was national and the nation was now controlled politically from the outside, by a centre most people felt to be remote. Hence the idea could take root of a developed or civil society – an order 'apolitical' with the meaning of distinct from political interference or state-prescribed law and order, yet 'autonomous' in the sense of self-regulating and having momentum of its own.
>
> Nairn (1997: 78)

However, as Nairn (1997: 79) notes, there was nothing autonomous or apolitical about civil society. Its unique situation was made possible by an imposed state-level arrangement. The Treaty of Union was not the result of socio-economic advancement but a by-product of political expedience. Civil society did not emerge in Scotland as a natural side-effect of improvement, but was an institutional endowment from a previous state and a new 'remote and wildly corrupt state authority; and then, after 1745–46, further military defeat and suppression, followed by heady colonial and mercantile expansion'. The post-national intellectuals of the Scottish Enlightenment reinterpreted civil society as autonomous and outside of the state, a 'diffuse assemblage of anything and everything which could be located somewhere in between politics and state power on the one hand and the family on the other' (Nairn 1997: 77).

Ferguson's (1966) ambiguous and *Janus-faced* concept of civil society was developed by Hegel who extended its scope into the first theory of civil society (Cohen and Arato 1992). All strands of the history of the conception of civil society meet in Hegel's *Rechtsphilosophie.* In this theory, Hegel attempted to unite a conception of ancient ethos with one of the modern freedom of the individual. Hegel's theory is also *Janus*-like in that it presents modern society as both a world of alienation and an open-ended search for social integration. A key theme of this understanding was that of capitalism as an antisocial force.

The second understanding of civil society comes from Marx where civil society is not only a field for the play of private egotistical interests, but is now a superstructure that camouflages the domain of commodities and a capitalist class. The notion of an autonomous plurality of institutions opposing and balancing the state is often interpreted by Marxists as masking the dominance of economic forces. However, Gramsci developed Marx's position and argued that civil society was the realm of political, cultural, legal and public life, situated between economic relations and political power. In the East,

> the State was everything, civil society was primordial and gelatinous; in the West, there was a proper relationship between State and civil society, and when the State trembled a sturdy structure of civil society was at once revealed. The State was only an outer ditch, behind which there was a powerful system of fortresses and earthworks: more or less numerous from one State to the next, it goes without saying—but this precisely necessitated an accurate reconnaissance of each individual country.
>
> Gramsci (1971: 238)

Gramsci (1971) not only appropriated and influentially redefined the idea of civil society, he also provided an ideal of a non-state, self-standing society under which capitalism and class rule might eventually be transcended. However, within the confines of capitalist society, there would never be the space for institutionalising a more inclusive universal sphere.

The third model for civil society comes from Tocqueville, who described it in terms of the voluntary association of a wide array of community, cultural and religious groups. Arato (2000) argues for the importance of this model in relation to the collapse of communism and rejects the more ambiguous notions of the first two models. To identify civil society with capitalism was to degrade its universalising moral implications and the capacity for criticism and repair that the existence of a relatively independent community implies. Howard (2003) reflects this model when he defines civil society as encompassing:

> a wide array of groups, associations, and organisations, including community and local organisations; human rights, peace, and environmental groups; educational or cultural activities; churches or religious organisations; sports or recreational clubs; and women's, veterans', youth, elderly, disabled, animal rights, health and self help groups.
>
> Howard (2003: 35)

Linz and Stepan (1996) outline five interacting and mutually reinforcing 'arenas' of democratisation: (1) civil society; (2) political society; (3) economic society; (4) the rule of law; and (5) state bureaucracy. This more schematic approach to civil society still uses the broad definitions of this third model and shares a common understanding of most scholars who write about civil society – however they may define or operationalise it – that is, the assumption that civil society has a positive or beneficial influence.

Another important argument about the conditions or even prerequisites for the development of civil society involves economics. This hypothesis predicts that a stable and functioning economic system, one that enhances the material well-being of its citizens, is necessary for a country's civil society. In relation to established democracies or democratising countries, the civil society relationship is much more interactive and reciprocal (see Cohen and Arato 1992). Howard (2003) also highlights the supportive role of the state in the West in strengthening civil society. In the case of Eastern Europe, however, the relationship between civil society and the state was viewed as two social forces in opposition, with civil society against the state. In the post-communist context, particularly in Russia, it is clear that the state has all too frequently not provided the necessary resources and support for the organisation of civil society. However 'primordial and gelatinous', civil society rapidly disappeared from the Russian political and scholarly agenda in the years following the period of mobilisation around the collapse of the communist regime.

Why then do post-communist citizens mistrust and avoid public organisations? What explains this distinctive pattern of weak civil society? Howard (2003) argues that the legacy of the communist experience of mandatory participation in state-controlled organisations, the development and persistence of vibrant private networks and the tremendous disappointment with developments since the collapse of communism have left most post-communist citizens with a lasting aversion to public activities. In the new post-Cold War era, in which many countries have embarked on various forms of democratisation, civil society has come to be seen as one of the main indicators of that process.

This conflict between the state and civil society in Eastern Europe has often meant that Western diplomacy interprets the idea of building a civil society in the East into the simple notion of ending state interference, state funding and state control. Society can only be civil in the absence of politics. The building of popular sovereignty, the establishment of links between voter preference and public policy or respecting expressions of public protest or strike action by citizens and workers form no part of this interpretation of civil society. 'Strong public protests against the kinds of privatisation favoured in the West or against increasingly unpopular examples of predatory Western buy-outs are to be ignored' (Gowan 1995).

Howard (2003) outlines an important problem with whether the definition of civil society is applicable to associations based on common interest where those interests are anti-liberal or anti-democratic. He explicitly excludes the mafia from civil society as, he argues, only those groups or organisations that accept the legitimacy of other groups, in a mutually recognised public realm, can be considered part of civil society. Groups belonging to civil society must follow the general liberal democratic principles that have long been associated with its development. This position is problematic on a number of counts, and to explore it further we must return to our first account of civil society.

Hegel's theory, outlined earlier, presents modern society as both a world of alienation and an open-ended search for social integration. Cohen and Arato (1992) argue that this contradiction runs through Hegel's analysis of civil society in the form of two interrelated questions: (1) Is *Sittlichkeit* or ethical life possible only as an inherited and unquestioned *ethos* to which individual subjects must conform in order for them to be consistent with their identity, or is it possible to think of ethical life in a truly modern form, permitting and even requiring its own questioning and criticism as well as a plurality of normatively valued forms of life? (2) Is civil society to be conceived as *Sittlichkeit* or *Antisittlichkeit*, or as a dynamic combination of both moments?

At the heart of the *Philosophy of Right* was an interpretation of ethical life and its relation to law and morality. Its intent was to make the abstractions of law and morality concrete, to provide his philosophy with what Harvey (1981) calls a 'political body'. Through this interpretation, Hegel describes a series of mediations necessary for individual consciousness to realise itself within ethical life. Hegel first describes the family as a sphere of ethical life. This sphere is characterised by personal altruism. In contrast to the family was civil society. This second sphere was one of 'universal egoism', characterised by market competition and the social division of labour. Here, individuals sought to use others as a means towards their own private ends. The tension between the two spheres, between the family and civil society, the private and the public, can only be resolved, according to Hegel, through the possession of a universalistic consciousness on the part of all. The objective expression of that consciousness could be realised only through the institutions of the modern state (Harvey 1981).

That ethical life could only be realised through the acceptance of the authority of the 'rational state' over the individual has led many authors to criticise Hegel's politics for being both conservative and authoritarian (Popper 1966; Marx 1975). This is a view confirmed for many by Hegel's description of the institutions of 'the rational modern state' as being reminiscent of the Prussian state of his own time. However, there is what Harvey (1981) calls an 'intriguing ambiguity'[3] that runs through Hegel's work which is also combined with a radical critique of modern institutions of the state that would belie such interpretations.

Hegel's ideal of the state was inspired by classical Greece and Rome. It was also a contemporary reaction against the 'nightwatchman'[4] state of liberalism, a state formation that was safeguarded by a contract between self-interested individuals (Beiser 2005); in other words, a state dominated by the realm of civil society and 'universal egoism'.

Hegel desired a political formation that synthesised the community and the individual, to bring together the classical freedom of democratic participation with the modern freedom of rights (Harvey 1981). Although rooted in the customs and practices of a community, these customs and ways of life should not be imposed on the citizens of a state, but must be reflexively accepted as an expression of the popular will. If the necessary communicative channels are not adequate and decisions are enforced by the state, they will lack legitimacy.

> Hegel starts from an ethical concept of individual freedom and derives from it the relative importance of formal right and of morality, mainly in order to show that they have necessarily to be included in the various communicative spheres which together represent the ultimate conditions for individual self-realisation; therefore, he believes that the legitimacy of a modern legal order depends upon its capacity to guarantee each citizen the chance to participate in those spheres, which have all at the same time to be secured in their distinct normative integrity.
>
> Honneth (2000: 60)

Hegel claims that the *rational* state as the 'actuality of the ethical idea' can transcend the dualities of private and public life and therefore heal the 'wound of the social body' (Žižek 2000: 95). In this way, Hegel presented a theory of ethical life that would enable people to live their lives rationally according to socially accepted aims and thus experience their life as meaningful. However, he was also profoundly aware of the constraints at the heart of modern liberal society that prevented this happening. Contrary to contemporaries such as Adam Smith, Hegel argued that 'negative liberty' and economic regulation by the market were not only defective means by which to achieve social harmony, but they also generated contradictions within social life. Hegel argued that self-interest and individual right based on property[5] were incapable of generating institutions that could lay the foundations for the ethical unity of the people. At the heart of these constraints was what seemed to Hegel an unavoidable aspect of liberal democracies: the inability of such societies to accord recognition to all its members. This aspect of liberalism not only meant that modernity was unable to solve the problems that it created[6] – the problems of poverty and increasing polarisation in the distribution of wealth and income – but it also excluded a significant number in those societies from the opportunity to develop a meaningful and self-determined life (see Hegel 1967; Avineri 1974; Honneth 2000; Harvey 2006; Arrighi 2007).

There is a paradox at the heart of Hegel's ethical life: although he argues strongly for the transcendence of civil society and for the state as the 'actuality of the ethical idea', he nowhere explains how this can be achieved within the constraints of the modern bourgeois state. Avineri (1974) points out:

> Few people around 1820 grasped in such depth the predicament of modern industrial society and the future course of nineteenth-century European history. What is conspicuous in Hegel's analysis, however, is

> not only his farsightedness but also a basic intellectual honesty which makes him admit time and time again – completely against the grain of the integrative and mediating nature of the whole of his social philosophy – that he has no solution to the problems posed by civil society in its modern context. This is the only time in his system where Hegel raises a problem – and leaves it open.
>
> Avineri (1974: 154)

As we will see later in the chapter, this will not be the only time that we find Hegel running against the grain of his own system.

In Hegel's own time, modern society had become fragmented by market competition and was based on 'universal egoism'. Individuals had become reified by abstract law in the form of an imagined social contract, and society had become polarised by wealth and power (Arrighi 2007). *Sittlichkeit* allows the exploration of normative questions on the level of the concrete, historically emergent institutions and practices that represent the institutionalisation or actualisation of freedom (Cohen and Arato 1992). It facilitates the production and self-production of social life through self-conscious action, yet as Taylor (1975, cited in Cohen and Arato 1992) states, it constructs 'the norms of a society's public life ... sustained by our action, and yet already there'. *Sittlichkeit* is its own antithesis, as mentioned earlier, a *Gegen-* or *Antisittlichkeit*. For Hegel, civil society was 'a system of ethical life lost in its extremes', a world of egotism and alienation.

Ethical life then is presupposed as intersubjective social bonds: it already exists; however, its realisation is constrained by the existing social/institutional structure of society. As mentioned above, although Hegel argues strongly for the transcendence of civil society, he remains trapped within the constraints of the modern bourgeois state (Avineri 1974). The intriguing questions that Hegel leaves open, however, concern the legitimacy of state institutions. Legitimacy, for Hegel, depended on the ability of those institutions to guarantee each citizen the opportunity to participate actively in civil society in a way that made possible their individual self-realisation; and it was only through this realisation of an 'objectively' possible reason – the rational potential already inherent in society's institutions, practices and everyday routines – that legitimation could be grounded. If the constraints mentioned above cannot guarantee citizens a free and self-determined life, then the intersubjective relations of 'ethical life' that Hegel envisaged are transformed. As Eagleton (2009: 124) points out, although ethical life can refer to the positive notions of a community – habitual virtue, local affections and kinship – it can also be used to describe the more negative, such as 'cultural conformism, unreflective custom, the blind coerciveness of tradition' – the result of a failure in the restructuring and expansion of the embryonic forms of ethical life. For Hegel, immersion in ethical life, the symbolic order, can also then be pathological. This pathological aspect of ethical life was reflected in Adorno's concept of 'ethical violence' (see Butler 2005).[7]

> [N]othing is more degenerate than the kind of ethics or morality that survives in the shape of collective ideas even after the World Spirit has ceased to inhabit them – to use the Hegelian expression as a kind of shorthand. Once the state of human consciousness and the state of the social forces of production have abandoned these collective ideas, these ideas acquire repressive and violent qualities.
>
> Adorno (2001: 17)

What Adorno is highlighting here is that moral questions do not always appear solely in relation to their current social context. The concrete universality of ethical life can take on repressive and violent forms and attempt to impose 'a false unity that attempts to suppress the difficulty and discontinuity existing within any contemporary ethos' (Butler 2005: 4). Žižek (1990: 50) highlights 'ethical violence' in the *Janus* nature of Eastern European transitions when he suggests that one of the reasons the West is so fascinated by civil society in Eastern Europe is in relation to the increasing signs of democratic hollowing out and crisis in the West. Lost in bureaucratic routine and publicity-style election campaigns, democracy is being rediscovered in all its freshness and novelty in Eastern Europe. In other words, the *Janus* gaze is 'the point from which the West sees itself in a likeable, idealised form, as worthy of love'. The reality, however, is more complex than this idyllic picture of the two mutually fascinated gazes. The 'emptiness' of the Western gaze is mirrored more accurately in economic rationality than in the finer points of constitutional development and social solidarity. As Adorno writes, once the state of the social forces of production has abandoned these collective ideas of constitutional development and social solidarity, these ideas acquire repressive and violent qualities. The politics of the new Eastern Europe cannot be adequately understood merely in terms of the severance of economics from civil society. The failure of civil society in East Central Europe cannot simply be reduced to internal failures, as Howard (2003) recounts above. As well as the failures brought on by the direct legacy of the communist experience, civil privatism and disillusionment, blame should also be directed against Western diplomacy and conditions of conditionality.

Ethical life can adopt, according to Hegel, pathological forms. As we have seen, for Hegel, law was both a mechanism of civil society and a manifestation of reason within ethical life. However, at the edge of his theory, Hegel acknowledged that civil society presented a darker dialectic that undermined the existence of ethical life by exposing it to deep-seated structural conflict. There exists here an antinomy at the heart of Hegel's theory of civil society, that is civil society as being beyond the spheres of self-interest: in other words, the view that societies are not governed by power alone or the pursuit of self-interest versus the view that civil society represents the self-interest of the most powerful. Therefore, the discourse of civil society can be as repressive as it is liberating, and legitimates not only inclusion but exclusion as well. In this way, civil society is the bifurcation of ethical life, as both *Sittlichkeit* and

Antisittlichkeit, where the unity of substantial ethical life is attained only in appearance (Cohen and Arato 1992). As Habermas (1992) indicates, the values and norms of ethical life become ideological in situations in which civil society does not exist. Personhood, justice and freedom become mere ideals, abstract norms whose very abstractness and universality serve to reinforce rather than inhibit or diminish domination and exploitation.

Gowan (1995) argues that the building of 'civil society', and the construction of democratic, legal and civil institutions, was derailed by the negation of existing institutions from above. This top-down approach was at the very heart of the operational priorities to subordinate the will of electorates and parliaments to the overriding priority of rapid systemic transformation to capitalism, downgrading constitutional development, social and political consensus-building and respect for minimal economic and social solidarity. These features of the drive have been most evident in the policy towards Russia and the former Soviet Union. The governing consideration is to swiftly create a capitalist class with strong entrepreneurial and proprietary instincts: in bandit or mafia capitalism, there was a solution.

> The West has urged that those who managed to accumulate money-capital under communism should form the core of the new domestic capitalist class. These people have been mainly currency speculators and black-marketeers as well as corrupt members of state administrations, especially in the import–export sectors. Such people have shown entrepreneurial spirit, albeit of a criminal kind. Lord Howe, appointed adviser to the Ukrainian government in 1991, was quite frank on this point. He urged the need for the development of what he called 'bandit capitalism' in Ukraine and drew a favourable parallel with the great robber barons of American capitalism in the nineteenth century.
>
> Gowan (1995: 230)

Yeltsin's 1992 Act liberalised the Russian economy in the absence of any controls. The prices that mattered to the majority – bread and rents – were liberalised; the prices that mattered to the minority were not – oil, gas, diamonds and metals. This gave birth within months to a new species of 'robber baron' – the Russian oligarch (Glenny 2008) and *krysha* (*krysha* means roof and is Russian for protection agency or mafia).

> This process of enrichment was quite simply the grandest larceny in history and stands no historical comparison. As the New Russia dressed itself up to look like a responsible capitalist economy that was attractive to foreign investment, its most powerful capitalists were riding its key commodities (mineral resources of almost incalculable value), trading them for dollars and then exporting these funds out of the country in the biggest single flight of capital the world has ever seen. As the IMF shovelled billions into Russia to stabilise the economy and prop up the

> rouble, the oligarchs sent even larger sums to obscure banks in every corner of the world, from Switzerland to the Pacific island of Nauru, to be swallowed almost immediately in bafflingly complex money-laundering schemes. The whole process was dramatic testimony to how venality and myopic stupidity are always likely to triumph in the absence of regulatory institutions.
>
> Glenny (2008: 72–73)

The secret services set up their own semi-legal commercial empires before the 'transition to capitalism', and then recruited the criminal underworld as protectors and enforcers of their monopolies. More often, though, it is intelligence agents who offer their services to organised crime, during periods when lawlessness reigns and political police forces are being purged or dissolved. Not only were institutional economic reforms coercively imposed by external institutions (IMF, World Bank) but the obliteration of existing constitutions created a 'legal gap' that allowed the decriminalisation of what would generally be understood as corporate and organised criminal activity.

Varese (2001) argues that organised crime is not just a criminal business, it is a criminal government. It is concerned with the monopolisation of illegal markets and the extortion and protection of those markets. There is a set of firms that provide extra state protection to consumers in both the illegal and the legal market sector. In this reading, organised crime may be understood not only as a response to a particular institutional demand by the nascent market economy, that is the need to protect property rights that are not satisfied by public protection and enforcement agencies, but also as playing the role of a civil society. A diffuse assemblage of services and networks between the market and state power:[8]

> Organised crime can be imagined only when the state and the system of justice it effectively enforces are in place.
>
> Volkov (2002: 22)

Mafias arise when market demand for extra-legal protection is met by supply. They originally arose as a response to the imperfect transition from feudal economic structures during the nineteenth century (Blok 1974; Gambetta 1996), a period when there was an increase in the number of economic transactions but no mechanism to control them. As we have seen above, in the former Soviet Union, the rapid transfer from a state command economy to a market economy during the late 1980s and early 1990s entailed widespread transfer of state assets into private hands. Because this transfer was not matched by either social norms or the state institutions protecting the integrity of market transactions and property rights, potential entrepreneurs were highly vulnerable to predators. This, in turn, presented these individuals with a considerable disincentive to engage in trade. In short, there was a widespread market demand for protection that was not being met by the state (Gambetta 1996; Varese 2001).

Conclusions

At the beginning of this chapter, the importance of civil society as a public sphere where values and institutions generate the capacity for social criticism and democratic and social integration was emphasised in relation to both transitions to democracy and criminalisation. However, it was also noted that the concepts used to interpret the transition to civil society in East Central European societies were problematic, particularly in relation to their normative assumptions. As Habermas (1992) pointed out, the bourgeois norms of personhood, reciprocity, justice and equality expressed in the conception of a juridically constituted state, although necessary to protect and nourish a public sphere within civil society, take on an ideological form in the absence of such a sphere. The chapter drew on Hegel's conception of civil society as the bifurcation of ethical life, as both *Sittlichkeit* and *Antisittlichkeit*, where the unity of substantial ethical life is attained only in appearance to explore the ideological force of civil society in some of the transition literature. This framework highlighted the antinomies of civil society during periods of imperfect transition, in which civil society lacks access to the violence monopolised by the state. In so doing, it developed an alternative conception of civil society where it was argued that the civil sphere can be as repressive and violent as it is liberating. The chapter focuses on Eastern European legal transitions and the failure of criminalisation to contextualise the relationship between civil society and 'violent entrepreneurialism'. It thus provides an alternative to general rule-of-law discourses on criminalisation.

Notes

1 Conventional criminality in this case can be translated as 'Western' definitions of the crime problem and strategies for policing (see Andreas and Nadelmann 2006) on the relationship between crime policy and EU enlargement).
2 See Benjamin's (1973) 'angel of history' – Benjamin views history as an immense negative process. His angel is blown backwards into the future by the storm wind and sees only the trail of destruction in its wake. The point of Benjamin's story according to Löwy (2005) is not to conserve the past, but to realise the hopes of the past. Benjamin's 'angel of history' is a refusal to regard the progress of knowledge and technology as identical with the progress of humanity. Progress consists of the struggle to resist the constant danger of regression and the possibility of avoiding complete disaster.
3 There is a debate among Hegel scholars as to whether he intended the later section of *The Philosophy of Right* to be a normative account of what ethical life should be, as facilitated by state institutions, or whether his work merely reflected the actual institutions of the state at that time. Although parts of Hegel's preface to *The Philosophy of Right* would suggest the latter, other sections contradict this interpretation (see Marcuse 1954; Marx 1975; Fine 1993; Norrie 1993; Honneth 2000).
4 The 'nightwatchman' state was based on 'negative liberty', i.e. doing as you pleased as long as you did not interfere with private property of others.
5 For Hegel, property was a form of recognition, 'subjects mutually recognise each other as bearers of legitimate claims to possession' (Honneth 1996: 19). The

'nightwatchman' state was not legitimate because those who lacked property were not accorded recognition, and were therefore denied rights.

6 Hegel showed in *The Philosophy of Right* that 'bourgeois society appears to be incapable of solving through internal mechanisms the problem of social inequality and instability that arises from its tendency to over-accumulate wealth at one pole and deprivation at the other. A "mature" civil society is thus driven to seek external solutions through foreign trade and colonial or imperial practices' (Arrighi 2007: 220).

7 Bourdieu (1977: 192) uses the term 'symbolic violence' in relation to 'socially recognised' domination (legitimate authority): 'symbolic violence, the gentle, invisible form of violence, which is never recognised as such, and is not so much undergone as chosen, the violence of credit, confidence, obligation, personal loyalty, hospitality, gifts, gratitude, piety … cannot fail to be seen as the most economical mode of domination, i.e. the mode which best corresponds to the economy of the system'.

8 An example of this is Milo Djukanovic's 'transit tax'. For most of the 1990s, Montenegro was the centre of a multi-dollar criminal industry that allowed the country to stay solvent (see Glenny 2008). Djukanovic claimed that the annual revenue from the tobacco trade was £20 million and from that he paid for most of the state's running costs; the estimated tax loss to the EU was £4–6 billion per year (mainly in the UK and Italy).

References

Adorno, T.W. (2001) *Problems of Moral Philosophy*, Cambridge: Polity.

Alexander, J.C. (1995) *Fin de Siècle Social Theory: Relativism, Reduction, and the Problem of Reason*, London: Verso.

——(2006) *The Civil Sphere*, Oxford: Oxford University Press.

Anderson, P. (1992) *A Zone of Engagement*, London: Verso.

Andreas, P. and Nadelmann, E. (2006) *Policing the Globe: Criminalization and Crime Control in International Relations*, Oxford: Oxford University Press.

Arato, A. (2000) *Civil Society, Constitution and Legitimacy*, Oxford: Rowman & Littlefield.

Arrighi, G. (2007) *Adam Smith in Beijing: Lineages of the Twenty-First Century*, London: Verso.

Avineri, S. (1974) *Hegel's Theory of the Modern State*, Cambridge: Cambridge University Press.

Beiser, F. (2005) *Hegel*, London: Routledge.

Benjamin, W. (1973) *Illuminations*, London: Fontana.

Bernstein, J.M. (1989) 'The Causality of Fate: Modernity and Modernism in Habermas', *Praxis International*, 8(4) January: 407–25.

Bideleux, R. and Jeffries, I. (2007) *A History of Eastern Europe: Crisis and Change*, Abingdon: Routledge.

Blok, A. (1974) *The Mafia of a Sicilian Village, 1860–1960*, Long Grove, IL: Waveland Press.

Bourdieu, P. (1977) *Outline of a Theory of Practice*, Cambridge: University of Cambridge.

Burawoy, M. (1992) 'The End of Sovietology and the Renaissance of Modernization Theory', *Contemporary Sociology*, 21(6): 774–83.

Butler, J. (2005) *Giving an Account of Oneself*, New York: Fordham University Press.

Cohen, J.L. and Arato, A. (1992) *Civil Society and Political Theory*, Cambridge, MA: MIT Press.

Eagleton, T. (2003) *Figures of Dissent: Critical Essays on Fish, Spivak, Žižek, and Others*, London: Verso.
——(2009) *Trouble with Strangers: A Study of Ethics*, Chichester: Wiley-Blackwell.
Ferguson, A. (1966) *An Essay on the History of Civil Society*, Edinburgh: Edinburgh University Press.
Fine, R. (1993) "The Rose in the Cross of the Present": Closure and Critique in Hegel's Philosophy of Right', in A. Norrie (ed.) *Closure or Critique: New Directions in Legal Theory*, Edinburgh: Edinburgh University Press.
Forbes, D. (1966) 'Introduction', in A. Ferguson, *An Essay on the History of Civil Society*, Edinburgh: Edinburgh University Press.
Fukuyama, F. (1993) *The End of History and the Last Man*, Harmondsworth: Penguin.
Gambetta, D. (1996) *The Sicilian Mafia: The Business of Private Protection*, Cambridge, MA: Harvard University Press.
Glenny, M. (2008) *McMafia*, London: Bodley Head.
Gowan, P. (1995) 'Neo-Liberal Theory and Practice for Eastern Europe', *New Left Review*, I/213 Sept/Oct: 3–60.
Gramsci, A. (1971) *Selections from Prison Notebooks*, London: Lawrence and Wishart.
Habermas, J. (1976) *Legitimation Crisis*, Cambridge: Polity Press.
——(1985) 'Modernity – An Incomplete Project', in H. Foster (ed.) *Postmodern Culture*, London: Pluto.
——(1990) 'What Does Socialism Mean Today? The Rectifying Revolution and the Need for New Thinking on the Left', *New Left Review*, I/183, Sept/Oct: 3–22.
——(1992) *The Structural Transformation of the Public Sphere*, Cambridge: Polity.
Harvey, D. (1981) 'The Spatial Fix – Hegel, Von Thunen, and Marx', *Antipode*, 13(3): 1–12.
——(2006) *The Limits to Capital*, London: Verso.
Hegel, G.W.F. (1967) *The Philosophy of Right*, Oxford: Oxford University Press.
Honneth, A. (1996) *The Struggle for Recognition: The Moral Grammar of Social Conflicts*, Cambridge: Polity Press.
——(2000) *Suffering from Indeterminacy: An Attempt at a Reactualisation of Hegel's Philosophy of Right*, Amsterdam: Van Gorcum.
Howard, M.M. (2003) *The Weakness of Civil Society in Post-Communist Europe*, Cambridge: Cambridge University Press.
Hui, W. (2011) *The End of the Revolution: China and the Limits of Modernity*, London: Verso.
Jameson, F. (1972) *The Prison-House of Language*, Princeton, NJ: Princeton University Press.
——(2005) *Archaeologies of the Future: The Desire Called Utopia and Other Science Fictions*, London: Verso.
Linz, J.J. and Stepan, A. (1996) *Problems of Democratic Transition and Consolidation; Southern Europe, South America, and Post-Communist Europe*, Baltimore, MA: Johns Hopkins University Press.
Löwy, M. (2005) *Fire Alarm: Reading Walter Benjamin's 'On the Concept of History'*, London: Verso.
Marcuse, H. (1954) *Reason and Revolution*, New York: Humanities Press.
Marx, K. (1975) 'A Contribution to the Critique of Hegel's Philosophy of Right, Introduction', in L. Coletti (ed.) *Marx Early Writings*, London: Pelican.
Nairn, T. (1997) *Faces of Nationalism: Janus Revisited*, London: Verso.

Norrie, A. (1993) 'Closure and Critique: Antinomy in Modern Legal Theory', in A. Norrie (ed.) *Closure or Critique: New Directions in Legal Theory*, Edinburgh: Edinburgh University Press.
Offe, C. (1996) *Modernity and the State: East, West*, Cambridge, MA: MIT Press.
Popper, K.R. (1966) *The Open Society and its Enemies. Vol.2: The High Tide of Prophecy. Hegel, Marx, and the Aftermath*, London: Routledge & Kegan Paul.
Taylor, C. (1975) *Hegel*, Cambridge: Cambridge University Press.
Varese, F. (2001) *The Russian Mafia: Private Protection in a New Market Economy*, Oxford: Oxford University Press.
Volkov, V. (2002) *Violent Entrepreneurs: The Use of Force in the Making of Russian Capitalism*, London: Cornell University Press.
Žižek, S. (1990) 'Eastern Europe's Republics of Gilead', *New Left Review*, I/183: 50–62.
——(2000) *The Ticklish Subject: The Absent Centre of Political Ontology*, London: Verso.

Part II

Criminalisation and decriminalisation

Modernising criminal law and regulatory strategies

3 Building justice through criminal law

Issues of criminalisation and trust

Nina Peršak

Introduction

Two decades ago, a group of European societies opted for change. When the Berlin Wall crumbled, it symbolically marked the beginning of the end of communism in Europe, announcing significant changes to be experienced by those countries in the years to follow. Changes that ensued were not only economic and political; sometimes – as was the case in Slovenia, a newly formed state in the aftermath of these changes – they encompassed changes in the very constitution or identity of the state. All these modifications and new creations obviously involved shifts in the value system, which, on the one hand, triggered the re-evaluation of the past, and stimulated certain new expectations and social goals, on the other.

Criminal law as a symbolic platform, describing standards of the 'ethical minimum' (Jellinek 1878) of a given society and expressing 'our shared beliefs of what is truly condemnable' (Robinson 2000: 1869), reflected those shifts, re-evaluations and new expectations. As such, it was and always is vested not only with values but also with societal fears and insecurities, all of which the analysis of criminalisation can help reveal. Because the transition (or transitions)[1] brought with it the above-mentioned specific elements, 'transitional criminalisation' makes a particularly interesting object of study.

This chapter will address this two-decade-long transition as reflected in Slovene criminal law, and distil its evolution and its principles as well as the influences of these changes and the current state of affairs. It will further discuss the problem of social trust, which enters into the debate on the proper scope of criminal law, affects criminalisation and plays a key role in people's perception (or social representation) of justice, i.e. of what is just. A contrast between trust in criminalisation as justice on the books and trust in the judicial application of criminal law as justice in action will be analysed alongside its repercussions. The chapter will conclude with some reflections on the implications and the symbolism of criminalisation, particularly for a society in transition, and on the transitional justice contained therein.

Processes of criminalisation

The 1990s

Processes of social differentiation, pluralisation and democratisation have slowly been taking place since the 1950s (see, for example, Jambrek 1992). These processes of liberalisation and democratisation have also been mirrored in jurisprudence and criminal legislature. The worst shortcomings of the former totalitarian criminal law, which violated the principles of the rule of law, had thus been abolished long before the 1990s, either through partial Criminal Code reforms or through the judiciary's active avoidance of, or non-engagement in, those criminal law provisions that violated those principles (Bavcon 1994).

Nonetheless, after the dissolution of the Socialist Federal Republic of Yugoslavia (SFRY) and with Slovenia gaining independence on 25 June 1991, so-called democratisation progressively ensued, which *inter alia* encompassed the changing of the existing laws that were mostly Yugoslav, socialist laws and replacing them with new Slovene, democratic laws. As soon as the country stabilised after declaring independence and surviving the ensuing conflict (the 10-day war), the drafting of the new Criminal Code (hereinafter CC) began. This is the statute that probably more than any others represents the core values of a given society and the nature of the existing state order. The Slovenian CC, first drafted in 1991 (Bavcon 1994: 290), was enacted in September 1994 and entered into force on 1 January 1995.[2] One change particularly worth noting is that the new general part of the Code took out the concept of 'social danger' from the abstract definition of the criminal offence. Social danger was one of the elements of the general concept of the criminal offence and was removed because it was considered a typical socialist invention, a remnant of the past that infringed the principle of legality and was prone to political abuses, and was replaced with the term *protipravnost* (wrongfulness, unlawfulness).[3] As a consequence, the former 'substantive-formal' (or 'material-formal') definition of a criminal offence, which defined the criminal offence as 'a socially dangerous act, which the law proclaims as a criminal offence and concurrently describes its characteristics',[4] became in 1994 a 'formal-substantive' (or 'formal-material') definition, defining the criminal offence as 'an unlawful act that is, owing to the danger it involves, so determined by the statute, the elements of which as well as the sentence are therein defined'.[5] However, the notion of 'danger', albeit not of 'social danger', thus remained (until it was finally excised in 2008 – see the discussion of this below in the section on the 2000s). Clearly, the danger was still the social one (danger to society): the explicit omission of the word 'social' was purely symbolic – the legislature was trying to avoid any vocabulary or terminology that would be reminiscent of the Soviet doctrine, which often led to dangerous results in the totalitarian Bolshevik regime.[6]

In this period, criminalisation was driven by two forces. One of them was the need to make a clean cut with the communist past, a clear separation from the former, Communist criminal law and produce Slovenia's very own,[7] new Criminal Code, reflecting parts of the new social identity that was being forged through processes of differentiation or disassociation with the Yugoslav Other. The other thrust was the desire to catch up as soon as possible with modern democratic systems within the EU, and therefore to have a comparable CC, a code that resembles other European Criminal Codes. The new social identity thus encompassed both the search for similarities with the EU and the processes of association with the European Other.[8] Here, German criminal law provided one of the handiest role models. The Slovene criminal legal system is traditionally part of the Germanic legal circle and hence shares a number of similarities with the German legal system, providing the modern German criminal law as an easy (and renewed) reference point, which increasingly began to inform Slovene criminal law theory.[9]

Both these driving forces were pulling in the same direction, but the first seems to have been a priority, a primary driving force in this initial period of transition, when justice was being built (or affirmed) through the establishment of a criminal law framework that would be different or disassociated from the former, with the hope that it would prevent the state abuses and human rights violations that were present under the previous political regime. The second driving force, however, gained prominence at the end of the 1990s and in the decade that followed.

The noughties

Concrete criminalisations (by amendments to the Code in 1999 (KZ-A) and 2004 (KZ-B) and the new CC in 2008) in this period represented, first, changes needed on the basis of our international obligations (implementation of the signed and ratified conventions, the Rome Statute of the International Criminal Court, etc.). Second, some changes were needed because of the EU's requirement that the accession state harmonise its laws with the existing *acquis communautaire.*[10] Third, some offences were amended as responses to social reality. For example, the crime of extortion was extended to extorting a debt,[11] and the crime of 'dodging alimony' changed to the crime of 'not paying alimony'.[12] Mostly, however, the changes reflected modern, European and global legislative trends with various new or improved, more detailed criminalisations of organised crime, of cyber crime and child pornography, etc. One important milestone for the criminal law was added in 1999 with the passing of the Liability of Legal Persons for Criminal Offences Act,[13] which not only followed similar trends in other European legislatures but also responded to the relevant crime policy needs (Novoselec 2003: 181),[14] fuelled by the transition from planned to market economy, as a result of the ensuing privatisation, denationalisation and the rise in white-collar, economic and organised crime (Bavcon 1994: 290, 291).[15]

At the end of the 1990s, we were already beginning to see a certain punitive turn. In 1999, some sentences were raised from 15 to 20 years' imprisonment, as the so-called 'special maximum' of imprisonment penalty was raised from 20 to 30 years (e.g. for war crimes). The new Criminal Code in 2008 took another punitive step by introducing – to a certain academic outcry, but a much lesser public outcry – so-called life imprisonment.[16] Article 46, para. 2 stipulates that a life sentence may be pronounced for crimes of genocide, crimes against humanity, war crimes and aggression and, under the condition that the court sets the penalty of 30 years' imprisonment for two or more criminal acts, also for certain crimes of terrorism, for murder, for manslaughter of the President of the Republic, for the killing of persons protected by international law, for the killing of hostages and for certain other felonies. On the other hand, the 2008 CC also introduced some new criminalisations that were perhaps long overdue, such as the mobbing-like[17] crime of 'vexation in the workplace' or the environmental crime of 'polluting of sea and waters from ships'. Some other new criminalisations include 'quackery' (pseudo-medical practices), 'domestic violence', 'illegal employment', 'illegal, biased and unjust trial', etc. Some old provisions were struck from the Code: most, however, were amended.

Furthermore, the general part of the new Code again changed the definition of the criminal offence. The criminal offence is construed as a 'human unlawful act which the law due to the necessary protection of legal values stipulates as criminal and concurrently defines its elements and the punishment for the guilty perpetrator'.[18] 'Danger' has thus been completely removed from the definition, replaced by the notion of legal values.

The general approach to criminalisation

The general approach to criminalisation remains casuistic, following only nomothetic rules and adhering to a few basic criminal law principles, which are 'formal' principles, whereas substantive principles of criminalisation, which would give instruction regarding the substance of that which is legitimate to criminalise, are lacking.[19] The formal principles are as follows. A principle of legality in criminal law is found in Art. 28 of the Constitution and in Art. 2 of the CC. In Art. 3, para. 2, reference is made to the principle of proportionality between the prescribed sentence, on the one hand, and the gravity of the offence and the perpetrator's guilt, on the other. The old, pre-2008 CC also explicitly mentioned the so-called repression-limiting principle (the *ultima ratio* principle), which deemed it 'legitimate to lay down criminal offences and to prescribe sentences only when, and to the extent that, the protection of human life and other basic values cannot otherwise be assured'. However, even this principle was removed from the new Code. What Slovenia currently has in addition to this is a small booklet, entitled *Nomothetical Guidelines*, written by the members of the Governmental Legislative Office, describing general rules for making laws, which are applicable to any type of drafting of laws and merely regulate the linguistic, methodological and structural aspects of the formation of laws. The guidelines, being purely formal, say nothing about what type of conduct should be criminalised through criminal law proper. They do, however, contain an interesting sentence regarding the drafting of violations (or regulatory offences, encompassed in the criminal law *lato sensu*),[20] extending beyond the formality of the guidelines, by declaring that '[i]t is very important that the prescribed conduct, whose infringement is stipulated as a violation, is by its nature such that it is sensible to make its infringement a violation ...'.[21] Unfortunately, the Guidelines remain silent on the issue of what 'sensible' is or what it should mean. Another legislative instrument, more recently adopted, is the so-called *Resolution on Legislative Regulation*,[22] which sets out general principles (again mostly formal) that drafters and the legislator should take into account when making laws, none of which is specific for criminal law. Among the principles cited here, one finds principles of necessity (of legal regulation), of self-limitation, of proportionality, of responsibility, the principle of *lex certa*, of accessibility, of simplification and of transparency.

What is needed at this juncture, I believe, is a principled normative approach to criminalisation, a set of substantive (rather than formal) principles, offering legitimate grounds for criminalisation or a coherent conception of justice.[23] An approach, as I suggest (Peršak 2007), based on actual harm, akin to the Anglo-American 'harm principle' (Mill 1991, orig. 1859; Feinberg 1984), could serve as a critical yardstick of legitimate criminalisation.[24] In the absence of any such substantive principle, the principle of legality has been used as a *passe-partout* principle to strike down any kind of deficient criminal legislation – which includes one that suffered from the lack of (a requirement of) harm. Owing to its over-use, however, the legality principle has lost much of its bite.

That some substantive principles would be welcome in the area of criminal law was acknowledged also by the Council of the EU, which on 30 November 2009 issued its *Conclusions on model provisions, guiding the Council's criminal law negotiations*, suggesting the model on which the future legislative proposals in this regard should be based. Paragraph 5 of these Conclusions suggests, for example, that

> [t]he criminal provisions should focus on conduct causing actual harm or seriously threatening the right or essential interest which is the object of protection; that is, avoiding criminalisation of a conduct at an unwarrantably early stage. Conduct which only implies an abstract danger to the protected right or interest should be criminalised only if appropriate considering the particular importance of the right or interest which is the object of protection.

This statement is very much in line with the basic tenets of the harm principle. Even more recently, the Hungarian Presidency of the Council of the EU

(2011), while recognising the sensitive nature of this enterprise at the EU level, reaffirmed the need for a more coherent and consistent approach to criminalisation, and for certain common minimum rules concerning the definition of criminal offences. The latter are undoubtedly easier to achieve if the EU member states agree on certain substantive criminal law principles.

A proper scope of criminal law and its proper application: a question of justice or trust?

Any narrowing down of grounds for criminalisation, any setting of limits on this process, brings us of course to the question of the proper scope of criminal law and, consequently, to the question of the criminal law's specific role and symbolism, which distinguishes it from other areas of law. Criminal law has always provided a sort of legal litmus test for societal 'basic' values. The changing or amending of the criminal law, and even the speed with which laws are amended, therefore also mirrors the changes in the societal value system. Moreover, it mirrors the changes in how 'others' are perceived and treated; it mirrors the levels of social trust. The less we trust each other (and institutions),[25] the more we rely on formal, written rules, contracts and laws, punishing those who violate our trust. As such, criminalisation can also be seen as a sort of coping technique for countering people's insecurities and fears from the 'bad', 'untrustworthy', 'unknown' and so on.

It is interesting to note that, despite the steady decline of social trust in the legal system and legal authorities,[26] the public trust in criminal law and its powers seems to have suffered no blows. With every shocking story, one can observe cries for changes in criminal legislation that can be heard on the streets, in the media and the parliament, trying to persuade us that, if only we raised the sentence for some particular crime, this crime would never happen again; this seems to attest to the astonishing trust of people, media and politicians in the powers of criminal law.

Aside from the issues of trust and populism,[27] there is, however, a normative question regarding the proper scope of criminal law. Just how much criminal law do we want to have? Should criminal law prohibit only the worst, the most harmful conduct or all socially undesirable conduct? How high a tolerance should a given society display towards socially unpleasant or unusual behaviour of some? Some believe that very little of 'the undesirable' should be tolerated, if at all. However, not all 'zero tolerance' or at least 'lower' tolerance perspectives can clearly be traced to their authors' plainly punitive views; some seem to stem from heightened sensitivity to the ill-treatment of others and the lack of good manners in society, and are often articulated in a human rights discourse. The latter often believe the proper role of criminal law lies in symbolic *declaring* of something as inappropriate and wrong, because only by doing that can the state clearly show that it is taking some social nuisance seriously.[28] Both groups, unfortunately, seem to see the solution in criminal law. Both attitudes, regardless of where they come from, usually lead to more, rather than less, criminalisation, where minor deviations – previously considered not serious enough to warrant criminalisation or nuisances that one should probably nevertheless tolerate in an urban, pluralist, late modern society – suddenly become criminal, thus contributing to the 'widening of the net' and to the 'thinning of the mesh' (Cohen 1985). When criminalisation is no longer seen as the last resort of state intervention but, rather, as Ashworth and Zedner (2008: 43) put it, 'as a routine system for managing disorder there is little inhibition in employing it liberally to regulate minor forms of offence'.

In Slovenia, such (minor) socially undesirable behaviour is often criminalised through the 'back door', i.e. through the law on violations, which together with the criminal law proper comprise the 'criminal law' in the broad sense. In 2007, Slovenia, for example, criminalised indecent exposure, intrusive offering of sexual services or having sexual intercourse in a public place, insofar as the mentioned conduct 'disturbs people, causes alarm or indignation'.[29] The similarity in phrasing of the British definition of anti-social behaviour[30] is striking. A trend that can be discerned here is that criminalisation is aimed at protecting people's emotions or rather protecting people from negative, unpleasant emotions (or emotional states), i.e. protecting them from offence rather than from harm. The question is, of course, whether this really provides a legitimate ground for criminalisation; further, whether all emotions or emotional reactions equally deserve criminal law protection,[31] and whether this is still criminalisation on the basis of some actual harm or rather offence or even legal moralism.[32]

An additional trust-related problem, which has repercussions for criminalisation, is an acute distrust in the application of (criminal) laws, i.e. distrust in courts – in those entrusted with the delivering of justice. This distrust has its role in the processes of criminalisation as well, because the sentiment that the penalties are small, and too lenient, usually drives people to appeal to politicians to 'fix' the situation through legislation – to criminalise X or prescribe higher sentences – whereas the cause of the problem might lie somewhere else.[33] Truth be told, the Slovenian judiciary does face some real problems, particularly with backlogs built up in the past, which have led some people to appeal successfully to the European Court of Human Rights regarding violation of their right to be tried within a reasonable time. However, many of the objections (e.g. lenient sentences pronounced, the piling up of backlogs) are no longer valid, yet people still hold this perception.[34] As regards trust, it is people's perception that counts, not the actual fact. This represents a problem because it affects the institution's legitimacy, the social representation (Moscovici 1976) of the judiciary and ultimately people's behaviour because, if they believe the courts to be corrupt, unfair or that it will take too long for justice to be served, they may decide not to sue or press charges, but instead prefer to take the law into their own hands or just to do nothing, just leave it be. Although not doing anything about it (e.g. not deciding to prosecute or sue) is less problematic than taking the law into one's own hands (vigilantism), it leads to growing cynicism or apathy and further decline in trust. Moreover, these representations are difficult to shake, which is probably tied to the fact that they are neither value neutral nor entirely evidence-based. Seeing justice delivered, believing justice is being served (or not) is to a great extent an emotional experience. Because trust is proverbially difficult to earn and easy to lose, it is that much more important to keep it, because at least a minimum of trust in institutions is needed to maintain their legitimacy in a democratic society.

Conclusions

Criminalisation, it seems, fulfils so many desires and goals that it represents a symbolic vent for the societal ills of the day. Keeping it unprincipled, *ad hoc* and piecemeal, i.e. resisting a principled approach that would necessarily restrict the expansion of the law and be less driven by ill-thought-out emotion, may therefore be useful to some. The constant changing of criminal law (including violations), furthermore, gives the impression of society's evolution, which is particularly important for a society in transition. Seeing the 'light at the end of the tunnel' getting bigger is comforting and for a transitional society to know that transition is approaching its end and that we are coming out at the right end, even more so. This is perhaps also one reason why – whereas the initial criminalisation (criminalisation at the beginning of Slovenia's transition period) was particularly wrought with a desire to declare the state's and criminal law's rupture with the socialist past – the later criminalisation could progressively assume a more 'associational' nature with amended and new criminalisations that mirror our EU and international obligations, other European criminal legislatures and global social reality.

Additionally, in a context in which judicial application of laws is distrusted, it seems so much more important that at least the enacted law, the law on the books, is 'in order'. This may be particularly applicable to criminal law, which more than others spotlights what is wrong and (implies) what is right, and punishes those (or at least appears to punish those) who do wrong. What is perhaps also important is that, whereas people cannot participate in or influence the application of laws (judging), they can and do participate in criminalisation in the sense that they can and do influence the legislator. Parliamentary representatives, as opposed to the judiciary, do not hold permanent office and as such are much more dependent on the influence of people's views and sentiments. In this light, criminalisation should be seen as a broader social, not just legal or crime policy, phenomenon.

Transitional justice as the coming-to-terms with the communist past can be reflected in various ways. It can be, and often is, reflected through the application of (criminal) law. Some claim that Slovenia, lacking high-profile cases that would have brought to justice those who used to hold power and committed crimes under the previous regime, moved 'beyond the crimes of the past without the benefit of "truth and reconciliation"' (Kotar 2009: 201) and that transitional justice, therefore, did not form part of Slovenia's transition (Kotar 2009: 216). However, it can be argued that another way for transitional justice to manifest itself is through criminalisation or 'justice on the books', which is perhaps a more abstract, forward-looking and less directly punitive justice.[35] In Slovenia, the reckoning with the communist past was certainly, at least to a certain extent, achieved through black-letter law, which also seems to enjoy more trust than the judicial application of laws and is consequently particularly vested with people's perceptions and notions of justice.

It is worth remembering, however, that the situation in Slovenia reflects a particular, in many ways unique, transition of one socialist and federal republic to a democratic, independent country – a path that was in many ways different from other South European and East European transitions because the very starting point differed. The type of socialism Slovenia had was less stringent than, for example, in Bulgaria, Romania or Czechoslovakia, which only much later managed to break their ties with the Soviet Union. Because the level of oppression in Slovenia and Yugoslavia was lower than in other communist states, it is reasonable to conclude that Slovenia's experience of communism as well as Slovenia's transition was and is dissimilar to many others, and cannot therefore be generalised. Nonetheless, precisely because of this, the Slovenian experience contributes a critical insight into the diversity of forms of transitions, encouraging us to see these as situational and historical, rather than a single phenomenon.

Notes

1 Although 'transition' is more commonly used to describe the period after the 'turn' from communist, authoritarian to democratic, post-communist states, the singular form is somewhat misleading. What several CEE countries, in fact, experienced would be better termed 'transitions', as there were several of them, distinguished by kind (political, economic, cultural, etc.) as well as by place and time.

2 Until then, the Criminal Code of the Socialist Federal Republic of Yugoslavia (hereinafter: CC SFRY) was in force, its validity extended by the Constitutional Act for the implementation of the Declaration of Independence of the Republic of Slovenia (in Art. 4) on 25 June 1991.

3 The prevailing theory understands this notion not merely in the formal sense of unlawfulness but also in the more substantive way, i.e. as wrongfulness.

4 Art. 8, para. 1 of the CC SFRY.

5 Art. 7 of the CC RS (KZ 1994, Ur. l. RS, no. 63/97, 70/94, 23/99 and 95/2004).

6 The concept of social danger was a convenient tool to retroactively define something as criminal. The grounding of criminal law on the concept of social danger also enabled the Criminal Code to become a 'mere governmental instrument for execution of crime policy it deemed desirable' (Bele et al. 2008: 58).

7 It is worth mentioning, however, that Slovenia in a way already had its own Criminal Code. In addition to the CC of Yugoslavia, each federal republic passed its own CC as well – an option, granted to each republic with the 1974 Constitution of SFRY. On the territory of the Socialist Republic of Slovenia (SRS), the criminal legislature of SRS, criminal code of SFRY and criminal law provisions of other statutes of SFRY were thus applicable. See Art. 2, para. 1 of CC SRS, 1977.

8 It was not until May 2004 that Slovenia acceded to the EU.

9 Socialist law in itself was considered as a special case of Romano-Germanic civil law.

10 See the Proposed Amendments to the Criminal Code of the Republic of Slovenia (26 December 2003) for a more detailed list of legal instruments, which prompted the amendments.

11 Owing to the courts' backlogs and consequently perceived inefficiency, some people who were owed money turned instead to private enforcers to extort the money from their debtors. The state, wishing to put an end to this behaviour, reacted by turning to criminal law, i.e. criminalising such conduct.

12 This was mostly a reaction to the growing problem of unpaid alimonies.

13 *Zakon o odgovornosti pravnih oseb za kazniva dejanja* (ZOPOKD), Ur. l. RS, no. 59/1999 (12/2000 corrected), 50/2004, 98/2004–UPB1, 65/2008.

14 In general terms, the criminal liability of legal entities was, however, already envisaged in the Criminal Code of 1994.

15 Other CEE countries were experiencing similar or even more acute problems, driving Gosztonyi (2005) to name crime as one of the 'costs of transition'.

16 Criminal law scholars who were hired to draft the new Code have claimed that, as Slovenia does not yet have a sentence of life imprisonment, such a sentence, when pronounced by the Permanent International Criminal Court, could not be executed in Slovenia and that, in view of the fact that Slovenia signed and ratified the Rome Statute, the reception of this type of sentence would be the only right thing to do as it would show 'a correct attitude toward [this] international treaty' (Jakulin, in Bele et al. 2008: 78). Other academics, on the other hand, strongly objected to any debate based on the Rome Statute, emphasising the fact that the Rome Statute in no way obliges the state to raise its penalties or prescribe life imprisonment. Professor Alenka Šelih, in addition, found it 'contradictory that in the former totalitarian system [Slovenia], despite having a death penalty, had not used it for 50 years and the maximum prison sentence was 20 years, whereas in the democratic system, which is supposed to be less repressive and less punitive, we have first received 30 years of imprisonment and now, furthermore, a life sentence' (from an interview by Čepin Čander 2009).

17 Mobbing is a term for psychological bullying in the workplace. See, e.g., Wikipedia. Online. Available http://en.wikipedia.org/wiki/Mobbing (accessed 19 July 2011).

18 Art. 16 of KZ-1 (CC-1), Ur. l. RS, no. 55/2008.

19 Slovenia is not an isolated case in this lack of a principled approach to criminalisation however. In Britain, Ashworth has similarly noted that 'criminal offences are tacked on to diverse statutes by various government departments, and then enacted (or often, re-enacted) by Parliament without demur. There is little sense that the decision to introduce a new offence should only be made after certain conditions have been satisfied, little sense that making conduct criminal is a step of considerable social significance. It is this unprincipled and chaotic construction of the criminal law that prompts the question whether it is a lost cause. From the point of view of governments it is clearly not a lost cause: it is a multi-purpose tool, often creating the favourable impression that certain misconduct has been taken seriously and dealt with appropriately. But from any principled viewpoint there are important issues – of how the criminal law ought to be shaped, of what its social significance should be, of when it should be used and when not – which are simply not being addressed in the majority of instances' (Ashworth 2000: 225). However, some countries have developed such a principled approach, most notably Finland and Sweden.

20 In the Continental criminal legal system of the Germanic legal circle, we distinguish two areas of law that both comprise the so-called criminal law in the broad sense: one is criminal law proper or *stricto sensu* (offences mostly contained in the Criminal Code), and the other is the law on violations. Violations fall somewhere between the criminal law and administrative law, and much has been written on

which area befits violations best; the majority, however, seem to conclude that, because of its penalties and similarities in procedure (subsidiary), it is a type of criminal law.

21 Služba Vlade RS za zakonodajo (2008: 43).

22 *Resolucija o normativni dejavnosti*, Ur. l. RS, no. 95/2009 from 24 November 2009.

23 In order to responsibly make as well as evaluate the existing laws, one must philosophically reflect on morality and justice, as Simmonds (1986) correctly reminds us.

24 The theory on harm and the harm principle could also contribute to the Continental theory on the legal good (*Rechtsgut*). The 'legally protected interest' – a building block in both the concept of harm and the concept of a (violation of a) legal good – could be perceived as the two systems' point of convergence and the theory surrounding both concepts as informative for each other. For more detail, see Peršak (2007: 104–18).

25 Some talk about the horizontal and vertical dimensions of trust, the latter being confidence in institutions (see, for example, Letki 2005: 6). Others distinguish between 'trust' and 'confidence', with trust being based on value similarity and confidence being based on performance. See Siegrist et al. in Breakwell (2007: 142).

26 This decline is not specific for Slovenia or other post-communist countries (see, for example, the European Values Study), even if transition and a communist past have contributed to it. Distrust and cynicism have, for example, been labelled as 'the predictable legacy of communist rule' and overcoming this legacy appointed an 'immediate problem' for the post-communist systems of Eastern and Central Europe. See Mishler and Rose (1997: 419).

27 Particularly the rise in penal populism and issues of populist punitiveness (Bottoms 1995), which are often directing criminalisation efforts today.

28 The criminal law obviously always 'declares' wrongs; any criminalisation is also a declaration. However, this is a descriptive statement, a statement that cannot – to avoid running the risk of being accused of committing a Humean fallacy – be confused with a normative statement.

29 Art. 7, para. 3 of the new Public Order and Peace Act (*Zakon o varstvu javnega reda in miru* (ZJRM-1), Uradni list Republike Slovenije, no. 70/2006; in force since 21 July 2007). The fine prescribed for such a conduct ranges from 200 to 400 Euros. They are all considered types of 'indecent behaviour', which is statutorily defined as 'individual or group behaviour which causes alarm, agitation or threatens other individuals or a group, or when with insulting words harms the reputation of an individual or of a group or of an official in the middle of conducting their official business' (Art. 2, point 5 of ZJRM-1).

30 The British government first introduced the so-called ASBOs (Anti-Social Behaviour Orders) in the Crime and Disorder Act 1998. ASBOs are imposed on an individual who acts in an improper, antisocial way, which in the UK means acting 'in a manner that caused or was likely to cause harassment, alarm or distress to one or more persons not of the same household as himself'. Because they are civil orders only, a civil standard of proof (a balance of probabilities) is required to prove that the defendant has acted in this way. The order can be issued to a child of at least 10 years of age and usually prohibits certain behaviour or access to certain places – anything described in the order – for a minimum of 2 years (no maximum). Despite being civil orders, they do have a certain criminal law dimension, because a defendant who breaches the terms of the order without reasonable excuse can be convicted of an offence and face up to 5 years in prison, for which a magistrates' court is not allowed to grant a conditional discharge. See Ashworth (2000: 231).

31 Bottoms (2006), when analysing the British Crime Survey 2003/04, for example, concluded that respondents' emotional reactions to disorder (annoyance, anger, worry) contain a strong element of resentment. If emotions are to be protected by

(criminal) law, does resentment deserve equal protection to fear? Does annoyance or anger?

32 On the offence principle and legal moralism, see, generally, Feinberg (1985, 1988) respectively.

33 For example, in that the judges pronounce the sentence in the lower third of the sentencing interval or too quickly resort to delivering conditional (imprisonment) sentences.

34 On contemporary representations of the Slovene judiciary, see also Peršak (2011). For a more detailed account of the transition in the Slovene judicial system, see Novak (2003) and Igličar (2003).

35 What 'transitional justice' is or should mean remains, in fact, a contested terrain, where different concepts and approaches can be found. For a nice example of such heterogeneity, see the edited collection by McEvoy and McGregor (2008). See also the discussion in the Introduction to this volume.

References

Ashworth, A. (2000) 'Is the Criminal Law a Lost Cause?', *Law Quarterly Review*, 116: 225–56.

Ashworth, A. and Zedner, L. (2008) 'Defending the Criminal Law: Reflections on the Changing Character of Crime, Procedures, and Sanctions', *Criminal Law and Philosophy*, 2(1): 21–51.

Bavcon, L. (1994) 'Nastajanje novega kazenskega prava v postsocialističnih državah', *Revija za kriminalistiko in kriminologijo*, 45(4): 290–98.

Bele, I., Deisinger, M. and Jakulin, V. (2008) 'Uvodna pojasnila h Kazenskemu zakoniku (KZ-1)', *Kazenski zakonik (KZ-1 in KZ-UPB-1)*, Ljubljana: Gospodarski vestnik.

Bottoms, A. (1995) 'The Philosophy and Politics of Punishment and Sentencing', in C.M.V. Clarkson and R. Morgan (eds) *The Politics of Sentencing Reform*, Oxford: Clarendon Press.

——(2006) 'Incivilities, Offence and Social Order in Residential Communities', in A. von Hirsch and A.P. Simester (eds) *Incivilities: Regulating Offensive Behaviour*, Oxford: Hart Publishing.

Breakwell, G.M. (2007) *The Psychology of Risk*, Cambridge: Cambridge University Press.

Čepin Čander, M. (2009) 'Akademkinja dr. Alenka Šelih: Človekove pravice so padle v drugi ali celo tretji plan' (interview), *Dnevnikov objektiv*, 14 August 2009. Online. Available www.dnevnik.si/tiskane_izdaje/objektiv/1042291037 (accessed 15 November 2009).

Cohen, S. (1985) *Visions of Social Control*, Cambridge: Polity Press.

Feinberg, J. (1984) *Harm to Others – The Moral Limits of the Criminal Law*, New York: Oxford University Press.

——(1985) *Offense to Others – The Moral Limits of the Criminal Law*, New York: Oxford University Press.

——(1988) *Harmless Wrongdoing – The Moral Limits of the Criminal Law*, New York: Oxford University Press.

Gosztonyi, G. (2005) 'Crime as the Cost of Transition – A Social Policy Perspective: The Blind Hole of the European Union', in Z. Kanduč (ed.) *Kriminaliteta, družbeno nadzorstvo in postmodernizacijski procesi,* Ljubljana: Inštitut za kriminologijo pri Pravni fakulteti v Ljubljani.

Hungarian Presidency of the Council of the EU (2011) *Towards an EU Criminal Policy: Non-Paper for 10 June Council – Justice Minister's lunch*, 11155/11, Brussels. Online. Available http://eurocrim.jura.uni-tuebingen.de/cms/en/doc/1542.pdf (accessed 30 June 2011).

Igličar, A. (2003) 'The Judiciary in Slovenia: A Profession in Ascendancy', in J. Přibáň, P. Roberts and J. Young (eds) *Systems of Justice in Transition: Central European Experiences since 1989*, Aldershot: Ashgate Publishing.

Jambrek, P. (1992) *Uvod v sociologijo*, Ljubljana: Državna založba Slovenije.

Jellinek, G. (1878) *Die Sozialethische Bedeutung von Recht, Unrecht und Strafe*, Wien.

Kotar. Z. (2009) 'Slovenia', in L. Stan (ed.) *Transitional Justice in Eastern Europe and the Former Soviet Union: Reckoning with the Communist Past: 1*, New York: Routledge.

Letki, N. (2005) 'Investigating the Roots of Civic Morality: Trust, Social Capital, and Institutional Performance' (conference paper). Online. Available www.qog.pol.gu.se/conferences/november2005/papers/Letki.pdf (accessed 15 November 2009).

McEvoy, K. and McGregor, L. (eds) (2008) *Transitional Justice from Below: Grassroots Activism and the Struggle for Change*, Oxford: Hart Publishing.

Mill, J.S. (1991, orig. 1859) *On Liberty and Other Essays*, Oxford: Oxford University Press.

Mishler, W. and Rose, R. (1997) 'Trust, Distrust and Scepticism: Popular Evaluations of Civil and Political Institutions in Post-Communist Societies', *The Journal of Politics*, 59(2): 418–51.

Moscovici, S. (1976, orig. 1961) *La psychanalyse: son image et son public*, Paris: Presses Universitaires de France.

Novak, M. (2003) 'The Promising Gift of Precedents: Changes in Culture and Techniques of Judicial Decision-Making in Slovenia', in J. Přibáň, P. Roberts and J. Young (eds) *Systems of Justice in Transition: Central European Experiences since 1989*, Aldershot: Ashgate Publishing.

Novoselec, P. (2003) *Ustreznost klasičnega kazenskega prava v pogojih tranzicije*, Ljubljana: Uradni list RS.

Peršak, N. (2007) *Criminalising Harmful Conduct: The Harm Principle, its Limits and Continental Counterparts*, New York: Springer.

——(2011) 'Managing Insecurities and Expectations: Social Trust and Judiciary in Transition', *Shaken Order – Working Paper Series*, Sofia: Centre for Advanced Study. Online. Available www.cas.bg/uploads/files/Shaken%20Order/N.%20Persak.pdf (accessed 7 June 2011).

Proposed Amendments to the Criminal Code of the Republic of Slovenia, 26 December 2003. Online. Available www.dz-rs.si (accessed 15 November 2009).

Robinson, P.H. (2000) 'Why does the Criminal Law Care what the Layperson thinks is Just? Coercive versus Normative Crime Control', *Virginia Law Review*, 86(8): 1839–69.

Simmonds, N.E. (1986) 'Introduction', in N.E. Simmonds, *Central Issues in Jurisprudence: Justice, Law and Rights*, London: Sweet & Maxwell.

Služba Vlade RS za zakonodajo (2008) *Nomotehnične smernice*, Ljubljana: Uradni list RS.

4 Exodus from Lithuania

State, social disenfranchisement and resistance in an era of austerity

Arunas Juska and Charles Woolfson

Our society more closely resembles [a country] afflicted by disintegrating 18th century feudalism than an evolving liberal society.

Krescencijus Stoškus (2011)

Introduction

Lithuania today is a society in crisis, not just economically but socially and politically. A massive outward migration triggered by the start of global economic recession and the collapse of the housing bubble in 2008 now threatens the future viability of the nation-state. As the economic crisis intensified, unemployment grew from a relatively low level of 4.1 per cent in 2007 to 18.3 per cent in the second quarter of 2010 with a concomitant increase in emigration from 26,600 in 2007 to 83,200 in 2010 (Statistikos Departamentas 2011a). This was the highest level of emigration since 1945 and comparable only with the extensive depopulation of the country during World War II. Since the restoration of independence in 1990, out of a population of some 3.7 million, 615,000 had left the country (Statistikos Departamentas 2011b); three-quarters were younger people (up to 35 years old), many of them educated and with jobs in Lithuania. By 2008, the emigration rate from Lithuania was the highest among EU countries (2.3 per 1,000), and double that of the next highest country, Latvia (1.1 per 1,000) (Statistikos Departamentas 2009: 7).

However staggering these numbers are for such a small country, there were substantial grounds for speculation that the actual number of people who had left the country was even higher, because official statistics substantially undercounted migration flows. A better accounting of migration by state agencies following the introduction of mandatory health insurance fees for those not declaring departure gave an increase of nearly four times from the previous year of those officially registered as leaving. As 2010 was already the second year of severe economic crisis in Lithuania, the scale of previous underestimates can perhaps be better calibrated to around 150,000 persons who had departed officially, and many more unofficially.

Forecasts for the period 2008–35 suggest a demographic decline by a further 10.9 per cent, one of the highest rates in the EU (after Bulgaria and Latvia) (Eurostat 2008). The 2011 population census seemed only to confirm these grim prognostications. Demographers had previously proved to have been too optimistic in their forecasts (the latest issued in 2010) and had overestimated the size of the Lithuanian population by about 200,000. Instead of the forecasted 3.24 million, the census found that, by 2011, Lithuania's population was only just over 3 million (3.054 million) (Saukiene 2011a).

The spectre of rapid depopulation exacerbated by deep economic recession has conjured metaphors of hopelessness and despair among commentators. For some, emigration *from* Lithuania was characterised as turning into an evacuation *of* Lithuania; parallels have been drawn between the historically high rates of suicide in Lithuania (among the highest in the world) and massive emigration from the country, both being interpreted as forms of 'self-destruction' of the nation (Kukulas 2010); still others have lamented that, even during the darkest years of Stalin's terror and deportations, the population had not declined as steeply as it has done in the years from 2008 to 2010.

How has this state of affairs come about? Can it really be said that recent flows of migration represent a migration that is qualitatively new? The contention of this chapter is that the mass 'exodus' of the population is not a simple reflection of rising unemployment, or far less of administrative changes in the registration system for those leaving the country. It goes beyond a simple response to economic adversity and signifies a deeper rejection by a significant proportion of the population of the very society into which they have been socialised.

In order to grasp the full measure of this crisis, the changing relationship between the individual, society and the state is examined. It is argued that austerity policies that were adopted by the Lithuanian government in response to global recession and the bursting of the housing bubble in 2008 reconfirmed significant changes in prevailing interpretations of the social compact between the state and society, between individuals and the wider polity. We trace the beginnings of this transformation to the *de facto* absence of criminalisation of entrepreneurial practices during the period of privatisation of state property in the early 1990s. Then we analyse the impact that the political crisis of 2003, resulting in the impeachment of President Rolandas Paksas for his ties to Russian criminal elements, had on the relationship between the individual, state and society. Finally, we outline how, since the start of the 2008 recession, an ongoing erosion in the social contract was compounded by a new wave of mass emigration from Lithuania and a growing trend towards *de facto* criminalisation of protest in the country.

For analytical purposes, two distinct meta-narratives are identified that describe state–society relationships in post-independence Lithuania. We interpret meta-narratives as systems of meanings used to describe social phenomena by offering a narrative that reveals and emphasises some aspects, while concealing and making invisible others. We argue that an ethno-national political paradigm was prevalent from the *perestroika* era in the late 1980s and until the first few years of independence in the 1990s. The strengths and appeal of this ethno-nationalist discourse as a binding ideology in the building of the new independent post-Soviet Lithuania are charted. Second, we describe the events of the late 1990s and the early 2000s that led to this socially optimistic meta-narrative being supplanted by a new discourse of 'social disenfranchisement' (*socialinis beteisiškumas*) as the expectations of the population were disappointed and political disillusion set in. Third, it is suggested that, as the most recent global economic downturn and economic crisis gripped the country, a popular perception of the oppressive nature of the state grew. This was associated with the imposition of austerity measures and the growing authoritarianism of the state as expressed in the militarisation of policing and the restriction and criminalisation of political protest. Growing authoritarianism in Lithuania, in turn, only intensified the 'social disenfranchisement' discourse, leading to claims that the state was being transformed into a 'feudal oppressor' imposing a 'social serfdom' (*socialinė baudžiava*) on the country, which, it was asserted, had become the impetus for an entirely new kind of migration, an 'exodus' from social and political bondage.

The ethno-national discourse

The term ethno-nationalism refers to both '… loyalty to a nation deprived of its own state and the loyalty to an ethnic group embodied in a specific state, particularly where the latter is conceived as a nation-state' (Conversi 2002: 2). It also refers to a primordial perception of the nation and nation-state as strongly related to ethnicity. The individual belongs to the ethnic group by birth and this belonging cannot vanish. Consequently, this means that nation is seen as an ethnically homogeneous group and constructs itself through a differentiation between 'We' and 'The Other' (non-ethnic Lithuanians or non-Lithuanians in general) (Rona-Tas 1996). The vision that only independent statehood would provide a guarantee of the ethno-national survival of the Lithuanian nation against the threats of denationalisation and Russification had been the driver of popular mobilisation in the struggles for political independence from the Soviet Union (Brubaker 1996). Independent statehood was also intended to allow the re-integration of Lithuania into Western Europe from which it had been forcefully 'torn away' by the Soviet occupation, as well as providing an opportunity for the socio-economic and political modernisation of the country within the framework of liberal democracy and a market economy.

Peculiar to this ethno-political vision was the presumed synergy or unity between the state and 'the people' or the *tauta* (ethnic Lithuanian people or *Volk*) (Klumbyte 2006b). Its roots were in the late nineteenth and the early twentieth-century formulations by Lithuanian intellectuals, who interpreted the state as the highest level of development of the nation as well as the precondition for its historical continuity and self-preservation. In this discourse, the role of the individual was subsumed under his/her membership of the nation (Krickus 1993; Valantiejus 2003). Although internal divisions among different socio-economic groups within the *tauta* existed (such as class, generation, occupation, region and, to some extent, gender), they were by far outweighed by the social solidarity produced by external (geo-political and ethno-cultural) threats to the survival of this small nation situated among the much larger and more powerful neighbours of Germany, Russia and Poland.

This vision was carried forward and developed during the late 1980s in the struggles for independence by the political movement of *perestroika* and the Lithuanian independence movement, the *Sąjūdis*. The search for a new unifying ideology was well articulated by one prominent spokesperson for the nascent Lithuanian independence movement: 'It is necessary for us to become citizens of Lithuania. It would be our common joy … we would have common duties and common concerns' (Juozaitis 1990: 1). Crucial to the consolidation of this constructed unified national identity of 'common duties' and 'common concerns' was the resurrection or re-invention of symbols of nationhood. This required the negotiation of an uncomfortable authoritarian (largely proto-fascist) legacy from the inter-war era of Lithuanian national independence. The resurrection of Lithuanian national identity also entailed the contemporary reinstatement of the primacy of the Lithuanian language over Russian, the rejected language of the Soviet 'occupier', although still the first language of a significant Slavic minority, especially of the working population (Russian, Ukrainian and Belarussian emigrants to Lithuania and their descendants, as a result of industrialisation policies pursued by Moscow in the region). With uncertain legitimising resources of past history, and consumed with the expurgation of its more contemporaneously imposed Soviet identity, the nascent independence movement in Lithuania resorted to the creation of a sometimes spurious vocabulary of symbolic national unity.

Following independence in 1991, previous discourses on the ethno-political contract between the state and the *tauta* underwent gradual transformation. In part, this happened because of the deep economic recession in the early 1990s, which saw living standards plunge; the appearance, for the first time, of mass unemployment; the dismantling of Soviet-style social benefits and widespread chaos in social and political life. Thus, after what had been an intense period of mass participation, the political demobilisation of society followed, as day-to-day economic survival became the single most important preoccupation of the citizenry. A decade later, with the integration of Lithuania into NATO, followed by accession as a new EU member state in the mid-2000s, unifying societal geo-political threats to independent statehood were declining. Moreover, the spread of consumerism and the coming of age of the first post-socialist generation born in independent Lithuania speeded up the decline of ethno-nationalism. Children of the last Soviet generation of Lithuanians neither personally knew nor cared much about their parents' sacrifices and concerns with the survival of the nation, which to them seemed increasingly irrelevant, out-of-date and even quaint. As Donatas Katkus, a prominent conductor and professor of music, succinctly put it, 'Lithuania had fallen out of fashion' (Katkus 2010).

At the same time, of even more importance to the erosion of ethno-political bonds between the *tauta* and the state were growing internal divisions among various groups within society, with conflicting and, in some cases, openly antagonistic interests. During the 1990s, these divisions focused on attempts to influence or even 'capture' the state by powerful interests, often with criminal associations, especially in the dubious process of privatisation of state property and restitution of land to its pre-World War II owners (Hellman et al. 2000). The implementation of privatisation and land reforms was characterised by underdeveloped and contradictory rules and regulations and their lax enforcement; widespread corruption; shady semi-criminal and criminal deals; and the rise (and very often overnight fall) of banks and their millionaire directors.

As the economic engine of the transition process to the market, according to its most enthusiastic proponents, privatisation of Soviet-era public property was supposed to make workers 'co-owners' and fulfil 'social justice' and equity objectives (Lithuanian Free Market Institute 2000). Yet within a matter of a few years, or sometimes even within months, the majority of privatisation vouchers handed out to workers in former state enterprises were sold on the black market for cash and ended up in the pockets of enterprise managers on extremely favourable terms, jarring with 'public expectations … strengthened by propaganda, promising high dividend rates, high profitability of the shares and higher living standards' (Maldeikis 1996: 3). So great was public unrest concerning 'corruption and the influence of organised criminal groups' over the process of privatisation that it was temporarily halted (Maldeikis 1996: 16). The distribution of assets before auctions, via 'payments to organised criminal groups for the right to acquire particular assets, selling of "insider" information by officials and their participation in [the] privatisation process', had a significant impact in producing a popular negative view of the whole process (Maldeikis 1996: 16). The stripping of business assets, insider-dealing, the creation of 'daughter firms', organised theft and nepotism thus produced a largely 'criminalistic', but not, as yet, 'criminalised', entrepreneurial class. The absence of criminalisation of those perceived as stealing public property proceeded concomitantly with the rapid pauperisation of large segments of the population who increasingly regarded their impoverishment by privatisation as *prichvatization* (slang for the Lithuanian version of the Russian word 'appropriation' or 'swindling') (Klumbyte 2006a). The rise of a discourse on *prichvatization* signalled a profound transformation in public understanding of the relationship between society and the state. During privatisation, the state had ignored not only the collective interests of the *tauta* but also basic principles of social justice, thus powerfully undermining social solidarity.

In 2003, populist anger, driven in part by the injustices committed during privatisation, led to the election of President Rolandas Paksas under the banner of restoring 'justice and law' in the country. However, he was quickly impeached for ties with Russian criminal elements and removed from office. For many of Paksas's supporters, the president's impeachment represented a blatantly illegal attempt by 'the elites' to dispose of a president intent on investigating and prosecuting shady deals of the privatisation era. In other words, for pro-Paksas loyalists, the majority of whom were pauperised former Soviet industrial and agricultural workers, impeachment seemed only to confirm their view of the state acting as an oppressive entity protecting the owners of the 'swindled' national property (Laurenas 2004; Juska 2007: 248–49).

Up until the onset of the deep economic recession in 2008, the discourse of social disenfranchisement of the *tauta* was confined mostly to less educated, older people and those residing in rural areas and provincial townships, the so-called 'losers' of transition (Wallace and Abbott 2007). However, the collapse of a housing bubble in 2008, the acute financial crisis and the imposition of harsh austerity measures by the government in 2009 led to a significant reinvigoration of the emergent discourse of social disenfranchisement. In an era of austerity, the critique of the state as oppressive and unaccountable, and serving the interest of the few, sharply intensified.

In particular, a growing *authoritarianism* on the part of the Lithuanian state was identified in two forms: first, in the undemocratic process in which crisis austerity measures were imposed by the *Seimas* (the Lithuanian parliament) 'in the dead of the night'; second, in the way in which the Lithuanian state responded to social unrest through an increasing militarisation of policing and a pronounced trend towards the *de facto* criminalisation of political protest. This growing state authoritarianism in turn fed into public perceptions of 'social disenfranchisement'. Some commentators began to argue that Lithuania had descended to the level whereby social relations had assumed a new quality – an oppressive 'social serfdom', almost feudal in nature and imposed upon the *tauta* by a hostile state. Thus came the peculiar rise among Lithuanian intellectuals, commentators and a broader public in the use of terminology associated with a *feudal* social order (Klisyte 2008; Saukiene 2010; Maslauskaite 2011; Sipaviciene 2011).[1] It was this new seemingly archaic metaphor that began to be used in constructing discourses on relationships between the state and society (Mickūnas and Savukynas 2011) and the economy (Ramanauskas 2010; Vaičaitytė-Cruz 2011). How then to explain the currency that this discourse of feudal oppression achieved? What do these amorphous terms 'social disenfranchisement' or 'social serfdom' signify in the public imagination?

The nation in state bondage: the 'social serfdom' mytheme

Following Lévi-Strauss (1967), we can identify these emerging discourses on social serfdom as 'mythemes' or myths. In ethnography, myths are defined as sacred stories explaining the origins of the world or how the world and the creatures in it came to have their present form. Myths represent a way by which societies transmit knowledge and values across generations, and orient us to what is, what could be and what should be. Therefore, the discourse of social serfdom could be interpreted as a mytheme or a lay explanation of the deep economic, social and political crisis in the country that was reaching existential proportions.

Lévi-Strauss argued that mythemes tend to be organised in terms of binary opposites (such as, in his examples, good/evil, raw/cooked, male/female), and that the myth taken as a whole functions to interpret and provide meaning to human experience. For present purposes, 'social serfdom' can be represented as a dramatic struggle between good and evil. The evil in such a narrative is constituted by the *valdininkija* or state bureaucrats who, in alliance with big business or the oligarchs, have all but captured the state and are using it for their own enrichment and aggrandisement. The good, in turn, is represented by the exploited, deceived, neglected Lithuanian nation or 'the people,' the powerless and abused victims of domination.

Within this mytheme, perceptions vary on just how 'evil' the state bureaucrats are: from cynical 'rent-takers' (using Marxian terminology), who take as much as they can everywhere they can, to a combination of rent-taking with simple incompetence and impotence, lack of empathy, inability to address practical problems and neglect, expressed in a superior and condescending attitude on the part of many bureaucrats that it is not they who are the servants of the public, but rather, the public is there to serve them.

Why has there come to be a preference for the use of conceptions such as 'social disenfranchisement' or 'social serfdom' rather than the plain, simple – and certainly more contemporary – notion of 'state corruption'? Arguably, during the early 1990s, the two most prominent issues that dominated public life in Lithuania were state corruption and crime. Why did corruption as a rallying point for criticism and protest not meet the need for a coherent narrative of the ills besetting the nation? Here, there are two sets of factors that need to be taken into account: first, the capacity of the Lithuanian political system to channel and dissipate political protest without addressing popular grievances; and second, a significant actual decline in corruption and increasing professionalism of the state administration more generally.

The last two cycles of elections in the country (in 2004 and 2008) produced major turnover in the political elites. In both elections, winning parties/blocks were formed a short time before the elections, and were swept to power by populist anger, only to disintegrate shortly after.[2] Despite the volatility of the political system, and a quick turnover of politicians in response to the profound dissatisfaction of the electorate, in the view of the public, there was little substantial improvement either in the way politics functioned in Lithuania or in the conditions of aggrieved segments of the population such as, for example, pensioners, teachers, librarians or police officers.

In pondering why this was the case, the philosopher Vytautas Rubavicius proposed to differentiate two types of democracy: the first being formal, procedural democracy, which he contrasted with the second, 'democracy of substance and culture' steeped in 'political decency and political responsibility' (Spraunius 2006). In Lithuania, the former currently prevails, in which the ruling elites have learned to successfully manipulate the media and elections using sophisticated public relations technologies; creating images, emotions and expectations among segments of the electorate, while at the same time appropriating the state institutions in their own interest and ruling the country through various types of insider-trading and 'back-room deals'. Thus, echoing previous popular disillusionment with privatisation, the failure of democratic politics is summed up in the brutal observation that 'there is no justice in Lithuania' (Bogdanas 2010).

The second reason why simple corruption fails to provide an adequate explanatory narrative results from a decline in this type of crime in Lithuania in general. Especially since Lithuania's accession to the EU in 2004, there has been a noticeable increase in professionalism and standards of state service (although, arguably, from a low initial benchmark and with notable exceptions such as the underfunded state medical care system). Despite complaints about corruption in the press (often mixed with complaints about incompetence, excessive bureaucratisation and/or impotence), the rule of law has significantly strengthened in the last decade in Lithuania. Consider the tax collection agency in Lithuania. Until now, there have been virtually no recorded high-profile cases of corruption involving revenue service personnel, although tax authorities tend to be among the most corruption-prone agencies worldwide. The very fact that, in 2004, the president was impeached for his dealings with the Russian mafia suggests that the rule of law was upheld in the country with all its drawbacks and inefficiencies – an unimaginable development in Soviet times or in most of the other former republics of the USSR, including Russia itself. Similarly, two other officials occupying the highest ranks in government and parliament – the former chairman of the Labour party and minister of the economy, Viktoras Uspaskich, and the former chairman of the *Seimas*, Viktoras Muntianas – were both prosecuted on corruption charges and removed from office. Finally, since 2009, there has been a noticeable increase in the number of economic crimes being prosecuted. An increasing emphasis on law enforcement in relation to white-collar crime has been part of a strategy pursued by the government in order to clamp down on the growing scope of the informal economy and tax evasion following the imposition of austerity measures. At the same time, new emphasis on prosecution of white-collar crimes was used by Kubilius's administration to legitimise its austerity policies in the eyes of the electorate, ostensibly by showing that the burdens of economic hardship and sacrifice were being 'equally borne' (ELTA ir Lrytas.lt 2009). Hence, the result has been neither criminalisation nor decriminalisation, but rather a real decline in crimes of financial corruption accompanied by an increased referral of such crimes to the criminal justice system.

Thus, instead of a discourse on corruption, there came about a prevalence of new discourses on social serfdom, social disenfranchisement and an emphasis on procedural democracy, all of which represented a moral and ethical critique of the ruling classes or *valdininkija*. The major problem with these discourses is that they denounce state functionaries as a class, but fail to identify these 'evil' state bureaucrats as individuals, and to identify which positions they occupy, who neglected their duties and who acted as 'overlords' of the 'Lithuanian nation', making it unlikely that they will be brought to justice and prosecuted. Instead, the framing of narratives of 'social serfdom' and 'social disenfranchisement' indicate an insidious subversion of the social contract between the state and the people, expressed in the humiliating dependency and the helplessness of citizens when dealing with state officials: pervasive obstructionism in issuing official papers and their condescending attitude towards ordinary people. In turn, this has strengthened a widespread perception that matters can only be resolved through friends and acquaintances rather than through official channels, propagating a general sense of pervasive social uncertainty and vulnerability and a deep mistrust of employers, courts and state institutions and indeed of authority in general (Markeviciene 2010). This then is the background to the dramatic explosion in social anger on the streets of the country as austerity gripped the nation.

January 2009 street riots in Vilnius

The shock of austerity was made all the more severe because it contrasted with several boom years between 2004 and 2007 in which economic growth at around 7 per cent of GDP per annum was among the highest in the EU. During the 'fat years', the Lithuanian population had come to believe in the miracle of a 'tiger economy' with vistas of unending prosperity. At one stage in 2007, property prices per square metre in the capital exceeded those in Stockholm. As the global economic crisis engulfed Lithuania, and the housing bubble burst, the economy entered a freefall that made the impact of recession in the Baltic region the most severe among the EU countries. In response, governments across the Baltic states introduced radical austerity measures: so-called 'internal devaluation', which included deep wage and social benefit cuts, significant cuts in public expenditure and extensive rewriting of protective labour legislation, all without popular or democratic consultation with representative bodies such as trade unions, small business representatives or organisations speaking for selected groups such as students and pensioners who were to be hardest hit by austerity measures. The result was unprecedented mass protests on the streets, which ended in rioting in the capital city in January 2009 and ongoing protests up and down the country (Mullett 2009; Thomas 2010).

Social disorder on this scale had never before been seen in the post-socialist period and in a fundamental respect was a turning point in the political development of the country since its independence from the Soviet Union. That it was a deep shock to the ruling authorities who had previously relied on the famed 'passiveness' of the Lithuanian population is probably an understatement. For the government of the day, only organised conspiracy on the part of 'Lithuania's enemies' could explain the scale and intensity of the disorder, which saw hundreds arrested and tear gas and rubber bullets used against demonstrators outside the *Seimas*. Yet, beyond conspiracy theories, which largely failed to gather traction, there emerged a new set of discourses, entirely incompatible with the unified assumptions of the previous ethno-nationalist discourse of an independent, democratic and free Lithuanian statehood.

The prevailing interpretation of the January 2009 rioting in the country's news media was couched in the new meta-narrative of 'social serfdom'. In this narrative, the individuals and/or the nation were represented as powerless victims of an oppressive state. Accumulated grievances, expressed in a form of powerless victimhood and provoked by the secretive imposition of severe austerity measures, had erupted in social disorder directed at the institutions of the oppressive state. More specifically, the clashes between demonstrators and police were interpreted as a 'lashing out' or as a spontaneous reaction of either supra-individual *tauta* or 'the people' or ordinary individuals who had snapped because of being subjected to prolonged and humiliating victimisation by the state; the state here considered as having been hijacked by arrogant politicians and state bureaucrats in alliance with the oligarchs and other big-business interests. The riots therefore represented a 'spontaneous eruption of detestation and loathing accumulated through the years by the people towards the Lithuanian government' (Leparskas 2009); 'natural reaction of ordinary people to … cynicism and isolation … natural expression of despair and distrust of the government [that constituted] the radical political stance of the *tauta*' (Paulauskas 2009); 'outburst of social anger' (Bartasevicius 2009); 'expression of protest by civil society against corrupt government which for 18 years pauperised, deceived, and exploited the people' (BSN 2009); and a 'spontaneous outburst of the disaffection pervasive in society' (Mazeikis 2009).

The other socio-psychological term used in analysing the unrest was that of 'alienation', expressed in two forms: 'either as falling on the knees and worshiping the next forthcoming saviour' (a reference to a succession of populist Lithuanian political leaders) 'or by hopeless resignation with curse words and a bottle on the table' (Aleksandravicius 2009). Finally, some commentators pointed to the psychological mechanisms of displacement, when the hatred and violence become directed at oneself (drinking, suicide, hopelessness, violence in the home, reckless driving leading to disproportionally high injury and fatality rates, etc.). These destructive impulses were (purportedly) displaced and expressed as hate of the government that just a few months ago was elected by the same people who were now rioting by throwing stones and spitting at the *Seimas* (Juskaite and Paskauskas 2009).

What is particular to these discourses on confrontation with the state is the absence of acknowledgement of any civic group or organisations that could mediate the collective interests of individuals or the people in their relationships with the state. Instead, individuals (the term 'citizens' is absent in press coverage; the preferred term being *zmogus* or fellow) or the *tauta* are depicted as being confronted by a towering Leviathan (the state). Even when groups and organisations are present, they are treated in the media as if they are either invisible and/or insignificant (like labour unions). With the exception of pronouncements by the leaders of the fringe Marxist and socialist groups, dismissed out of hand because they sounded too much like the discredited Soviet-era slogans about workers' power and socialism, etc., there was little record in the press of protesters, including labour union leaders, calling citizens to organise, unite and try to collectively address their grievances.

There were demands for social justice, but these demands were for social justice for *tauta* and/or for respect for the dignity of the individuals who were literally swindled in broad daylight by the government that each had elected. Those who were protesting were described not as representatives of organised or communal interests (such as labour unions) but as representatives of social–demographic categories such as pensioners (especially evident in the depiction of elderly ladies throwing stones at the *Seimas*, which could be considered as the epitome of the wrath of the *tauta*, the nation, in its righteousness), small business owners, students, workers and unemployed people. It is in this context that we can understand the *de facto* criminalisation of protests that was about to take place.

The slide to authoritarianism

Following the 16 January 2009 riots, authorities across the country, and particularly in Vilnius, increasingly attempted to curtail, restrict and criminalise public protests. Thus, a growing number of arbitrary administrative prohibitions and restrictions on political protest were put in place that in some cases resembled a virtual bureaucratic sabotage of rights to free speech and public assembly. As a result, in the last 2 to 3 years, litigation and resort to court action have become an almost routine necessity for civic groups and political parties wishing to obtain permits for public rallies in the face of hostile municipal authorities, which now routinely delay, drag out, restrict and prohibit demonstrations. The often clumsy and heavy-handed way in which the authorities began to restrict political rights guaranteed by the constitution only further strengthened the perceptions of growing 'social disenfranchisement' among the public.

Reasons given for denying permits for protests have tended to be twofold: the high likelihood that protests might threaten public safety and security; and the supposed presence of messages on the internet instigating protesters to turn to violence (Kranauskas 2011). Failure to obtain a permit and the holding of an unauthorised public event was punishable by a fine from 500 to 2,000 Lithuanian Litas (approximately \$200 to \$800) or administrative arrest for up to 30 days (LR ATKP 188–7 1994).

For example, when the Vilnius municipality declined a permit to the Socialist People's Front (SPF), a relatively small leftist organisation, to hold a rally in front of the *Seimas* on 16 January 2010 to commemorate the first anniversary of the previous episode of unrest, the court reversed the decision of the local authority. Facing hostile courts, the municipality changed its strategy in dealing with permits and chose to drag out and delay decisions on petitions so that little time would be left for applicants to appeal rejections and for the courts to review the ensuing complaints. Thus, on 15 January, the SPF was finally issued with court permission to hold its rally the following day. However, this gave insufficient time to prepare for the event, thus blunting the effectiveness of the protest (Gabrilaviciute 2010).

Similar developments occurred a year later. On 22 December 2010, the main confederation of labour unions, the Lithuanian Confederation of Labour Unions (LPSK), had filed the required papers at the municipality requesting permission to hold a rally in front of the *Seimas.* Vilnius municipality offered the unions the option of relocating the rally either to the suburbs or to the city park, which at that time of the year was covered in a layer of snow up to a metre thick. The union leadership felt that such suggestions of alternative locations constituted a thinly veiled mockery and refused to reconsider their request for a central location in front of the *Seimas.* In response, the municipality delayed issuing a negative decision on the rally until 5 January 2011, although according to law it should have been processed within three working days. The labour unions contested the municipality decision in court and won. On 14 January, the court ordered the municipality to issue a permit to the labour unions to enable them to organise the rally. However, it took three more days, until 17 January, for the municipality to issue a permit for a rally that was to have been held a day earlier, on 16 January.

When confronted by journalists about why it took so long to comply with the court order, the mayor's office produced complicated logs of faxes sent and telephone calls made, including arguing (in self-justifying bureaucratic speak) that the court ruling was issued after the time of day (4pm) when the municipality offices were still open to process public business. To the protest organisers, this exchange with journalists was suggestive of arrogance and condescension by the city's bureaucrats, who effectively denied their legitimate request through an administrative manoeuvre, by claiming that in closing their offices clerical staff were simply acting 'according to the laws of the Lithuanian Republic on work hours …' (Samoskaite 2011).

This scenario was repeated in February 2011, but with a new absurd twist. In early December 2010, the trade union confederation applied for, but was denied, a permit to hold a rally on 16 January 2011. The rally was to demand an increase in the minimum wage, reversal of cuts in pensions, the introduction of progressive taxation and subsidies for the poor to cover increased heating and water expenses. Instead, a permit was granted for a rally to be held on 19 February in front of the *Seimas*, but with a stipulated maximum of 2,249 individuals. The municipality claimed that this was the number of participants that the square could safely accommodate.

Meanwhile, the unions had recruited close to 1,500 of their members throughout the country to attend the rally and had made arrangements for their transportation and stay in Vilnius. However, three days before the rally, a prominent national poet had died. In order to accommodate the funeral, the unions announced a change in the time of their own proposed event. On 17 February, just two days before it was due to take place, Vilnius municipality unilaterally rescinded the labour unions' permit for the rally. Humiliating pleas by union leaders to the town hall functionaries that such large-scale events with more than 1,000 participants were costly for unions to organise and required time to prepare (i.e. buses were already hired, speakers lined up, voice amplification equipment rented, stage prefabricated, demonstration paraphernalia prepared) were of no avail. After pleading to be allowed to exercise their civil rights, in the end, the unions were forced to acquiesce to the municipality's decision and reschedule the event for March (ELTA 2011a).

Nor was this the first time that local authorities had tried to set limits on the number of protesters in a seemingly arbitrary manner. For example, just a year before, Vilnius municipality had issued a permit for a protest rally in front of the *Seimas* to a coalition of groups '[f]or high quality and affordable higher education in Lithuania' but had limited it to only 300 participants (Delfi 2009).

Furthermore, public protest actions such as pickets are only permitted without prior permits if they are restricted in numbers to 10 persons or fewer. For civic and political groups organising public protests, such impositions of limits on numbers increasingly appear to be one more way in which the authorities have progressively sought to restrict rights of assembly guaranteed by the constitution. Recently, the major national daily newspaper commented that, if the trend towards imposing new restrictions on public protests were to continue, then 'soon we will need to acquire [individual] tickets from authorities in order to participate in rallies' (Ignatavicius 2011).

What is particularly troubling and what tends to strengthen perceptions of a regime of 'social serfdom' are the attitudes of the authorities towards political protest in general. These attitudes are rooted in the country's political culture inherited from and shaped by the legacy of the Soviet era. As tensions and discontent in society increased, so did the authoritarian reflexes of the authorities, especially with regard to public protests; these are treated not as an expression of the long-lamented absence of the civic engagement of various groups in society, nor as a form of civic activism, dialogue with the authorities and an exercise of constitutional and human rights. Instead, the authorities, from the prime minister and the speaker of the *Seimas* down to local municipalities, tended to regard these localised protest actions as disturbances, as annoyance, as superfluous noise, to be pushed out of sight to remote suburbs. There was also a tendency to demonise protesters as 'an enemy' which by the very fact of gathering in public had declared 'a war' on authorities, and thus delegitimised this form of democratic participation as gatherings of boorish, uncultured and easily manipulated simpletons (ELTA 2011b).

This perspective was best summed up by the speaker of the *Seimas*, comparing the proposed labour union rally to protest against austerity measures with the onslaught of Soviet troops on the Supreme Council of Lithuania during the last days of the Soviet Union (Saukiene 2011b). These protests were characterised by the prime minister as 'calls for disturbances', which he refused 'to dignify with a response' (Zelniene 2011). One *Seimas* member even went so far as to ponder openly that 'we already had [*Seimas*] windows broken; if people do not understand that it is inappropriate, then [protest rallies] should be banned' (Kranauskas 2011).

Para-militarisation of policing

The authoritarian attitudes that strengthened social disenfranchisement also found their expression in the increasing centralisation and militarisation of policing of political protests in Lithuania. For example, King and his colleagues argued that, by the mid-2000s, police reforms initiated a decade earlier and directed at depoliticisation, demilitarisation and decentralisation of the police, including institutionalising democratic and international standards which adhered to the law and due process, had stalled. Instead, there was a notable progression towards the militarisation of police units, strategy and tactics (Koci 1998; King et al. 2007).

In the press, this trend was dubbed a drift towards the 'Belarussification' of policing: the increasing use by authorities of repressive strategies and tactics similar to the ones employed by the authoritarian leader Alexander Lukashenko in neighbouring Belarus (Paulauskas 2011; Vasiliauskiate 2011). Today, participants in protests are regularly confronted with centrally coordinated and directed detachments of police dressed in military-style fatigues, wearing masks and helmets and armed with batons, rams, tear gas and rubber bullets. Thus, in preparation for a rally organised by labour unions in October 2009, the police established barricades with entry posts to check the rucksacks and holdall bags of participants. Mounted police and special riot units were present, dressed in military fatigues with flak-jackets and accompanying police dogs. Extensive visible surveillance and video-recording of the 371 participants in the rally was conducted. Mostly, the participants comprised kindergarten staff, school teachers and doctors. To the watching public and to the participants in the demonstration, it appeared that the oppressive police presence was an attempt at intimidation, there being almost as many police personnel present as protesters (Vysniauskiene 2009).

Similar intensive surveillance scenarios have occurred at other demonstrations, involving even quite small groups of protesters. In Kaunas, a protest organised by the right-wing Lithuanian Freedom League on 23 January 2009 saw 300 police officers guarding about 400 protesters (Karaliunas 2009). On 4 February, a rally organised by the leftist Socialist People's Front outside the *Seimas* saw around 500 police officers in bulletproof apparel and with (anti-barricade) battering rams guarding around 200 protesters (Traceviciute 2009).

At times, these scenes were eerie in their resemblance to Soviet-era policing tactics, when intimidation by overwhelming force and extensive surveillance was used against small groups of protesting dissidents. By early 2011, the police had created a special fenced-in area near the *Seimas* with manned security check points and a command and control headquarters from which the police and the interior ministry leadership were able to watch live video feeds from multiple surveillance cameras around the *Seimas* buildings.

These developments represent a shift towards policing by threat of violence rather than policing by consent and therefore could be interpreted as a constituent element of a broader trend towards 'social disenfranchisement' in Lithuania. Militarised policing is derived from and resembles war-fighting tactics, with military-style intelligence and equipment provision and training geared to achieve battlefield success. This militarisation is also expressed in the strengthening of what was, in essence, the military ethos of police officers, especially in their interaction with citizens, publicly manifested in military-style deployments and strict subordination and obedience to superiors, with the goal to attack and destroy. Virtually absent from both the discourse and the practice of austerity public order policing has been the core democratic acknowledgement that protesters were not 'the enemy' and that demonstrations and rallies were not 'hostile operations' to be either disrupted or prevented altogether; far less that these demonstrators are also citizens exercising their constitutional rights and the role of policing is to enable them to do so in safety and security.

It is hard to quantify the cumulative effects of routine denial and bureaucratic 'run-around' for civic, labour and political groups wishing to publicly express their disagreement with the authorities when this is combined with an increasingly militarised style of policing political protest. Such trends are a matter for serious concern in a democratic society. This was reiterated by the minister of internal affairs, Raimundas Palaitis, who was highly critical of what he called 'bureaucratic games' played by various government and municipality officials with the citizenry. Forcefully stating that the wishes of the general public to hold protest rallies 'do not constitute a threat to public order', he warned that denials by 'the bureaucrats' of the rights of citizens to publicly protest against decisions taken by their government could have 'serious negative consequences for public order' (Palaitis 2011). The alternative to the legitimised voice and participation is the individualised exit of the disillusioned and disenfranchised. It is this social mood that underlies the current cataclysmic outward migration previously detailed.

Conclusions

This chapter has charted the changes in discourses in contemporary Lithuania from the ethno-national political unity of state and the nation into that of 'social serfdom'. It has been suggested that the full symbolic meaning of the January 2009 riots lay in marking the end of the post-socialism era and the beginning of a new period in Lithuanian history marked by a deep crisis of national confidence, the disintegration of social solidarities and existential questions of national survival. The exhaustion of the political project of independence has become interwoven with a deep loss of confidence by the people in the elites and in their capacity to assure even the basic (demographic) survival of the nation. Austerity and the imposition of draconian cuts in living standards have provided the economic basis for a rupture of the social fabric.

Austerity has also produced a purported crisis of public order in which political protest has been increasingly obstructed by the forces of state power and administratively proscribed by the apparatus of government. A *de facto* criminalisation of protest developed through a combination of arbitrary administrative obstruction of legitimate protest coupled with the intimidation of protesters through militarising policing. This slide towards authoritarianism represents a denial of democratic voice, which has fed into perceptions of an absence of social justice in society and reinforced already existing feelings of social disenfranchisement. The unprecedented riot scenes in Independence Square in January 2009 with crowds attacking the *Seimas* while at the same time chanting *Lietuva, Lietuva!* (Lithuania, Lithuania!) presented a troubling paradox of both simultaneous loyalty and disaffection. Arguably, awareness that these events signified the end of a period in Lithuanian history and a beginning of something new could not be entirely disguised. More specifically, these protests drew a line under what could be considered the era that had started with *perestroika* in the late 1980s, and had as its ultimate goal the re-creation of the independent statehood of Lithuania.

Thus, what could be called a unified 'nationalising' project had been irretrievably fractured. The state as the ultimate embodiment and guarantor of the survival of the Lithuanian nation that had been re-established by the enormous sacrifices of the Lithuanian people had turned against them as a hostile force. The same *Seimas* building that unarmed people in 1990 and 1991 had surrounded to protect from the possible onslaught of the Soviet Army was now deeply despised and pelted with stones and eggs. Nationalism as a unifying idea that had driven the country since the late Soviet period seemed to be, if not discredited, then certainly antiquated and exhausted; deep antagonistic divisions in society were (at least for that moment) revealed; the idea of the state as the ultimate expression of the solidarity of the nation had evaporated; and the vacuum that was left behind was filled by outpourings of bitter disappointment and recriminations, widespread cynicism, apathy and withdrawal. It seemed as though Lithuania was standing at the beginning of a new uncharted era of increasing social tensions, turmoil and open conflicts.

As the discourse of ethno-national unity between the *tauta* and the state had been important in shaping political mobilisation during the *perestroika* era, so today are discourses on social disenfranchisement and social serfdom in influencing societal reactions to austerity measures imposed by the government since 2009. It is in these contexts that we must understand the changing Lithuanian definitions of the criminal, not through formal changes in law but rather, first, through the differential application of administrative law and the altered focus of policing and criminal justice practices and, second, through a critique and rejection of the symbiosis between a 'criminalistic' (in origin) but manifestly not criminalised entrepreneurial class and the country's political elites. This interpellation of state-sponsored authoritarianism and elite delegitimation has resulted in the perception of an imposed 'feudal' domination over society in which the prevailing social system is experienced by many as harsh, arbitrary and unjust.

Contemporary Lithuanian migration speaks to fundamentals of systemic socio-political failure: the denial of democratic voice, the dissipation of social trust, the disintegration of previous solidarities, the atrophy of reserves of social resilience and, above all, the socially destructive outcomes of a failed post-Soviet experiment in neo-liberal free market reconstruction. However, it also speaks to these 'absences' in a 'silent manner' in which root causes remain concealed, as the migrants depart one by one. Lithuania seems to be a society in *dis*integration in which economic crisis and austerity have created a tipping point for a population now increasingly *dis*located within both polity and society and uprooted by a mass migration of unprecedented proportions.

This haemorrhage of the population raises key issues for the future sustainable development of the country. It occurs against a background of serious demographic decline and a post-crisis economic prognosis for eventual recovery that is at best uncertain. Yet, the most profound cost is levied in the regressive loss of a social dimension to human existence. Lithuania has found itself as a nation with severely diminished reserves of social solidarity to solve its common problems. Viewed in a wider prism of European integration, the eastern enlargement of the European Union was intended to permit the cross-border migration of people within the Community. In the case of Lithuania as a new member state, it has done so, but in a paradoxical manner. Free movement is not realised as a beneficial result of the consolidation of the single market, even though that market had offered (at least for a brief period) seemingly unlimited access to sought-after material goods. Rather, Lithuania's embrace of the free market has paved the way for movement of an 'unfree' population in which migration has become an 'exodus'.

Notes

1 Most recently, the term 'legalisation of social serfdom' was used by critics of the new labour legislation, which was to significantly increase the discretion of employers in hiring and firing employees and making decisions on compensation (Paleckis 2010; Tvirbutas 2010). There are now criticisms of 'serfdom' in the higher education system; workers voice their protests against 'serfdom' imposed on them by their employers; and Catholic clergy are arguing about 'spiritual serfdom' prevalent in society.

2 In 2004, the majority of votes were won by Victoras Uspaskich's newly created Labour Party (LP). Its leader was a charismatic self-made millionaire who immigrated to Lithuania from Russia just before the collapse of the USSR and transformed himself from a machinist on the factory floor to a paternalistic (to his

workers and their families) owner of factories and farms and a trader in oil and gas. Journalists christened him 'duke of Kedainiai' because he was able to convert an economically depressed township into a struggling but bouncing back 'company town'. A number of high-profile millionaire-businessmen joined Uspaskich, thus making the LP the 'party of entrepreneurs'. However, the LP quickly fell apart because of internal infighting and corruption scandals as arrest warrants were issued against two top LP figures – Uspaskich himself and the speaker of the *Seimas* Victoras Muntianas. In the 2008 elections, the LP was swept out of power by the newly created National Resurrection Party led by TV personality A. Valinskas. The NRP came second (after the conservatives), and Valinskas became the speaker of the *Seimas*. Valinskas had become internationally known when he organised a 'Miss Prison of Lithuania' live competition in one of the Lithuanian prisons. There were copycat programmes of 'Miss Prison' in other countries as well. In both cases, this shake-up of Lithuanian politics demonstrated the power of rising segments of the elite in the country: *nouveau riche* capitalists-turned-populists and media personalities/magnates (on the Lithuanian scale). However, in less than a year, the NRP became embroiled in bitter infighting and split apart, while Valinskas, after some outrageous statements and public disagreements with the President, was removed from the *Seimas* speakership in a no-confidence vote.

References

Aleksandravicius, E. (2009) 'Neapykanta valdziai kyla is neapykantos sau', *Delfi.lt*, Vilnius, 16 February. Online. Available www.delfi.lt/archive/print.php?id=20590891 (accessed 10 August 2011).

Bartasevicius, V. (2009) 'Naudinga, bet ar teisinga', *Lietuvos Rytas*, Vilnius, 9 February. Online. Available www.lrytas.lt/print.asp?data=&k=news&id=12341294971232894795 (accessed 10 August 2011).

Bogdanas, R. (2010) 'Vsio zakono, arba tvirtablauzde nasle', *Delfi.lt*, Vilnius, 27 September. Online. Available www.delfi.lt/news/ringas/lit/rbogdanas-vsio-zakono-arba-tvirtablauzde-nasle.d?id=36952117 (accessed 10 August 2011).

Brubaker, W.R. (1996) *Nationalism Reframed*, Cambridge: Cambridge University Press.

BSN (2009) 'Visuomenininkai skelbia prisiimantys atsakomybe uz riauses', *Delfi.lt*, Vilnius, 5 February. Online. Available www.delfi.lt/archive/print.php?id=20433979 (accessed 10 August 2011).

Conversi, D. (2002) 'Conceptualizing Nationalism. An Introduction to Walker Connor's Work', in D. Conversi (ed.) *Ethnonationalism in the Contemporary World. Walker Connor and the Study of Nationalism*, London: Routledge.

Delfi (2009) 'Dideliems mitingams Vilniuje – raudona sviesa', *Delfi.lt*, Vilnius, 24 February. Online. Available www.delfi.lt/news/daily/lithuania/dideliems-mitingams-vilniuje-raudona-sviesa.d?id=20712233 (accessed 10 August 2011).

ELTA (2011a) 'Anuliavus leidima, profsajungos ruosiasi nesankcionuotam mitingui', *Delfi.lt*, Vilnius, 17 February. Online. Available www.delfi.lt/news/daily/lithuania/anuliavus-leidima-profsajungos-ruosiasi-nesankcionuotam-mitingui.d?id=42122195 (accessed 10 August 2011).

——(2011b) 'Protesto kulturos nebuvimas uzkerta kelia tikrosios demokratijos link', *ATN.LT*, Vilnius, 10 February. Online. Available http://politika.atn.lt/straipsnis/73487/protesto-kulturos-nebuvimas-uzkerta-kelia-tikrosios-demokratijos-link (accessed 10 August 2011).

ELTA ir Lrytas.lt (2009) 'Nusikalstamumas Lietuvoje auga, sparčiausiai daugėja finansinių nusikaltimų ir nelegalios prekybos atvejų', *Lietuvos Rytas*, Vilnius, 28 July. Online. Available www.lrytas.lt/print.asp?data=&k=news&id=12487746651247040151 (accessed 10 August 2011).

Eurostat (2008) 'Population Projections 2008–60', 26 Brussels. Online. Available http://europa.eu/rapid/pressReleasesAction.do?reference=STAT/08/119 (accessed 10 August 2011).

Gabrilaviciute, L. (2010) 'Prie Seimo gincijosi mitinguotojai ir policininkai', *15min.lt*, Vilnius, 15 January. Online. Available www.15min.lt/naujiena/aktualu/lietuva/prie-seimo-gincijosi-mitinguotojai-ir-policininkai-56–79966 (accessed 10 August 2011).

Hellman, J., Jones, G. and Kaufmann, D. (2000) *'Seize the State, Seize the Day' State Capture, Corruption, and Influence in Transition, Volume 1*, Washington, DC: World Bank. Online. Available http://econ.worldbank.org/external/default/main?pagePK=64165259&theSitePK=469372&piPK=64165421&menuPK=64166093&entityID=000094946_00091405494828 (accessed 10 August 2011).

Ignatavicius, T. (2011) 'I busimus mitingus – tik su bilietu?', *Lietuvos Rytas*, Vilnius, 9 February. Online. Available www.lrytas.lt/-12972302331296824670-%C4%AF-b%C5%ABsimus-mitingus-tik-su-bilietu.htm (accessed 10 August 2011).

Juozaitis, A. (1990) 'Statement of Member of the Sąjūdis Initiative Group', *Lituanus, Lithuanian Quarterly Journal of Arts and Sciences*, 36(2). Online. Available www.lituanus.org/1990_1/90_1_06.htm (accessed 10 August 2011).

Juska, A. (2007) 'Discourses on Rurality in Post-Socialist News Media: The Case of Lithuania's Leading Daily "Lietuvos Rytas"', *Journal of Rural Studies*, 23(2): 238–53.

Juskaite, J. and Paskauskas, J. (2009) 'Ekspertai: Situacija blogesne nei atrode', *Delfi.lt*, Vilnius, 16 January. Online. Available www.delfi.lt/news/daily/lithuania/article.php?id=20119210 (accessed 10 August 2011).

Karaliunas, A. (2009) 'Trims protestuotojams teko vienas tvarkos saugotojas', *Lietuvos Rytas*, Vilnius, 23 January 2009.

Katkus, D. (2010) *Lietuva išėjo iš mados. Pokalbiai su Donatu Katkumi*, Vilnius: Laisvos Valandos.

King, M., Koci, A. and Bukauskas, A. (2007) 'Policing Social Transition: Public Order Policing Change in Lithuania' *Policing*, 1(4): 428–37.

Klisyte, R. (2008) 'Migruojantys zmones', *Moteris*, September.

Klumbyte, N. (2006a) 'The Alchemy of Cynicism: Authority, Power, and the Post-Socialist State in Lithuania', *Defining Region: Socio-Cultural Anthropology and Interdisciplinary Perspectives. Acta Historica Universitatis Klaipedensis XIII, Studia Antropologica*, Part 2(II): 31–46.

——(2006b) 'Ethnographic Note on Nation: Narratives and Symbols of the Early Post-Socialist Nationalism in Lithuania', *Dialectical Anthropology*, 27 (3–4).

Koci, A. (1998) 'Reform of the Police in Hungary and Lithuania: Empirical Findings on the Policing of Public Order', *Innovation*, 11(3): 307–14.

Kranauskas, L. (2011) 'Mitingu menuo (ne)patekejo', *Atgimimas*, Vilnius, 18 February. Online. Available www.atgimimas.lt/Diskusija/Mitingu-menuo-ne-patekejo (accessed 10 August 2011).

Krickus, R. (1993) 'Lithuania: Nationalism in the Modern Era', in I. Bremmer and R. Taras (eds) *Nations and Politics in the Soviet Successor States*, New York: Cambridge University Press, 157–81.

Kukulas, V. (2010) 'Gelbekite savo zmogiskuma uzsieniuose', *Delfi.lt*, Vilnius, 13 September. Online. Available www.delfi.lt/news/ringas/lit/vkukulas-gelbekite-savo-zmogiskuma-uzsieniuose.d?id=36466159 (accessed 10 August 2011).

Laurenas, V. (2004) 'Politine krize Lietuvoje 2003–4 metais', *Politologija*, 35(3): 1–34.

Leparskas, A. (2009) 'Kodel sausio 16-toji – reiksminga diena Lietuvos istorijoje?', *Lietuvos Rytas*, Vilnius, 19 January. Online. Available www.lrytas.lt/-1232387269123 1091455-kod%C4%97l-sausio-16-oji-reik%C5%A1minga-diena-lietuvos-istorijoje.htm (accessed 10 August 2011).

Lévi-Strauss, C. (1967) *Structural Anthropology*, Garden City, NY: Anchor Books.

Lithuanian Free Market Institute (2000) *Privatization in Lithuania, Analysis*. Online. Available www.freema.org/Research/Privatisation.phtml (accessed 10 August 2011).

LR ATKP 188–7 (1994) 'Lietuvos Respublikos administraciniu teises pazeidimu kodeksas 188–7 straipsnis', *Lietuvos Respublikos Seimas*, Vilnius, Online. Available www.infolex.lt/ta/103787:str188–7 (accessed 10 August 2011).

Maldeikis, E. (1996) 'Privatisation in Lithuania: Expectations, Process, Consequences', CERT Discussion Papers, 96/3, Edinburgh: Heriot-Watt University. Online. Available www.som.hw.ac.uk/cert/wpa/1996/dp9603.pdf (accessed 10 August 2011).

Markeviciene, E. (2010) 'Gelbėjimo ratas migrantu rankose', *Kelias*, Vilnius, 8 July. Online. Available www.delfi.lt/archive/article.php?id=34259167 (accessed 10 August 2011).

Maslauskaite, A. (2011) 'Žmonės nebenori gyventi priešiškumo kupinoje aplinkoje', *Bernardinai.lt*, Vilnius, 14 January. Online. Available www.bernardinai.lt/straipsnis/ 2011-01–14-pagyre-virsininkas-kazkas-ne-taip/55973 (accessed 10 August 2011).

Mazeikis, G. (2009) 'G. Mazeikis: taikus mitinguotojai buvo uzmirsti', *Delfi.lt*, Vilnius. Online. Available www.delfi.lt/archive/print.php?id=20273830 (accessed 10 August 2011).

Mickūnas, A. and Savukynas, V. (2011) 'Kiek Europos yra Lietuvoje?', *Lietuvos Rytas*, Vilnius, 5 August. Online. Available www.lrytas.lt/-13125171431312315936-kiek-europos-yra-lietuvoje.htm (accessed 10 August 2011).

Mullett, A. (2009) 'Vilnius Protesters Clash with Police', *The Baltic Times*, Riga, 21 January.

Palaitis, R. (2011) 'Ministras: Pasekmiu gali tureti ne protestai, o draudimai juos rengti', *Delfi.lt*, Vilnius, 13 January. Online. Available www.delfi.lt/archive/print.php? id=40770163 (accessed 10 August 2011).

Paleckis, A. (2010) 'Darbo santykiu liberalizavimas – kelias į socialine baudziava', *Kontrastai*, Vilnius, 1 June. Online. Available www.balsas.lt/naujiena/392544/darbo-santykiu-liberalizavimas-kelias-i-socialine-baudziava/rubrika:naujienos-lietuva-politi kutribuna (accessed 12 December 2011).

Paulauskas, D. (2009) 'Riauses ziniasklaidoje', *Delfi.lt*, Vilnius, 20 January. Online. Available www.delfi.lt/archive/print.php?id=20192578 (accessed 10 August 2011).

——(2011) 'Protestas ar gedulas?', *Delfi.lt*, Vilnius, 13 January. Online. Available www. delfi.lt/news/ringas/lit/dpaulauskas-protestas-ar-gedulas.d?id=41004741 (accessed 10 August 2011).

Ramanauskas, T. (2010) 'Ekonominė baudžiava XXI amžiuje', *Veidas*, Vilnius, 16 July. Online. Available www.veidas.lt/ekonomine-baudziava-xxi-amziuje (accessed 10 August 2011).

Rona-Tas, A. (1996) 'Post-Communist Transition and the Absent Middle Class in East-Central Europe', in Victoria E. Bonell (ed.) *Identities in Transition: Eastern*

Europe and Russia after the Collapse of Communism, Research Series/Number 93, Center for Slavic and East European studies, University of California at Berkeley.

Samoskaite, E. (2011) 'Leidima mitinguoti sausio 16-aja isdave sausio 17 d', *Delfi.lt*, Vilnius, 19 January. Online. Available www.delfi.lt/news/daily/lithuania/leidima-mitinguoti-prie-seimo-sausio-16-aja-isdave-sausio-17-d.d?id=41018363 (accessed 10 August 2011).

Saukiene, I. (2010) 'Emigrantai: patriotizmas baigiasi, kai prasideda skurdas', *Delfi.lt*, Vilnius, 12 December. Online. Available www.delfi.lt/archive/print.php?id=39618591 (accessed 10 August 2011).

——(2011a) 'Pagal prognozes po 50 metu Lietuvoje nebus ne 2,5 mln. gyventoju', *Delfi.lt*, Vilnius, 17 July. Online. Available www.delfi.lt/news/daily/lithuania/pagal-prognozes-po-50-metu-lietuvoje-nebus-ne-25-mln-gyventoju.d?id=47694043 (accessed 10 August 2011).

——(2011b) 'Profsajungos jauciasi izeistos I. Degutienes kalbos, bet mitingo atsisako', *Delfi.lt*, Vilnius, 14 January. Online. Available www.delfi.lt/news/daily/lithuania/profsajungos-jauciasi-izeistos-i-degutienes-kalbos-bet-mitingo-atsisako.d?id=40813445 (accessed 10 August 2011).

Sipaviciene, A. (2011) 'Blogiausia, kad, užuot kovoję dėl savo teisių ar bandę kažką keisti Lietuvoje, lietuviai emigruoja', *Veidas*, Vinius, May 21. Online. Available www.veidas.lt/blogiausia-kad-uzuot-kovoje-del-savo-teisiu-ar-bande-kazka-keisti-lietuvoje-lietuviai-emigruoja (accessed 10 August 2011).

Spraunius, A. (2006) 'V. Rubavicius apie lyderi ir lietuviška demokratija', *Delfi.lt*. 31 January. Online. Available www.delfi.lt/archive/article.php?id=8652988 (accessed 10 August 2011).

Statistikos Departamentas (2009) *Lietuvos Gyventoju Tarptautine Migracija 2008. International Migration of the Lithuanian Population 2008*, Vilnius: Statistikos Departamentas.

——(2011a) *Deklaruotos ir nedeklaruotos emigracijos srautai. Požymiai: amžius, statistiniai rodikliai ir metai*, Vilnius. Online. Available http://tinyurl.com/723oudy (accessed 10 August 2011).

——(2011b) 'Statistikos Departamentas: per 7 men. emigravo 33 139 Lietuvos gyventojai', *Delfi.lt*, Vilnius. 18 August. Online. Available www.delfi.lt/archive/article.php?id+48679343 (accessed 10 August 2011).

Stoškus, K. (2011) 'Savivalė prieš neteisingumą, arba pilietinio neįgalumo anatomija', *Delfi.lt*, Vilnius, 27 July. Online. Available www.delfi.lt/archive/print.php?id=47957977 (accessed 10 August 2011).

Thomas, L., Jr. (2010) 'From Lithuania, a View of Austerity's Costs', *The New York Times*, New York, NY, 1 April.

Traceviciute, R. (2009) '"Fronto" svogunai atsirugs biudzetui', *Lietuvos Zinios*, Vilnius, 4 February.

Tvirbutas, S. (2010) 'Dabartine valdzia kurpia baudziavos istatymus', *Valstietis*, Vilnius, 26 May. Online. Available www.valstietis.lt/Pradzia/Naujienos/Lietuvoje/Dabartine-valdzia-kurpia-baudziavos-istatymus (accessed 10 August 2011).

Vaičaitytė-Cruz, L. (2011) 'Lietuvos ekonomikos apyaušris', *Atgimimas*, Vilnius, 8 August. Online. Available www.atgimimas.lt/Komentarai/Lietuvos-ekonomikos-apyausris (accessed 10 August 2011).

Valantiejus, A. (2003) 'Early Lithuanian Nationalism: Sources of its Legitimate Meanings in an Environment of Shifting Boundaries', *Nations and Nationalism*, 8(3): 315–33.

Vasiliauskiate, N. (2011) 'Apie viesas erdves, Sajudi ir Nauja Kaire', *Delfi.lt*, Vilnius, 31 January. Online. Available www.delfi.lt/news/ringas/lit/nvasiliauskaite-apie-viesas-erdves-sajudi-ir-nauja-kaire.d?id=41475635 (accessed 10 August 2011).

Vysniauskiene, B. (2009) 'Kiekvienam piketuotojui – po ginkluota policininka', *Lietuvos Rytas*, Vilnius, 22 October.

Wallace, C. and Abbott, P. (2007) 'Talking about Health and Well-Being in Post Soviet Ukraine and Russia', *Journal of Communist Studies and Transition Politics*, 23(2): 181–202.

Zelniene, L. (2011) 'A. Kubilius: mitingas – ne vieta deryboms', *Diena.lt*, Vilnius, 7 February. Online. Available www.diena.lt/naujienos/ekonomika/a-kubilius-mitingas-ne-vieta-deryboms-331078 (accessed 10 August 2011).

5 The reform story of the Finnish penal code

Ideological turns and waves of modernisation

Kimmo Nuotio

Eastern Europe has experienced major ideological shifts in how crime is considered in legal terms. Socialist views differed significantly from Western liberal traditions in which the focus was on the individual rather than the state and society. The various chapters in this book address the issues of justice in transition, examining what happened to criminal laws in the processes of transition. Criminal law is an interesting field in this regard, because it reflects political circumstances and state ideologies, while also constituting a structure as well as a social practice, both of which seem to develop slowly and resist sharp turns. History and tradition impose many limitations on reform and change.

This chapter examines the development of the penal code of Finland. One could say that Finland does not belong to this grouping of transitional societies because it has undergone a linear and gradual development. Finland has had a relatively long history of democratic governance, especially since the beginning of national independence in 1917. Finland did not experience such significant upheaval during those critical years after the fall of the Iron Curtain when Eastern European states underwent the most fundamental changes brought about by the collapse of state socialism (see Eser and Arnold 2000). In one sense, this is correct. The case of Finland differs from that of the new democracies. However, what makes the Finnish case interesting is that profound changes and redefinitions which have had a significant impact on criminalisation and the criminal law occurred nevertheless.

I will not focus on political transitions and how they leave traces in criminal law. Rather, I will look at other kinds of transition, such as when criminal law is being rethought and reframed and when its functions are being negotiated. General social modernisation and the development of legal and political culture are reflected in the conscious reform of criminal law as well as in the perhaps unconscious processes of cultural adaptation and adjustment.

I will look specifically at the comprehensive criminal law reform that was started in the early 1970s and has now been completed. Over almost four decades, this project had to adapt to various events and circumstances that led to a situation in which the end product was far from that foreseen by the early visionaries and drafters of the code.

The law reform project could be likened to the story of the building of the Cathedral of Siena. The building plan was great and ambitious, but the Black Death led to a halt in its construction. The long nave of the church was thus never finished, and a smaller nave had to serve the function originally destined for the bigger one. One wall stands alone outside. Nevertheless, the cathedral is a magnificent piece of architecture. It may be that today the time for such comprehensive reforms is over, as late modern society no longer seeks to address such comprehensive issues, focusing on small-scale problems instead.

The classical penal code of 1889

Like building the cathedral, the penal code project was also an ambitious one, and its failure to complete the original design envisaged for it is no cause for embarrassment. In the case of the penal code reform, the intention was that a large and concise penal code would be written that would contain all the central pieces of penal legislation. Its starting point in the 1970s was the awareness that the existing code (from 1889–94) was simply very much outdated, as was manifested in its underlying values, which were representative of the nineteenth-century legal and political context. In one sense, the aim of reform was to reproduce the ideas of the old code and restore its respect and its validity by revising it completely, ensuring that it could continue its life for another 100 years.

The situation in the 1970s resembled the experience of a century before when the governing Swedish code of 1734, which had been regarded as badly outdated, led to a very ambitious project of recodification of Finnish penal law. The old Swedish code was very harsh and religiously inspired, even Mosaic, in its values; it was conceptually based upon the authority of the absolutist monarch rather than on enlightened ideas. Gustavus III introduced some minor adjustments in the late eighteenth century, but the body of the original law still prevailed. Originally, it was not a codification in the modern sense; rather, it was a proto-codification. Execution was demanded for dozens of crimes, a penalty abolished in practice in the 1820s.

During the first part of the nineteenth century, the legislature had been at a standstill for political reasons. Finland was clearly behind Sweden in this respect. The striving for reform after the mid-nineteenth century led first to the preparation of minor but very significant partial law reforms in 1866. This finally led to complete reform and the adoption of what is still the current penal code of 1889 (in force since 1894). During the nineteenth century, the prison system was enlarged and the system of punishment was widely debated. Prison sentences at that time were based upon so-called 'progressive' ideas of reform and rehabilitation. Humanistic and philanthropic ideas circulated in academic writings (Blomstedt 1964). Towards the end of the century, such beliefs vanished and in practice only the 'desert' principle was left.

This nineteenth-century reform project was informed by German and Scandinavian criminal law scholarship. The two main architects of the new penal code were the Hegelians, Professors K.G. Ehrström and Jaakko Forsman. Of these two, Ehrström was more inclined to emphasise rehabilitation as the goal of punishment (Wahlberg 1989). The spirit of the code was classical, and the more sociological insights of the von Liszt school, for instance, remained very limited (especially in comparison with the Norwegian penal code of 1902 or the Danish code of 1930). Forsman supported so-called absolute theories of punishment, according to which the punishment can only have its basis in the offence committed (Forsman 1900: 26). He had been a key figure in the second drafting committee preparing the new code. Forsman's job was also to sell the code to the general public by ensuring that it was not radical, which rendered it easier to gain public support (Ylikangas 1989: 26–29).

It was also a matter of timing that the penal code did not imbibe as much influence as it might have done from the sociological school and its criminal policy orientation. During the late 1880s, scholars were not yet familiar with these new ideas. Forsman, for example, denied the merits of determinist approaches to criminal law and penal policy. The reform of the penal code became an important national issue because the Russian authorities did not like the idea that the Grand Duchy of Finland might have a penal code of its own, especially one that had been prepared by the Finnish authorities without any significant contribution from the imperial authorities. This controversy caused delays in the political processing of the code, but did not finally prevent the code from being implemented (Tyynilä 1989).

The Finnish penal code can be described as classical in style. As is often found in such codes, it was divided into a 'general' part (setting out the principles and doctrines governing the whole of the criminal law) and a 'special' part, which sets out and defines the specific crimes. The system of sanctions was simple, with very few exceptions, and reflected the 'desert' principle. Formal values of legal certainty prevailed. Corporal punishment was abolished, with imprisonment and fines being the main penalties. The death penalty remained but was subsequently abolished. The death sentence had already been replaced in peace time by deportation to Siberia.

The focal point of the code was the crime, not the criminal, although reduced capacity led to a formally reduced punishment, and minors (despite having penal liability starting at the age of 15) could plead their minority as a mitigating circumstance. The general part of the code was rather limited because the legislature did not wish to provide fuel for what it saw as 'unnecessary' academic debate. The legislature, it was felt, should only build on doctrine that was academically settled. Nonetheless, new types of offences were devised to adapt to new needs and societal transformations. A new category of generally dangerous offences (*Allgemeingefährliche Straftaten*) was created following the Prussian model, addressed by a new Chapter 34. Blasphemy was no longer the most heinous of crimes and offences against religion were downgraded in significance. The penal code also meant the end of *Polizeirecht* (police law), because minor breaches of various church and other rules were accorded sanctions in a specific part of the code, and no longer elsewhere. In the continental tradition, the boundaries between the broad concept of police law and that of penal law had been blurred, something of which Enlightenment thought had been critical (Nuotio 2010). The Finnish penal code was an effort to distinguish between criminal law proper and the lesser offences.

The first period of reform

The first part of the twentieth century was marked by new trends. Deterministic views gained the upper hand *vis-à-vis* those of the classical school. In the 1920s, Allan Serlachius prepared a comprehensive proposal for criminal law reform, but this did not lead to actual reform. During the first decades of the new code, the criminalisations in the special part were not profoundly altered, because most of the reforms addressed issues concerning the system of sanctions. A day-fine system was introduced in 1921, but the reasons behind this were more practical than ideological, as high inflation rendered this reform necessary. According to the day-fine system, the blameworthiness of the offence is expressed in the number of day-fines, in which the unit is always determined to be proportionate to the income and wealth of the individual. This system had already been discussed for some decades in academic circles, but Finland was the first country to implement it. Conditional imprisonment had also already been introduced in 1918. This reform was motivated mainly by the post-civil war context, a more lenient sanction than a custodial sentence being needed specifically for responding to the offences of the defeated rebels (on this development, see Das finnische Strafgesetz 2006).

The long-term incarceration of recidivists on the basis of 'dangerousness' was introduced in 1931, a sign that the sociological school was gaining significance. The sociological school had argued that the system of sanctions should be designed according to the dangerousness of the offender in question. Typically, a two-track system was proposed. Juvenile criminal justice was developed as a special legislative system for young offenders, and legislation was enacted during the war years in 1940. This did not, however, go so far as to introduce juvenile courts, although a separate prison for juveniles was introduced. This approach belonged to the Nordic model, which aimed to keep child welfare and criminal justice separate. Finnish criminological research also started to develop in the 1930s (Marttunen 2008).

The second period of reform

The mid-twentieth century can be described as more prevention-oriented than earlier times. So-called special prevention was emphasised. This treatment ideology was based on the belief that criminal justice works. And if it does not work, at least it controls dangerous individuals. Medicalisation was one of the key forms of treatment in closed institutions and was the general model for treating various forms of illness and deviant behaviour. The crucial criminological presupposition appeared to be that 'bad people' commit crimes, which need to be responded to, whereas 'ordinary people' are not criminals. Biological explanations of criminality were emphasised to a greater extent than individual or even social causes of crime. Criminal justice was regarded as a very natural thing, a natural reaction of society to the challenges posed by crime. The general political climate was also predominantly conservative as a result of the civil war, in which the Red Guards had been so overwhelmingly defeated, and even after World War II, it took time for Finnish society to recover. It was not until after World War II that the socialist and communist parties returned fully to political life (the Communist Party, in particular, had been prohibited after the civil war).

A tension was created by the challenges that sociological insights posed for the underlying basis of a code whose criminological origins lay in the nineteenth century. The focus on the 'just desert' of the classical school was an insufficient basis for addressing phenomena such as 'habitual offenders', 'deviant minors' and 'insane criminals'. By the 1960s, preventive interventions had reached their high point. However, recidivism was treated harshly, with hundreds of people convicted of theft being incarcerated and labelled as 'dangerous' recidivists.

In the Finnish model, which had a classical legalist inheritance, the treatment ideology was never really powerful and most of the potential excesses of that model were avoided. The neighbouring countries, Sweden and Denmark, which were the most immediate reference points, had gone much further down that line. The reasons why Finland did not follow had more to do with their different national histories than any ideological factors. Finland had undergone a civil war in 1918 and two exhausting wars against the Soviet Union in 1939 and 1941–44. The post-war increase in crime rates resulted in much greater repression in Finland than the Nordic average. It was not until the late 1960s that these differences started to alert academic scholars in Finland (Lappi-Seppälä 2009: 335). In Finland, social development was rapid from the 1960s onwards. Urbanisation and industrialisation progressed rapidly, and the educational system grew together with the augmentation of social welfare structures. A certain radicalisation affected social and political life, which also reflected European trends such as the student movement.

The modern period of reform

During the 1960s, the older generation of legal academics continued to support and generally approved of the existing approaches to criminal law, but the emerging younger generation started to challenge them, putting forward other reform models. The new generation of reformers fought against both the treatment ideology and general populist harsh penal ideologies. The ideological weapon of the reformers was an emphasis on traditional virtues and principles of justice, such as legality, act-proportionality and predictability. This new ideology was called neo-classicism, because it sought to re-establish the heritage of the classical school, adapting it to the new circumstances. The reform of the sentencing principles (Chapter 6 of the code) in 1976 is one of the clearest examples of this spirit. The impact of reoffending on sentencing was heavily restricted under this principle.

These critical voices became louder from the 1960s. Criminological findings had cast doubt on the belief that 'ordinary people' do not commit crime. Generally, criminology started to play a bigger role than before. The *Dunkelziffer* (dark figure) of crime became an important concept: not every instance of crime becomes known to the authorities and is registered. Faith in the efficacy of prevention had collapsed, and this had particular significance for prison sentences. For the first time, social movements started to address issues of the state's reaction to crime, not of criminality. The Nordic point of reference was of increased importance, because Finland wanted to be seen as part of the Nordic countries (Melander 2007; on the Scandinavian penal exceptionalism, see Pratt 2008).

In the early 1970s, the time was ripe for the establishment of a committee at the Ministry of Justice to elaborate the principles on which the forthcoming penal code should be built, thus preparing for the comprehensive reform of Finnish criminal law. The entire effort was proof of the power of radical social criticism. Interestingly, lawyers were generally regarded as conservative, and the desire for social insights therefore ensured that social scientists would be deeply involved in the work of the committee. Because the social scientists were on the frontline of attacks against the treatment ideology, the strong presence of social scientists on the committee ensured the victory of the anti-treatment camp.

Post-war criminal legal thought had defended a form of legal moralism, whereas the autonomy of the individual became increasingly important as time went on. Sexual offences were redrafted in order to clarify protected legal interest and to differentiate them from the legal moralism that had previously defined such offences. Sexual self-determination was to be taken as the basis, illustrating the rise in the rights of the individual. The Criminal Law Committee published a key report in 1977 (Rikosoikeuskomitean mietintö 1977) whose perspective on criminal law was heavily based on a social policy orientation.

During the working life of the committee, social and political divisions in Finnish society had been sharp and were manifested within the committee in the divide between the socialist and non-socialist factions. As an expression of this, the report contains many dissenting opinions on various points. Political ideologies did not, however, prevent the committee agreeing unanimously on all the most crucial points concerning the role of the criminal law and the principles of punishment. The new generation could agree on certain principles despite political disagreement, with generation being more important than political stance.

The sociological view of the role of criminal justice was apparent in several statements concerning the role of the criminal justice system. Criminal justice was not regarded as a good vehicle for directing social change. The prevalence of criminality was regarded as being determined by factors other than the threat of punishment, a perspective that encouraged a minimalist approach to criminal law. The social costs of crime control were to be included in the calculations when the role of criminal justice was being assessed. No society can function without criminal justice but, in this reduced role, the broadly understood preventive effect was regarded as decisive. Some room was left for so-called individual prevention; for example, prison laws have to take rehabilitation aims as the starting point (Anttila and Törnudd 1992: 12–13).

Drafting the new code

The first step was to draft the special part of the new penal code. Some key principles to be embedded in it were concentration and synthesising. The code was to be precise, simple and understandable in its formulations, and all relevant aspects of criminal law were to be included. This meant that a lot of *Nebenstrafrecht* regulations had to be examined and transferred to the penal code (by *Nebenstrafrecht*, we mean penal law provisions that were distributed throughout the legislation). The level of abstraction of the provisions had to be raised because otherwise the code would have grown immensely. The statutory provisions on offences were organised so that a general definition for each offence was given first, followed by definitions of an aggravating and usually also of a privileged form of the offence, that is, a lesser form. The chapter structure was organised anew, and many new chapters were proposed and later amended.

One of the primary aims of the committee was to start from scratch, allowing all criminalised conduct to be systematically reassessed. The intention was that specific spheres of life, such as the environment, traffic or housing, would provide a systematic context for the assessment, thus replacing the earlier systematisation which was built on protected interests (*Rechtsgut*) (Rikosoikeuskomitean mietintö 1977; on this concept, see Nuotio 2010).

Traffic law provides an important example of the need for rethinking the use of criminal law. Drink-driving regulations were outdated, a medical test was usually needed on an individual basis, and the only cases to be brought before the court were generally those in which someone had been injured in a car accident. The new approach called for the introduction of a fixed and general per milligram limit for road traffic and other forms of traffic. Routine checks were introduced, exploiting such devices as hand alcometers. Implementing these reforms in the mid-1970s resulted in a transformation. Sociological risk thinking was particularly appropriate to dealing with mass phenomena, with traffic being a perfect example. Since then, drink-driving regulation has been based on the presumption that a certain level of blood alcohol concentration suffices to establish the dangerousness of driving, a presumption that is effectively irrefutable. This model of regulation has spread all over Europe and beyond.

The work of the committee was very successful despite some academic criticism that was voiced when the report was released for public debate.

However, the committee had incorporated the theoretical approaches circulating in the academic spheres, which left very little room for serious criticism and contestation. No influential alternative models were produced.

In the 1980s, the reform process was directed by the perceived need to address a set of the most pressing matters, among which was the economic criminal law in its totality, including the law on tax offences. The preparations for these reforms had started already, operating parallel to the working of the committee. The first large reform package focusing on these issues came into force in 1991, followed by a second in 1995. The second reform package addressed a broad range of issues, setting out a number of chapters that either addressed traditional crimes, such as crimes of violence, or tackled new social concerns, such as environmental offences or data and communications offences. The old chapter on generally dangerous activities was reformed so that a new offence of sabotage not only covered the former activity of arson, but included other similar actions.

The third phase was not a single package, but several different reform projects that were carried out separately. In this third phase, the general part of the penal code was reformed, focusing on prison laws and several remaining chapters and sections of the so-called special part.

The reform project has been seen as a success story. The preparatory work of the committee and the academic discussions that took place had laid the foundation for a shared understanding of the difficulties in addressing criminal justice reform. Although the reform work had been organised under the Ministry of Justice, academic scholars had been heavily involved. Generous financial support had been available. Most of the criminal law experts in Finland had been involved in one way or another, which had ensured that no serious opposition could emerge. In fact, even during the later years, the project itself had not been seriously contested.

This attitude towards reform has been called pragmatic, and the project was a child of the large reform enterprises of the 1970s. In Finland, several other ambitious law reform projects were started simultaneously in areas such as consumer law and constitutional law.

The belief in the value and feasibility of careful planning diminished relatively soon after the actual reform work of the penal code had started however. The preparation of an entire code in one piece was simply too much. The task had to be cut into smaller pieces. It very quickly became clear that the project was unlikely to finish soon.

The pragmatism could be regarded as a virtue. The flexible attitude towards the committee drafts also created room for necessary adjustments and adaptations. In some respects, however, it could be concluded that the committee had gone too far. For instance, it had expressed the view that criminal liability for negligently causing harm was unfounded, and its conclusion that such cases should be treated as crimes of endangerment soon proved less realistic. Some of the insights from the social sciences, such as that concerning the various spheres of life, were simply forgotten when the work of addressing conventional areas of crime started. The reform of the criminal law was in many ways less radical than had been foreseen. Decriminalisations, for instance, turned out to be very rare.

Nonetheless, the criminal law reform project provided a context that may have helped take other reforms forward. It was not always clear to outsiders what was done in the name of the project and what was ordinary law drafting. In any case, many new agendas were proposed after the 1970s. For instance, community sanctions later gained a much larger foothold in the system of sanctions than had been foreseen. Community service was instituted as an alternative to short-term custodial sentences. A special juvenile punishment was developed which shared some of these community service elements. Both these ideas depart from the neo-classical spirit of the 1970s, and testify to the rise of concerns focused on individual prevention. Likewise, victim–offender mediation started growing in importance in the 1980s, and later became a feature of the mainstream criminal justice responses. These examples tell us not only about international influences, but also about the sociological and criminological insights developing within Finland itself, going beyond what the committee had proposed. The range of criminal justice grew correspondingly, but it simultaneously became more difficult than before to cherish the liberal virtues of predictability and act-proportionality. The new sanctions were tailored according to the needs and circumstances of the offenders, and were difficult to understand from the point of view of narrow neo-classical virtues.

Another similar point was that neo-classical thought had emphasised that treatment and punishment should be kept strictly apart. Punishment should never be masked as treatment. This led to two problems: first, punishment was almost useless, because it could not really be defended as an adjunct to treatment. Second, justice data analysis revealed that many imprisoned offenders were suffering from addictions and illnesses. This provided the justification for rethinking the role of treatment and punishment. Community-based interventions were introduced and, in some cases, referral to treatment could mean that criminal charges were dropped or avoided.

The development of these ideas may be seen as a sign of pragmatism and as indicative of an open society. In my view, if we take a look at these innovations with the hindsight of some decades, the weak point of the first reforms was that the resulting code in its initial form was so ‘home-grown’, so internally focused on a national perspective, that the growing international and European influence was not sufficiently strong to be taken into account. The times really were changing however. In 1990, Finland joined the Council of Europe and ratified the European Convention for the Protection of Human Rights and Fundamental Freedoms. The Finnish constitutional provisions on fundamental rights were reformed soon after in 1995. The significance of fundamental rights grew rapidly, and constitutional law started addressing questions of criminal law. The original spirit of the committee’s approach had resulted in reforms that did, in most cases, respect the later constitutionality requirements, but the force with which the rights of the individual grew in the entire legal order was unforeseeable.

The emergence of an international regime of law addressing core crimes has also been quite unforeseeable. The Finnish criminal law had some minor pieces of law to build on, but basically the regulation of those crimes had to be done almost from the beginning. In the 1970s, the first provisions on genocide and war crimes, for instance, were included in the penal code.

Reforming the general part

Reform of the provisions on general doctrines took much longer than planned. This is an area in which both European and international developments should have been addressed much earlier. For instance, when the drafters addressed the issue of organised crime in the context of sentencing law, they continued to look at the world through the eyes of the 1970s. Many things had happened in the meantime. The Vienna Convention of 1988 addressed drug offence regimes. The Palermo Convention of 2000 dealt with organised crime and defined the key concepts. Later, several EU framework decisions incorporated international and European law definitions, but this led to fragmentary amendments in Finland. As a result, for example, the code now operates with two or three different understandings of what a criminal organisation is (Nuotio 2009: 1170–74).

Preparations for reform of the provisions concerning the general doctrines of penal liability had begun in the 1980s but, during the 1990s, that part remained relatively untouched. When penal liability was addressed again, the times had changed, but the reform initiative could no longer be reopened. The special part being the main point of emphasis, the general part had to wait. The committee had already expressed itself on matters concerning the general part, and here the legislature had to be creative and avoid causing harm to established legal practice. For a number of years, the Supreme Court had to take the lead, which again meant that the legislature had to respect the *status quo* when returning to these issues. A dialogue or an interplay has thus emerged. The constitutional role of the Supreme Court has hence grown as it has reduced its broad appellate function and emphasised its directing role as a court producing precedents. The reasoning of the Supreme Court has, as a result, become more principle-based over recent decades (Matikkala 1998).

It would appear that the edifice of the penal code was not finished in quite the way the original drafters had intended. The systematic nature of the code was not entirely lost, but it suffered some losses. New concerns arose that sat uncomfortably in the full package. An obvious and powerful example, information technology criminality, touches upon several topics that are spread across various parts of the code. One systematic key excludes other alternatives. The original structure narrowed down options that could be followed in rethinking the systematic structural solutions.

Today, it would be unthinkable that anyone would have the time and resources to reform such comprehensive totalities simultaneously. Instead, everyday legal drafting focuses on prescriptive detail and amends the existing material little by little. More than half the new legislation originates from either international obligations or European law. The fragmentation of international law and European law reproduces itself in the way in which member states implement the laws they produce.

From the 1960s until the 1990s, criminal law reform continued more or less under the conditions of general consensus. From the 1990s onwards, this is no longer so clearly the case. The feminist critique has addressed issues of domestic violence and sexual criminal law. Abolitionists have raised their voice criticising the resort to criminal law, speaking from reasons of principle. The victim movement has gained some ground. The neo-classical emphasis on the offence of a perpetrator has come under sustained attack. During the 1990s, the severity of punishment for some violent crimes was increased. Reduction in the number of people serving a custodial sentence has continued to be an important goal, but this goal is no longer fully uncontested. Voices such as the victims' rights movement and the feminist movement have challenged the established policies and been influential, at least in particular instances.

Emerging challenges for the modernisation project

Today in Finland, crime policy is increasingly influenced by both public opinion and economic resources. The media home in on individual cases which attract media attention. Surveys are no longer a privilege of academic researchers. The role of social media has grown, as a result of which minor law amendments are sometimes passed as an immediate reaction to some marginal matter. Recently, for instance, the sending of text messages of a disturbing nature was rendered criminal as part of the protection of domestic peace. This amendment was a result of a Supreme Court decision in which the court had refused to apply the existing provision for such behaviour.

Criminal law also seeks to address issues on a broader front than previously. For instance, not only is physical violence addressed under the law, but now bullying and harassment are as well. Responding to organised crime requires tackling networks and contexts, not just individual acts, and finding means of regulating these activities as such. Crime policy has moved from wholly national to transnational and international forums. The establishment of a regime for terrorist offences has required an enormous amount of regulatory effort. Both the EU and the Council of Europe have raised their profile in criminal justice affairs. The economic aspects of crime have increased in significance, as organised crime in particular generates considerable profits whatever the substance trafficked and handled is. As even terrorism requires economic resources, efforts to prevent and combat this crime are supported by cutting away its financial support.

When looked at in the larger setting, the Finnish criminal law modernisation project, which started with visions of maintaining the unity and coherence of criminal law in an ideological sense, turned out to be something else. Both tendencies, the one of coherence and the other of fragmentation, are equally present in the structure and processes of the criminal law today. Its neo-classical heritage accounts for the fact that reform has been consciously geared towards increasing the clarity and simplicity of the criminal law materials. The structures basically facilitate this aim, but cannot entirely guarantee final success. The structures of liability are, unavoidably, much more complex than they were before.

One of the features of modernisation is that modern challenges such as environmental issues, work, traffic, taxation and other economic crimes figure significantly in the new penal code. As such, they present obvious challenges for the legislature in many ways. The offences in themselves are much less concrete and need to be carefully adumbrated. Most often, the link with supervisory authorities is clear: these crimes are seldom reported to the police by ordinary citizens. The authorities need actively to monitor the appropriate field of action as the essence and nature of these crimes relates to larger settings and functions of social life. They do not often just occur at a certain point in time, like theft and assault, but have a longer duration and long-term effects. Environmental offences are typical examples of this.

In fact, environmental criminal law in Finland was a key driver when penal liability for legal persons was introduced in 1995; enterprises are not regarded as being composed of the actors themselves, but the enterprise may be penally liable and sentenced to pay a community fine when the legal person can be linked to the offence in a specific way. Since then, the significance of corporate criminal liability has increased because this specific form of punishment is also provided today for many other economic and workplace safety offences. Another significant change is that previously corporate penal liability was not mandatory; rather, the prosecutor and the court could exercise discretion concerning whether to press such charges. Today, corporations are required to face charges if the legal requirements for liability are satisfied.

When thinking about the waves of modernisation that Finnish criminal law has faced during recent decades, I believe we can distinguish two that possess somewhat different features. The first relates to the features highlighted above: addressing issues such as economic crime and environmental crime, and introducing and recognising them at the level of the penal code. This development is a normal aspect of the modernisation of legal order, without which the criminal law would have been left to the tasks of the nineteenth-century nightwatch state, when the penal codes heavily protected the interests of the individual (as well as those of the state). Protection of collective interests is more typical of modern criminal law and, in this regard, criminal law is not very different from modern constitutional law. In fact, the year 1995 in Finland was a milestone for both criminal and constitutional law reform. Environmental interests figured in both reforms (Nuotio 2007).

This wave of modernisation of the criminal law required significant adaptation of criminal law at many levels. The regulatory framework had to be adjusted, and this concerned not only criminal law in the narrow sense, but the substantial regulation of the field in question as well. Environmental law serves as a good example here too. In the Finnish context, the idea was not so much to emphasise the efficacy of criminal legal controls on the industry, but rather to create a legal frame that enabled the authorities to press charges for such occurrences in an adequate manner so that the true character of the offence was properly recognised.

Reform was a matter of regulatory need and instrumental aims, but also about symbolic action, because it had come to be believed that criminal law could not exclude such areas without losing its credibility. The neo-classical inheritance could be said to have stressed the necessity to react in regulatory terms, but without believing that such regulation would utterly change the world. Criminal law was just one element in the toolbox, an element that was regarded as useful and even unavoidable. Modernisation of the criminal law drove the legal framework as well as criminal law theorising and doctrinal rethinking forward, but this modernisation did not wholly break up the tradition. Tensions were there, however, as we can see; for example, in that the reform discussion began over whether the general doctrines of criminal law were still fully general and applicable across the whole of the criminal law. An instance is whether intent in homicide means the same as intent in economic offences. This is a sign of the threat of criminal law fragmenting into different sub-areas each following their own internal logic. The force of a common penal code does not suffice to guarantee full generality. In my view, most of this part of the reform still finds room under the common umbrella and does not seriously threaten the generality and coherence of the criminal law as such. Hence, the values of legal tradition including the values of neo-classicism could be carried further and respected under these new circumstances.

As a second wave with somewhat different implications, I would list the high profile of security in criminal law that became apparent perhaps for the first time in the drugs crime reform of the early 1990s, and then included issues of organised crime and eventually terrorist offences. The novelty of this has partly to do with new conceptualisation. The organisational context is a crucial aspect of organised crime, for instance. Such an approach challenges the classical view that crime is a static occurrence in time and space which has observable features rather than a vague sequence with loose contours.

Instrumentalism in both criminal law regulation and crime policy has reached new levels as the international and European regimes have developed. The fight against terrorism includes the mobilisation of criminal laws and criminal justice to an extent that brings criminal justice quite close to issues of military intelligence, and even war. The system of criminal law is also interwoven into a complex regime of security governance. This efficiency-oriented approach is much more openly hostile than the liberal, neo-classical traditions, and it requires another type of rethinking and balancing (Nuotio 2006, 2008a).

Influences from the European Union regime

Security-driven concerns such as the fight against organised crime, drugs crime and terrorism have been particularly important for developments at the

EU level. These developments call into question classical criminal law doctrines and principles and require thoroughgoing adjustments of national laws. To some extent, these laws go beyond classical criminal law principles. The security orientation represents an extreme model of the modernisation of criminal laws, as well as increasing the fragmentation of criminal law in the national setting by adding a new layer.

The criminal law profile of the EU shares features of both these waves, but the security context is particularly obvious. This profile has also been severed by the underdeveloped legal safeguards of a human rights and constitutional fundamental rights character. The recent Lisbon Treaty seeks to improve the situation by taming the dominance of security and efficiency agendas by introducing both internal fundamental rights protection and external human rights controls (Nuotio 2011.) In this way, it may be hoped that constitutionalism could play the role of a counterforce to this extreme model of modernisation.

Influences from the international legal regime

Beyond the European regime, international criminal law has developed significantly over recent years, affecting the core crimes regime and the treaty crimes regime equally. Finnish criminal law was revised after the Rome Statute of the International Criminal Court entered into force in 2002. In particular, war crimes and crimes against humanity were conceptualised anew, because the old provisions did not capture the essence of these crimes according to the modern understanding.

One interesting development here is the law on torture. Finnish criminal law had an old provision regarding torture for the purposes of extracting a confession (on the previous history of such regulation, see Pihlajamäki 2007). This provision was abolished during the course of the criminal law project in the mid-1990s. Curiously enough, the UN Torture Convention from 1984 required the recognition of torture as a separate offence. The international development, generally, and the one concerning core crimes regimes, specifically, also led to a growing need to have torture criminalised separately. After some hesitation and because of pressure from supervisory bodies and non-governmental organisations (NGOs), the government undertook reform and introduced a new provision. The Nordic countries had usually claimed that international law did not legally require such a move, and had repeated this claim even here (Nuotio 2008b).

International criminal law certainly could be regarded as part of the high-security criminal law narrative. Simultaneously, the story could also be read the other way round in that the development of international criminal law shows that the principle of legality in criminal law can be applied to new forms of criminalisation without sacrificing the general legal safeguards of the accused. Perhaps, therefore, we should not classify the modernisation phenomena from one side only too hastily. We might say the same about terrorist offences. If international terrorism is not regarded as a crime, the alternative might be to treat it as an act of war, an option that gives terrorist offenders much less legal protection. In this sense, high-security criminal law is often a mix of various regimes, with criminal law clawing ground from other regimes.

Conclusions

During the course of this chapter, we have considered aspects of the modernisation of Finnish criminal law during recent times. It seems that the agendas are today much more set at international and transnational levels in comparison with the initial period of criminal law reform. What is and is not to be criminalised has been rethought profoundly during a time span of more than a century. Casuistic provisions have been replaced by more general and abstract ones. New types of collective interest have found their way into the criminal law: we only need to mention environmental offences and tax offences. Criminal law has been adjusted to the needs and values of the late modern society. This process is still under way – perhaps it always will be – as many social processes make their presence felt. Increased multiculturalism and religious pluralism, for instance, call for rethinking of the role of criminal law.

So far, we have witnessed very few examples of decriminalisation in Finland. As an example of one curiosity, we might mention the decriminalisation of bigamy in 1999. It was no longer regarded as necessary to maintain this criminalisation because of the comprehensive records of people's marital status: as these files will be consulted, the risk of bigamy was considered to have been removed.

In practical terms, the project has not been completed yet. Formally, the code of 1889 is still in force, although its main provisions have been revised. It is likely that the Ministry of Justice will soon prepare a law reform package that would reorganise all the provisions so that the current code too could finally be made history. If the reform reopens larger debates and addresses more issues of principle, the remaining task may be significant and demanding.

Finnish criminal law is under pressure in many ways because of changing domestic ideology and an international legal regime, which have increased and expanded expectations. Although criminal law has more and more work to do, it can deliver less and less. This narrative of the aggressive spread of criminal law as an instrument is, however, somewhat counterbalanced by the values of legality and legitimacy, which are anchored in constitutional values themselves. It must be against the *passe-partout* of the rule of law and legality, however, that the developments in the criminal law can be measured and analysed. The modernisation process has required criminal law to adapt to new circumstances but, in essence, criminal law has still remained the same.

One special feature of the national penal code is that it enjoyed very special democratic legitimacy in much the same way as a constitution should. Today, the forces behind modernisation sometimes escape democratic controls. We in Europe have seen the establishment of constitutional frames of legality arising from the erection of human rights and fundamental rights regimes at a transnational level. A more difficult challenge will be to resolve issues of democratic participation when European laws and policies are being produced. Hope may rest in the principle of European regulation, which builds on the idea of shared regulatory competence, thus leaving room for national legislatures. Within these somewhat restricted limits, the legislature may seek to continue the Finnish narrative of the modernisation of criminal law (Nuotio 2011).

We should now return to the metaphor of the Cathedral of Siena we took up earlier. Is the Finnish penal code as it stands comparable to that achievement? In some sense, we could say it is. The code was redrafted over a long period of time, and the law reform project had to be adjusted to new circumstances during the construction work. At any rate, even as it stands now, it represents a valuable piece of carefully rethought law. The story of criminal law does not end with the drafting of legislation. Rather, it starts when the new laws are being applied by the courts. Progress, too, is of course a relative concept in a legal setting. Compared with the old code, however, the reformed one, even when we consider its problems and deficiencies, still provides a much better foundation for the development of Finnish criminal law by all the relevant actors involved in the enterprise.

References

Anttila, I. and Törnudd, P. (1992) 'The Dynamics of the Finnish Criminal Code Reform', in R. Lahti and K. Nuotio (eds) *Criminal Law Theory in Transition. Finnish and Comparative Perspectives*, Helsinki: Finnish Lawyers Pub. Co.

Blomstedt, Y. (1964) *Rikoslakireformin ensimmäiset vaiheet vuoden 1866 osittaisuudistuksiin saakka. Historiallinen arkisto.*

Das finnische Strafgesetz, Rikoslaki, Strafflag, nach dem Stand von 1.10.2005 (2006) *Deutsche Übersetzung und Einleitung von Karin Cornils, Dan Frände and Jussi Matikkala*. Berlin: Dunker & Humblor GmBH.

Eser, A. and Arnold, J. (eds) (2000) *Criminal Law in Reaction to State Crime*, Freiburg i. Br.: Max Planck Institute.

Forsman, J. (1900) *Straffrättens allmänna läror (utg och anteckningar enligt hans föreläsningar av L Wasastierna)*, Helsingfors: Juridiska studentfakultetens förlagsrörelse.

Lappi-Seppälä, T. (2009) 'Imprisonment and Penal Policy in Finland', in *Criminal Law, Scandinavian Studies in Law*, vol. 54, Stockholm.

Marttunen, M. (2008) *Nuorisorikosoikeus: alaikäisten rikosten seuraamukset kriminaalipoliittisesta ja vertailevasta näkökulmasta*, Dissertation, Helsinki: Oikeuspoliittinen tutkimuslaitos.

Matikkala, J. (1998) 'Rikosoikeuskomitea ja rikosoikeuden kehitys', *Lakimies* 8/1998: 1325–40.

Melander, S. (2007) 'Nordic Criminal Justice Policy: Single Path of Separate Ways?', in J. Husa, K. Nuotio and H. Pihlajamäki (eds) *Nordic Law – Between Tradition and Dynamism*, Antwerp: Intersentia.

Nuotio, K. (2006) 'Terrorism as a Catalyst for the Emergence, Harmonization and Reform of Criminal Law', *Journal of International Criminal Justice*, 4: 998–1016.

——(2007) 'Eurooppalaistuvan rikosoikeuden ääriviivat', *Lakimies*, 2007/7–8: 1102–22.

——(2008a) 'Umsetzung internationalrechtlicher Vorgaben zur Terrorismusbekämpfung in Finnland', in J. Schwarze (Hrsg.) *Globalisierung und Entstaatlichung des Rechts,* Teilband 1: Beiträge zum Öffentlichen Recht, Europarecht, Arbeits- und Sozialrecht und Strafrecht. Verlag Mohr Siebeck.

——(2008b) 'Zur Kriminalisierung der Folter im finnischen Strafgesetz', in *Nullum ius sine scientia, Festschrift für Jaan Sootak zum 60 Geburtstag am 16 Juli 2008*. Tallinna: Der Juura Verlag.

——(2009) 'Rikosoikeuden koherenssi ja fragmentaatio: esimerkkinä järjestäytyneen rikollisuuden määrittely', *Lakimies*, 2009/7–8: 1154–74.

——(2010) 'Theories of Criminal Law and the Limits of Criminal Law: A Legal Cultural Approach', in R.A. Duff et al. (eds) *The Boundaries of Criminal Law*, Oxford: OUP.

——(2011) 'European Criminal Law under the Developing Constitutional Setting of the European Union', in N. Walker, J. Shaw and S. Tierney (eds) *Europe's Constitutional Mosaic*, Oxford: Hart Publishing.

Pihlajamäki, H. (2007) 'The Painful Question: The Fate of Judicial Torture in Early Modern Sweden', *Law and History Review*, Online. Available www.historycooperative.org/journals/lhr/25.3/pihlajamaki.html (accessed 10 August 2011).

Pratt, J. (2008) 'Scandinavian Exceptionalism in an Era of Penal Excess, Part I', *British Journal of Criminology*, 48: 119–37.

Rikosoikeuskomitean mietintö (1977) KM 1976: 72, Helsinki (Report of the Criminal Law Committee).

Tyynilä, M. (1989) 'Rikoslaki Suomen Venäjän-suhteiden kompastuskivenä', in *Rikosoikeuden juhlavuonna*, Helsinki: Suomalainen Lakimiesyhdistys.

Wahlberg, M. (1989) 'G.W.F. Hegel ja K.G. Ehrströmin rangaistusteorian ykseydestä eroavuudessaan', *Rikosoikeuden juhlavuonna*, Helsinki: Suomalainen Lakimiesyhdistys.

Ylikangas, H. (1989) 'Jaakko Forsman – lainlaatija ja poliitikko', in *Rikosoikeuden juhlavuonna*, Helsinki: Suomalainen Lakimiesyhdistys.

6 Criminalisation, decriminalisation and post-communist transition

The case of the Russian Federation*

Peter H. Solomon, Jr

What impact does the end of communist rule and a state-owned and administered economy make upon the content and scope of the criminal law? What kind of changes does post-communist transition imply for criminal law? The variety of transition experiences suggests that there is no uniform answer, but there may be tendencies and commonalities. At the same time, there remain sources of criminalisation and decriminalisation that have little connection to changes in political regime or economic system, including the perennial problem of the borders between less serious crimes and administrative offences and the use of criminal law to respond to new challenges. Criminalisation in response to new demands (domestic or international) may not involve extensive implementation, so that the change in the law performs symbolic rather than instrumental functions (Gusfield 1963). A temporary liberalisation of politics may also open the door for overdue responses to social change.

Specifically, what impact on the criminal law might democratisation or a shift to a market economy produce? One would not expect changes in the core of crimes, which in the pithy words of Sir Leon Radzinowicz reflects the 'core of human needs and greeds'. Rather, the changes would take place 'on the margins' (Radzinowicz and King 1977: 101–25, quotation at 105). These might include changes in crimes relating to politics (crimes against the state), to reflect a broader conception of acceptable political action and speech, and changes in crimes relating to business activity and organised labour once capitalist forms of ownership become normal. After the initial changes, what patterns might emerge? An authentic democracy, with an alternation of parties in power, might feature a politics of law and order, in which rival contenders promise expansions in the law (and harsher punishments). A chorus of voices in North America and Western Europe bemoans such expansion of the criminal law, because it fails to meet normative standards of rationality and economy of repression, and this process could be replicated in new democracies (Husak 2008). At the same time, a new study of democracy and decriminalisation in the United States argues that many states (although not the federal government) balance criminalisation with regular rounds of decriminalisation, especially of obsolete offences, but also in response to social change. Moreover, some state legislatures build into their operating procedures expert review of proposals for new crimes and do a reasonable job of avoiding excessive criminalisation (Brown 2007).

This chapter analyses the experience of the Russian Federation (RF) in its first two decades, along with the last period of the Soviet Union. In comparison with countries of Central and Eastern Europe, many of which joined the European Union, the 'transition' in Russia has produced neither democratic accountability nor a market economy in which the state adequately protects private business. For now, and perhaps the long haul, Russia has settled into a form of authoritarianism that includes elections but no real competition for power, and where regional governments also display a kind of subnational authoritarianism (Gelman and Cameron 2010). The economy has assumed a form of state capitalism, and even fully private entities require goodwill from relevant political authorities as a counterweight to insufficiently developed legal protection. In short, Russia has deserted communist politics and economics but not adopted the European models scripted in modish teleology as the end points of transition. This means that the way Russia has used its criminal law is unlikely to typify what has happened in post-communist countries that have fulfilled the dreams and promises of transitology. Still, the experience of Russia may have a lot in common with other countries that have not made these transitions.

Two preliminary observations are in order. First, the most contested aspect of the criminal law in post-Soviet Russia turned out to be its use in regulating business, which, as we shall see, had a serious negative effect on the business climate in Russia. The years 2009–11 witnessed an extraordinary, although so far unsuccessful, attempt to remedy the situation, especially through wholesale decriminalisation of business offences. Second, under President Medvedev, potential changes in the criminal law were treated as part of criminal justice reform more generally and, as a result, discussed in the context of changes in punishment and even criminal procedure.

Here, I start with an overview of criminalisation and decriminalisation in Russia, 1988 to 2010, its main patterns and phases. I turn then to a discussion of three different areas or types of change in the criminal law: business crime; the boundaries of common crimes; and responses to new challenges, both instrumental and symbolic in their effects. I conclude with examination of President Medvedev's initiatives to humanise and modernise the criminal law (from 2009 to 2011), including conflict over the proposals to decriminalise business offences (Poslanie 2009; Solomon 2009, 2010).

The Russian story

In the initial period of movement from communist politics and economy, Russian criminal law registered such necessary changes as the repeal of the prohibition on 'anti-Soviet agitation and propaganda' (1989) and the crime of 'speculation' (early 1990s) and related crimes. The policy of *glasnost* (openness) pursued from 1986 made the prosecution of critical speech obsolete, as the emerging market economy did the same for making profit through buying and selling (the crime of speculation). The liberal, reform-oriented atmosphere, which had profound effects in the area of judicial reform, also facilitated changes in criminal law, including the adoption in 1991 of new Fundamentals of Criminal Legislation by the government of the USSR. In effect the general part of the republican criminal codes, the new Fundamentals represented a deep and thoughtful reworking of the principles of criminal law and reflected nearly a generation of discussion among criminal law scholars in the USSR. They included, for example, narrowing the responsibility of managers and entrepreneurs for negative consequences of decisions that might be considered 'justifiable risk' (Solomon 1992; Naumov 1997). Another example of liberal reform was the decriminalisation of 'sodomy' among consenting adults, which was included in reform legislation that also narrowed the application of the death penalty. Suggestions for removing this from the criminal law started in 1979, were openly discussed from 1989 and came close to happening in late 1991. Actual decriminalisation came in 1993, reflecting both domestic and international factors. This fell on to the agenda of specialists drafting new versions of the criminal code in the early 1990s (Kon 1997; Noble 2010; and Noble's chapter in this volume).

The 1996 Criminal Code of the Russian Federation (RF), the first post-Soviet code, while incorporating the Fundamentals of Criminal Legislation from 1991 (including its sophisticated grouping of crimes into four levels of seriousness and matching punishments accordingly), did far more criminalising than decriminalising. Some of the additions represented new ways of protecting personal rights and civil liberties. These included: coercive taking of human organs; (mis)placing a mentally sound individual in a psychiatric institution (from 1988); infecting a person with AIDS; gathering or disseminating information on a person's private life without consent; refusal by an official to furnish documents relating to a citizen's rights and freedoms; and violations of equality rights (on grounds of gender, race or ethnicity). The code contained whole new sections on environmental crimes, computer crimes and crimes against the peace and security of mankind, with the last reflecting Russia's new international obligations (Naumov 1997). But the most significant new crimes are found in the new Chapter 22 entitled 'economic crimes' (really crimes relating to business), to be discussed separately. These offences reflected the urge of state officials to craft tools for regulating private business activity, and perhaps also finding ways of sharing in its rewards. At the same time, such regulation had considerable support from a public that resented the new differences in wealth and viewed even legitimate business figures as criminals (Radchenko 2007).

The adoption of a new criminal code, typically the result of extensive discussion among experts and politicians alike, might in some countries and times have resolved outstanding conflicts and resulted in a period of stability for the criminal law. But, in post-Soviet Russia, the opposite proved to be the case (just as it had been after the Bolshevik promulgation of the 1922 Criminal Code). Between 1988 and 2010, the legislature passed and the president signed 88 different laws changing the criminal code, many of which were omnibus bills containing multiple changes (Lopashenko 2010). The 35 laws adopted up to 2004 (including a major one in December 2003), introduced more than 600 changes, and the frequency of criminalisation measures outnumbered decriminalisation by almost threefold (Luneev 2004; Klebanov 2006). Some of these changes reflected new challenges, whether international or narrowly Russian in nature. It became a crime for an employer to fail to pay wages or pensions; for any authority to cut off the supply of energy or electricity; for an employer to use slave labour; or for anyone to engage in human trafficking (which includes male workers, as well as women and children in the sex trade). But many changes struck leading Russian criminologists (Luneev, Kuznetsova, Gilinskii) as unjustified, at least in combination, and they resented the way that these new crimes came into being (Klebanov 2006; Lopashenko 2009: 214; Kashepov 2010). The readiness to change the criminal law did not taper off; 2010 recorded 14 pieces of legislation introducing changes in the criminal law (Lopashenko 2010), most of which were not connected to the initiatives of President Medvedev.

The wave of criminalisation in Russia during the past 15 years was based not on a grand design, or any evidence provided by criminological research. Instead, it reflected the spontaneous and disorganised work conducted by the State Duma and the efforts of law enforcement personnel to counter attempts to liberalise policy on crime and punishment. To be sure, criminal policy-making in other countries, democratic and authoritarian alike, often suffered from similar defects. But the extreme frequency and sometimes capricious nature of the changes in the criminal law of the RF between 1996 and 2010 made Russia unusual.

Various Duma members, especially in the relevant committees, sought to add new crimes to please their popular constituencies or what they imagined the public would appreciate; others simply represented the interests of law enforcement. In fact, for every change in the criminal code that was adopted, there were many further proposals that were set aside, if only because the Duma did not have the last or only word (Luneev, in Klebanov 2006). In its normal pattern (inherited from the Brezhnev era), lawmaking in Russia involves a number of screening points. The full process that is used unless powerful people choose to bypass it requires either the legislative or the executive branch to send draft laws to relevant groups and collect comments (law enforcement agencies and regional governments among them). Draft laws must be reviewed by the Ministry of Finance for their financial implications, and people within the presidential administration (especially in the State Legal Administration) usually add their comments, at least before the President decides to sign; and in recent years, draft laws are also checked for their potential for corruption (e.g. any new and unnecessary discretion for officials). If such a procedure had not been pursued, the number and scope of changes to Russian criminal law between 1997 and 2008 would have been even greater.

Although vetting could eliminate egregious proposals, it was no substitute for systematic, considered and even scientific analysis of current practices of criminal justice and proposed changes. As we shall see, lawmakers in Russia took decisions that had serious consequences that they had not anticipated, and were to reverse themselves more than once, leaving both police and public confused.

Business crimes

Even the most liberal market economy requires regulation, and regulation includes the use of the criminal law to deal with actions that threaten the health of the economy. In the Russian case, the repertoire of business crimes developed during the early and mid-1990s is broad in scope and includes many offences that are not well defined in the Criminal Code of 1996, and reinforce a stifling system of licences and permissions that itself gives officials tools for pursuing firms that do not contribute to their personal enrichment. Moreover, legal obtaining of credit is defined narrowly, making it difficult for businesses to expand. Between 1996 and 2010, Chapter 22 of the code was changed two dozen times and, in the process, an additional 10 new business-related crimes were added, alongside only three examples of decriminalisation. As of 2010, Chapter 22 contained 35 Articles (up from 32), and many of these include two or three degrees of liability (qualifications).

The most knowledgeable scholars in the RF on business crimes and criminal law in the 1990s insist that Chapter 22, part of whose content was introduced into the earlier Russian Soviet Federative Socialist Republic (RSFSR) Criminal Code between 1992 and 1994, reflected only the good intentions of lawmakers, who assumed that regulation of the economy through the criminal law was necessary and who borrowed individual offences from foreign legislation based on forecasting of how the new capitalist economy in Russia would develop: an exercise that was difficult if not impossible to do accurately. Among other things, the lawmakers were not able to determine which objects or relationships within the economy the criminal law ought to protect. Nor did they coordinate their efforts with the parallel development of other areas of law, especially in the civil realm. But, according to Lopashenko, the resulting use of business offences for predatory actions by police was an unintended consequence of the legislation, which had to be corrected (Lopashenko 2010; Naumov 2010).

Many of the articles in Chapter 22 make criminal the violation of rules or regulations on particular subjects, the contents of which are not specified in the criminal law. At the top of the list, business firms and their managers face criminal prosecution for 'illegal entrepreneurship' (Article 171): that is, the pursuit of business activity without registration or in violation of the rules of registration; failure to provide necessary documents; providing false information on documents; and failure to obtain a licence where required – with enhanced liability wherever large sums of money or organised crime is involved. The rules and requirements of registration and licences change often, and vary from one region to another. Moreover, officials are known to use their discretion in providing licences and registration in a timely fashion as a lever for extracting payments. The threat of criminal prosecution for failure to obey these rules only strengthens the hands of the officials. Arguably, the pervasive shadow economy in the 1990s made crimes of this kind into an important tool for compelling businesspeople to report some of their operations and pay taxes, but they still did so only as much as necessary, and often complied with the letter more than the spirit of the law. Other crimes of a similar vagueness included: illegal banking; illegal obtaining of credit; illegal use of a brand; registering an illegal land deal; illegal exports; and failure to pay taxes. Extortionate prosecutions of business offences are sometimes commissioned by rival businesses, and offences in Chapter 22 can be combined in creative ways to threaten major damage to businesses and their owners (Firestone 2010). A good indicator of the self-interested manipulation of prosecutions for economic crimes is the small proportion of cases that ever make it to court and lead to convictions (about 20 per cent of cases opened between 2002 and 2006; the rest are stopped during the pre-trial phases (Volkov et al. 2010a)).

Chapter 22 also included crimes connected to deceit or fraud, such as the creation of fake firms, fictitious bankruptcy and acquisition or disposition of property through criminal means. But high-level prosecutions (such as that of Mikhail Khodorkovsky) often make use of the standard article on 'fraud' in another section of the code, as opposed to new specific ones. Naturally, there were also new prohibitions on money laundering, the favoured way of combating organised crime worldwide.

Prosecutions according to Chapter 22 offences reached a high of 165,090 crimes and 132,695 offenders in 2001 (8.07 per cent of convictions), and then declined to 97,793 in 2007 (by that point 2.1 per cent). The decline resulted in considerable part from the 2003 removal from the code (decriminalisation) of the offence of 'deceiving customers', a common crime from Soviet times that was used against storekeepers more than against businesspeople (Lopashenko 2009: 209ff). Some of the decline may also relate to the clarification of tax obligations in the early Putin years.

Broadly defined crimes are especially open to new uses, and allow, if not encourage, criminalisation through law enforcement practice. Thus, the master crime of 'illegal entrepreneurship' started to be applied in a brand new way in the autumn of 2009 against the owners and managers of gambling businesses. The July 2006 law on gambling restricted the operation of casinos and slot machines as of July 2009 to four remote locations within the country and, after that date, the police started forcing the closure of the many casinos in Moscow and other large cities (Zakon 2006). Naturally, some operators went underground, using both physical locations and the internet to continue operating. So there began a series of criminal prosecutions, notwithstanding the fact that the criminal code did not mention gambling. The most common charge turned out to be 'illegal entrepreneurship' (Article 171), which for some especially profitable casinos led to fines that could be endured. Yet, according to one legal commentator, a strict reading of Article 171 would not allow its use against gambling operations because there was no longer a requirement for their registration once they were illegal (Zabeida 2009).

The identification of overcriminalisation of business activity as a problem and the misuse of the criminal law *vis-à-vis* business got a big push with the establishment in March 2009 of the Centre for Legal and Economic Studies at the Institute for Social Development and its assignment by President Medvedev in November 2009 of the task of writing a 'Conception of Modernisation of Criminal Law in the Economic Sphere', a document that makes a strong argument for decriminalisation. I discuss this document, along with the efforts to realise its recommendations, in the context of Medvedev's other initiatives in the criminal sphere.

Adjusting the lower limits of common crimes

The most dramatic changes in statistics on crime in Russia, and in the number of people there who end up with criminal records, result not from new notions of what is deviant. They come instead from shifts in the definition of crimes already in the code, which in turn affect enforcement. Often, an element of decriminalisation is involved, but rarely legalisation, because the conduct removed from the criminal law may remain illegal and subject to administrative proceedings, or subject to qualification as a different criminal offence.

Post-Soviet Russia witnessed three stories of major changes in the lower limits of crimes, involving a lot of decriminalisation, albeit some of it only temporary. The changes involve what were (once) three of the most common crimes – hooliganism, theft and possession of illegal drugs.

Throughout the Soviet period, hooliganism was the favoured all-purpose offence used against those who misbehaved in public, covering everything from drunk and disorderly conduct to physical attacks, even with weapons. In 1970, there were 173,043 convictions for hooliganism, close to 20 per cent of total convictions, and earlier the rate was even higher. There were always overlaps between assault and the administrative offence of 'petty hooliganism', and changes in the law and law enforcement produced major oscillations in regular hooliganism convictions (as low as 42,853 in 1989, then back up to 129,505 in 1997 and 114,052 in 2003). From 1997, a charge of hooliganism required light bodily blows or harm to the victim's health and no longer covered simple drunk and disorderly behaviour (Ivantsova 2004).

The dramatic change came in December 2003 when hooliganism was redefined to cover only 'crude violations of the public order ... committed with a weapon or object used as a weapon'. This narrow definition led to a massive drop in hooliganism convictions (from 114,052 in 2003 to 24,810 in 2004, 20,360 in 2007 and 1,907 in 2010). To be sure, convictions for blows or assault (Article 116) rose from 40,211 in 2003 to 60,924 in 2004 and then increased steadily to 118,134 in 2007, no doubt picking up many of the same incidents that would previously have been qualified as hooliganism. In the next few years, there was a major drop in convictions for both offences, but the new proportions stayed the same: hooliganism fell to 1,907 in 2010 and petty assault to 24,002 (in the same three year period, petty hooliganism dropped by nearly a quarter as well (Sudebnyi Department 2010)). As it happened, threatening to use force in public was actually legalised, because this conduct was not included in the offence of petty hooliganism in the Code of Administrative Procedure (Gavrilov 2008: 10; Lopashenko 2009: 489–94). What prompted the narrowing of the definition of hooliganism is not clear, but this action pleased criminal law scholars who always disliked broad and overlapping offences.

In July 2007, the definition of hooliganism was enlarged again so that the charge could be deployed against 'extremism'. The crime came to include crude violations of public order on the basis of political, race, ethnic or religious hate or hostility or such, directed at a particular social group (Kibalnik and Solomonenko 2008). I do not (yet) know how often this new version of hooliganism is being used, or its share in the tiny number of convictions for hooliganism, or what role it is playing in the modest confrontation with extremist groups. Hooliganism is not mentioned in current police data or on Supreme Court reviews of extremist crimes (SOVA Center 2011).

Similar repeated changes took place in the crime of theft. The lower limit for the crime of theft became the object of changes back and forth within one year. In July 2002, with the passage of the new Code on Administrative Violations, the administrative offence of 'petty theft' was enlarged to include stealing of up to five MROTy (the minimum daily wage) from its previous level of one MROT, so that thefts in the range of one to five MROTy were no longer criminal offences. On 4 November 2002, the legislature reversed its position and made offences of this kind into crimes once again. During a mere four months, 350,000 incidents of theft were effectively decriminalised, that is treated as administrative rather than criminal offences, and the change affected cases processed over the next year or two as well. But this was not all. First, the changes in November 2002 eliminated entirely any minimum amounts for the crime of theft whenever a group was involved. Second, in June 2007, the legislature changed the lower level once again by setting the maximum amount for petty theft at a mere 100 roubles (or US$4)! A year later, the amount was raised back to 1,000 roubles, still well under the original limit of one MROT (Gavrilov 2008: 49–50; Lopashenko 2009: 485–89).

To place the lower limit of theft at one MROT (around US$85 at the time) meant treating as criminal almost any instance of misappropriation; even five MROT (about US$425) would strike many observers as too low. But according to a former judge in Russia, the moral sensibilities of ordinary Russians required incarceration for anyone who stole, even the smallest amounts (Radchenko 2009: 8)! A legal scholar asserted that extending the crime of theft to small values was necessary to protect the most vulnerable members of society, pensioners and the working poor, for whom the loss of US$100 had great significance (Lopashenko 2009: 488). The overall effect of such a low limit was the continuation of high levels of convictions for theft, far and away the most common charge in Russian crime statistics. At the same time, many of these people were sentenced to incarceration because of the failure to develop most of the alternative punishments mentioned in the criminal code – a shortcoming that the Medvedev humanisation initiatives were meant to address. Many of these offenders were also held in pre-trial detention, because they were not residents of the city where they committed the offence, a fact that made a custodial sentence *de rigueur*.

A similar pattern of waffling with resulting instability in the law is found in the definition of the crime of possessing narcotics without intent to traffic. An amendment to the criminal code in 2003 limited criminal responsibility for possession to situations in which the accused was found to have large or especially large quantities of narcotics. The amounts were to be determined by the Ministry of Health and the police, with 'large' referring to 10 minimum average doses and 'especially large' to 50. The purpose of the amendment was to move towards treating some users as victims rather than criminals through decriminalisation of simple possession of reasonable amounts. But this did not suit the interests of the police (MVD and the federal drug agency alike), whose record of success in the fight against narcotics depended upon the prosecution and conviction of ordinary users, whose convictions ensured high rates of clearance and overall productivity. The result was that the minimum average dose amounts were set very low, so low as to generate protest from scholars, the Ministry of Justice and the Presidential Commissions on Human Rights. A fresh effort to develop realistic standards led to a new table of doses that operated from May 2004. The minimum average dose of heroin in the table was raised from 0.0001 gram to 0.1 gram. But officials in the federal drug agency did not accept this liberalising restriction on the prosecution of addicts and, along with leaders of the church, lobbied the Duma, even collecting 200,000 signatures in favour of the prosecution of simple users. As a result, amendments to the criminal code in February 2006 shifted responsibility to absolute amounts of drugs in the possession of the accused rather than minimum average doses, and produced a scale more likely to result in prosecutions. Thus, a large dose of heroin was set at 0.5 gram and especially large at 2.5 gram. This level still allowed for a modest decriminalisation compared with the 2003 level. However, the total number of narcotics crime cases (involving five different offences) rose from 83,685 in 2007 to more than 100,000 in 2009 (Sudebnyi Department 2007, 2009; Orlova 2009).

The oscillations in the amount of drugs needed to make possession a crime reflected an ongoing conflict among different agencies and groups of officials that supported different understandings of the problem of drug use and how best to combat it. It is likely that the changes in the definitions of hooliganism and petty theft also had their origins in similar conflicts, but these stories remain to be uncovered.

Responses to new challenges

Another source of criminalisation in Russia has been the normal need to respond to new challenges. Sometimes, the problem is strictly domestic, or Russia's alone; at other times, it has an international dimension (clearly the case with the offence of trafficking), and criminalisation may be necessary to satisfy external pressures. In both situations, criminalisation does not necessarily imply enforcement, which depends upon the capabilities and interests of the various police agencies. The passage of time may reveal that the introduction of new crimes ends up serving symbolic purposes alone, and does not address the underlying problem. As examples, I will refer to three new crimes or groups of crimes – crimes against the administration of justice, infecting a person with AIDS and human trafficking.

As part of the first efforts to address revelations about incidence of outsiders attempting to influence judges, Soviet lawmakers added articles to the criminal code criminalising 'interfering with the resolution of court cases', threatening a judge and insulting a judge. Versions of these crimes continued in the 1996 Code as part of a chapter on crimes against the administration of justice that includes more common offences such as false testimony by a witness, false evidence from an expert, refusing to give evidence and paying or forcing a person to give evidence. Prosecutions of the new crimes did not become common. Convictions for obstructing the administration of justice (which replaced interference with the resolution of cases in the 1996 Code) occurred 22 times over the four-year period of 2000–03. In the six years 1997–2003, there were 17 convictions for attempts on the life of a judge (the actual number of incidents was at least four times greater). Disrespect, or contempt for the court, resulted in 20–40 convictions a year between 1997 and 2003 (Galakhova 2005). The relatively small number of cases under these charges suggests that the prohibitions had more symbolic significance than operational. In autumn 2009, the chief of the High Arbitrazh Court proposed that judges themselves be given the power to bring cases against those who engaged in improper leverage, because procurators failed to respond to complaints from judges (Butorina 2009).

One of the achievements of the 1996 Criminal Code was the inclusion of a new crime relating to the transmission of AIDS, namely to knowingly place another person in danger of being infected with HIV (Article 122). This prohibition may well have reflected international pressures. Actual prosecutions under this article have been few and far between – convictions for this crime and infecting a person with venereal disease totalled 39 in 1999, 26 in 2000 and 23 in 2001. The main function of this criminalisation has turned out to be declaratory and symbolic. The criminalisation has reportedly had no effect on the frequency of the sharing of syringes among drug addicts. Moreover, the criminalisation may also have had a negative impact on HIV testing and access to HIV prevention and care services, not to mention the right to privacy (Butler 2003: 52).

A major social problem in post-Soviet Russia (and Ukraine) has been the trafficking of women, children (and even men), often on the basis of force or deception, for use as slave labour, especially in the sex business. In December 2003, after fits and starts, the RF joined other countries in criminalising both the use of slave labour and trafficking itself (defined in a broad way). This move reflected pressure and input from abroad, as well as the need of Russian police for better legal instruments for confronting trafficking than the earlier law on prostitution (McCarthy 2011).

During the 1990s, the issue of trafficking gained international attention, culminating in 2000 with the UN Trafficking Protocol as part of the Transnational Convention on Organised Crime. The protocol called upon member states of the UN to criminalise trafficking and prosecute traffickers; provide social services to victims; and engage in preventive measures. With the moral and political authority of the protocol in hand, Russian non-governmental organisations (NGOs), usually with foreign connections and funding, became active in the early 2000s in media awareness campaigns relating to both trafficking and prevention activities. The sources of the criminalisation of trafficking date back to a Duma roundtable organised with foreign help in 1999. After a period of neglect and pressure exerted by negative publicity in US State Department human rights reports, in 2002, the Duma formed a working group that introduced a far-reaching bill on trafficking a year later. After months of neglect, the president finally decided to support a weak version of the bill, allegedly because of threats of more negative publicity for Russia from the legal adviser at the US Embassy in Moscow. The lining up of necessary support owed much to the efforts of one legislator, Elena Miziulina, also a key figure in the passage of the new Criminal Procedure Code in 2001 (Solomon 2005). The failure to adopt the stronger version of the bill developed by the working group was allegedly due to its budgetary implications, for example paying for new rehabilitation centres (McCarthy 2011).

The initial enforcement of the new prohibitions was not impressive. In 2006, for example, police conducted 125 trafficking investigations, leading to 53 prosecutions and 13 convictions. The cases concerned mainly sexual exploitation, often targeted non-Russians and resulted in light sentences. The prejudices of policemen charged with enforcement account for these practices, and Russia's status as a state whose role in the international project of combating trafficking lacks bite (Johnson 2009: 119–46).

The Medvedev initiatives: humanisation and business offences

In his annual address to the parliament in November 2008, President Medvedev announced that Russia's system of crime and punishment had become too severe and too costly and he called for its humanisation (Solomon 2009). A year later, the president repeated the message and provided more details on the measures that he was supporting (Poslanie 2009). Days later, Medvedev commissioned a group of jurists and economists constituting the Centre for

Legal and Economic Research (LECS) at the Institute of Contemporary Development (INSOR) to examine the use of criminal law in business regulation and make recommendations for its reduction (Centre for Economic and Legal Research 2011). Both these presidential initiatives involved potential decriminalisation of offences. Although each had a separate logic and history, the playing out of the initiatives became increasingly connected.

The humanisation initiative was aimed especially at extending the real repertoire of alternatives to imprisonment, lowering the range of punishment for some offences and the decriminalisation of some petty offences, by shifting them to the administrative sphere or eliminating them altogether. Leading a team in the Ministry of Justice in developing proposals and writing draft legislation was retired First Deputy Chairman of the Supreme Court of the RF, Vladimir Radchenko, who went out of his way to present his ideas to the public and relevant groups such as the Defense Bar (Radchenko 2008, 2009). By winter 2010, the draft legislation had been completed and sent to other government agencies for review of its financial implications and corruption potential.

The draft criminal legislation stemming from the humanisation initiative promised to broaden the range of non-custodial alternatives to incarceration through the extension of corrective work to those already employed (as was the case in Soviet times), to expand the use of bail as a restraint on accused people and to make early release more common. At the same time, a series of decriminalising measures were being planned, including: insulting an authority, illegally obtaining and distributing public documents (to become an administrative offence); and all offences pursued through private accusations (e.g. insult). Criminal responsibility for failure to pay taxes would be eliminated for situations in which the suspect, individual or firm paid up when asked, and would be possible only after an accused had already been subject to administrative responsibility once before; that is after an 'administrative prelude' (Prava cheloveka v Rossii 2009; Rodin and Samarina 2009). The decriminalisation of basic violations of income tax rules was taken out of the larger package and a version (without the administrative prelude) became law at the end of 2009 (Nalogovye prestupleniia 2009).

During 2010, the draft humanisation law was reviewed by various agencies, including from law enforcement, and in late summer discussed by a working group at the presidential administration. It became clear that some of the suggested changes, especially relating to decriminalisation, encountered resistance from other agencies. As a result, in September, the Minister of Justice Alexander Konovalov decided to divide the proposed reforms into two separate packages, the first of which would deal only with punishments, and the second address the more controversial matter of decriminalisation (Lenta 2010). As we shall see, this decision opened the door for considering business offences in the now separate draft law.

In fact, the very week in September 2010 when Konovalov reported on the resistance to decriminalisation of some petty offences, the group of economists and lawyers connected to the Centre for Economic and Legal Research presented their analysis of criminal law and business at special hearings of the State Duma (Novikova et al. 2010; Centre for Economic and Legal Research 2011). In less than a year, which included a major roundtable discussion in April entitled 'The Decriminalisation of Business', this group (which included distinguished jurists such as retired Supreme Court justices Zhuikov and Radchenko, retired Constitutional Court justice Morshchakova, top criminal law scholars Lopashenko and Naumov, leading lawyers such as Reznik and brilliant well-connected economists such as Grigoriev and Novikova, the coordinator of the group) had drafted a 'Conception of Modernisation of Criminal Legislation in the Economic Sphere' (hereafter 'Conception'), along with suggestions for changes in the law. This long and detailed document argued convincingly that: (1) in the RF, the criminal law was over-used and misused in the regulation of business activity, involving violations of legal principles, and reflected not only in laws and court decisions but also in the practice of law enforcement; and (2) the sanctions applied by courts in Russia were inappropriately harsh not only for business crimes but also for property crimes of all kinds, including theft. In addition, the Conception itself, as well as analytical articles published with it (including one by the author of this chapter), described in detail the common practice of police officials starting prosecutions for business offences as a way of extracting rent or pursuing the interests of rival firms that would benefit from prosecutions. The documents also laid out the huge economic losses sustained by Russia as a result of the harassment and persecution of business through the criminal law (Novikova et al. 2010; Solomon 2010).

The recommendations put forward by the authors of the Conception included the removal from the criminal code of some 15 articles, about half of Chapter 22, including those on 'illegal entrepreneurship' and 'self money laundering'. Other recommendations called for changes in the general part of the code that affected how the articles on business crimes were interpreted. Thus, the authors called for the addition of: (1) a ban on broad interpretations of the law, except to reduce responsibility or punishment; (2) a requirement that terms used in the criminal law be understood as they were in civil or other areas of law, and not in specialised ways; and (3) the principle that doubts and contradictions in the criminal law must be interpreted in favour of the accused (Solomon 2010).

During the period of preparation of the Conception, in April 2010, the president decided to introduce a dramatic change in the handling of business offences, namely a ban on the use of pre-trial detention for those suspected of business crimes. Despite resistance by law enforcement and incomplete implementation, this ban led to a dramatic fall of at least one third in the overall number of prosecutions opened for business crimes overall, including of 65 per cent for illegal entrepreneurship (Article 171) and 80 per cent for money laundering (Article 174.1). The drop in prosecutions reflected the reluctance of police officials to start cases when they could no longer use release from custody to get businessmen to pay for stopping the case (Diatlikovich 2011; Nikitinskii 2011; Peshkova 2011).

The Duma hearings on the Conception of September 2010 produced major support for decriminalisation of business offences among both the members of the Duma and the press, which was reinforced by another discussion at a Duma committee in February 2011 but, as might be expected, the law enforcement agencies opposed many of the changes in the strongest terms, and expressed their reservations during meetings of the Working Group on the humanisation legislation. The Minister of Justice Konovalov joined them, claiming that decriminalisation of business offences was unnecessary because of low levels of conviction (Samarina 2010; Samarina and Rodin 2010). He ignored the fact, as Radchenko and others have emphasised, that tens of thousands of prosecutions for business crimes were started by police officials, only to be stopped before they got to court. Konovalov insisted that high fines would be preferable to decriminalisation. In the end, the Working Group on the humanisation legislation did consider the inclusion of some of the recommendations contained in the Conception with the other decriminalisation initiatives but, as we shall see, rejected almost all of them.

Spring 2011 was framed by the passage into law of the package of changes to punishments (7 March 2011) and the presentation to the Duma (and first reading) of the draft law on decriminalisation in early June, known as the second and third 'pakety' of the humanisation programme. The punishment reform included not only the revitalisation and extension of applicability of alternatives to imprisonment (both corrective work and obligatory labour) but also the removal of the lower limit on punishment for a long list of common offences. The result was a major increase in the discretion of judges in awarding punishment. This discretion could be used to shape punishment to individual needs, to reward those who opted for special procedures (plea bargaining) and to extract bribes. The draft law on decriminalisation included the expected removal from the criminal law of minor offences such as insults and slander, violations of equal rights of citizens, illegal trade in precious metals and, most dramatically, violations of the rules of customs (so-called 'kontrabanda'). Unlike most countries, Russia had made the import of goods of any kind without customs approval into a crime (as opposed to the import of illegal goods such as weapons or narcotics). The discovery by customs officials of mistakes in documentation of imported goods and failure to pay full duties provided a basis for opening or threatening to open prosecutions, which became another way for officials to extract bribes. The draft law of June also forbade the use of imprisonment for first convictions for non-serious crimes and changed the definition of this category to include all offences with a maximum of up to three years' imprisonment (up from two years) (Kulikov 2011; Proekt Federalnyi zakon 2011; Trunov 2011).

For the proponents of decriminalisation of business offences, however, the new draft law was a disappointment. Apart from the new definition of contraband, almost all the business offences that the Conception reformers wanted eliminated from the criminal code remained in place, but with a new provision that offenders could escape conviction by repaying any losses plus a fine of five times the loss (the idea that the Minister of Justice had promoted the previous autumn). This provision was to apply to those accused of illegal entrepreneurship (Article 171) and other business crimes. In the eyes of some observers, this provision seemed to provide a new basis for corrupt activity (Petrova 2011).

The political struggles over decriminalisation of business crimes were far from over. To begin, the Conception reformers organised a series of public discussions, including a roundtable with businesspeople on 25 May, a roundtable with government officials on 29 May and another meeting on 2 June (Centre for Economic and Legal Research). Members of the group also subjected the new draft law to a blistering critique, describing it as a set of half-measures, even pseudo-reforms that ran the risk of creating the impression of genuine change ('Eksperty TsPES' 2011a; Radchenko and Zhalinskii 2011a, 2011b). They also started promoting a wide-scale amnesty for businesspeople previously convicted of business crimes, continuing an initiative started in April ('Eksperty TsPES' 2011b; Morshchakova 2011; 'Obrashchenie ekspertov' 2011). In both these efforts, reformers warned in Cassandra-like fashion of the damage to the economic future of Russia that failure to enact real reforms would entail. They cited dramatic data on the emigration, current and planned, of businesspeople from the RF, and shocking statistics on the steady rise in the closure of businesses in the country (in 2010, four times the level of eight years earlier), so that for the first time the number of businesses closed exceeded the number opened! They attributed this development mainly to the inhospitable climate for business activity created by criminal liability and the actions of law enforcement officials.

The second and third readings of the decriminalisation law in the State Duma took place in the autumn of 2011, and the Bill became law in December 2011. The reformers tried once again to get the decriminalisation of business offences (beyond contraband) added to the bill (Popravki 2011), but without an intervention from the top of the political system (unlikely in the context of the upcoming parliamentary and presidential elections), the broad decriminalisation of business offences promoted by the Conception reformers seemed doomed to failure, notwithstanding the fact that President Medvedev alluded to it at a meeting of the United Russia party on 23 September (NEWSru.com 2011). However, even the controversial elements included in the draft law, such as the reform of contraband and the option for businessmen to avoid criminal responsibility through large payments, were adopted ('O vnesenii' 2011).

The processing of President Medvedev's initiatives to humanise crime and punishment in Russia in response to the post-Soviet harshness and widen the net covered by the criminal law reveals a lot about the distribution of power within the Russian government. Medvedev proved all too willing to have his initiatives subjected to the full impact of bureaucratic review, in which the agencies of the state (especially in policing) had not just a strong voice but also an effective veto power. Perhaps they had their own allies at the top of the political pyramid whose preferences made it difficult for the president to realise his objectives.

If so, notwithstanding particular instances of decriminalisation (and a potentially major change in punishments, including a significant drop in custodial sentences), the criminal law of the RF was likely to remain over-extended, and in comparison with the Soviet period especially bloated. And a similar situation obtained with the Code of Administrative Violations! The combination suggested a post-Soviet and post-communist political and economic order with increased regulatory capacity or, with inconsistent execution, more opportunity for rent-seeking.

Conclusions

When a post-communist regime pursues democratisation and movement towards a market economy, such changes are bound to have an impact on the criminal law. But the effect may involve not only decriminalisation that accompanies political and social liberalisation but also new forms of crime associated with regulating a capitalist or market economy, and their application may have strange effects. In countries where the process of political change stalls or the form of capitalism adopted gives pride of place to the state and its officials, liberalising tendencies are likely to end and be replaced by more extensive criminalisation. In addition, the sources of change in the scope of the criminal law that are common in stable regimes or states not involved in political transitions continue to matter. These include both the pressures to reduce the volume of criminal offences through shifts to administrative jurisdiction and the need to adjust the criminal law to meet new challenges, domestic or international in character.

All these generalisations are supported by the experience of the RF in its first 18 years. But Russia's experience with criminal law has other features too – an unusual degree of instability, with constant changes in multiple directions, itself reflecting a political process in which political benefits and special interests, including those of the police and prosecution bodies, almost exclude policy-making based on scientific research, not to speak of reasoned understanding of the practice of law enforcement and criminal justice.

Among the interests starting to exert influence in criminal policy in the second decade of the new millennium is the Russian Orthodox Church, which opposes Western-style juvenile justice (as a threat to the family!) and has become a promoter of new restrictions on abortion, which could involve criminalisation of the performance of abortions under many circumstances. As of summer 2011, the Duma Committee on Questions of the Family, Women and Children was developing a draft law on the rights of the unborn child that promised drastic restrictions on a woman's right to have an abortion (only in the first trimester, only with permission of a partner or parent and only for medical reasons). The consideration of this initiative reflects a deep-seated view that the criminal law should reflect moral values, even if they are shared by only a minority of the population (Shkel 2011).

Just as Russia's 'transition' is far from paradigmatic, so its experience with criminalisation and decriminalisation may diverge from that of at least some post-communist countries, especially the Visegrád group and the Baltic States which entered the EU relatively early.[1] It would also be useful to compare the development of the criminal law in Russia with its counterparts in Ukraine, Belarus and Kazakhstan. One might expect considerable convergence of experience within those states because of shared values and the strong influence of law enforcement agencies in all of them.

Notes

* This chapter benefited from comments on previous drafts by Kathryn Hendley, Lauren McCarthy, Alexei Trochev, Lucan Way and participants in the conference on which this volume was based.

1 A comparative study of patterns of legislative change and stability of laws in post-socialist Europe argues that, in some countries such as the Czech Republic, Slovakia and Hungary, laws are much more stable and better defined than they are in Russia and Ukraine (Volkov et al. 2010b). In contrast, a Hungarian criminal law scholar has criticised 'the incessant amendment of the Penal Code' during the 1990s and beyond. This 'panic of law-making' led to far more criminalisation than decriminalisation (Nagy 2007).

References

Brown, D.K. (2007) 'Democracy and Decriminalization', *Texas Law Review*, 86(2) (December): 223–75.

Butler, W.E. (2003) *HIV/AIDS and Drug Misuse in Russia: Harm Reduction Programmes and the Russian Legal System*, London: International Family Health.

Butorina, E. (2009) 'Sudebnaia arifmetika. Predstaviteli Rossiiskoi Femidy vyskzalis o svoei reforme', *Vremia novostei*, 2 December.

Centre for Economic and Legal Research (2011) Centre for Economic and Legal Research Website. Online. Available www.lecs-center.org (accessed 26 September 2011).

Diatlikovich, V. (2011) 'Svoboda kak politika', 19 April. Online. Available http://rusrep.ru/article/2011/04/19/freedom (accessed 26 September 2011).

'Eksperty TsPES' (2011a) 'Analiticheskaia zapiski o proekta federalnogo zakona o vnesenii izmenenii v UK RF', June 2011. Online. Available www.lecs-center.org (accessed 26 September 2011).

——(2011b) 'Amnistiia predprinimatelei', June. Online. Available www.lecs-center.org (accessed 26 September 2011).

Firestone, T. (2010) 'Armed Injustice: Abuse of the Law and Complex Crime in Post-Soviet Russia', *Denver Journal of International Law and Policy*, 38(4) (Fall): 555–93.

Galakhova, A.V. (2005) *Prestupleniia protiv pravosudiia*, Moscow: Norma.

Gavrilov, B.Ia. (2008) *Sovremennaia ugolovnaia politika Rossii: tsifry i fakty*, Moscow: Prospekt.

Gelman, V. and Cameron, R. (eds) (2010) *The Politics of Sub-National Authoritarianism in Russia*, London: Ashgate.
Gusfield, J. (1963) *Symbolic Crusade: Status Politics and the American Temperance Movement*, Urbana: University of Illinois Press.
Husak, D. (2008) *Overcriminalization: The Limits of the Criminal Law*, Oxford: Oxford University Press.
Ivantsova, N. (2004) 'Perspektiva khuliganstva – ego dekriminalizatsiia', *Zakonnost*, 11.
Johnson, J.E. (2009) *Gender Violence in Russia: the Politics of Feminist Intervention*, Bloomington: Indiana University Press.
Kashepov, V.P. (2010) 'Kontsepsiia razvitiia ugolovnogo zakonodatelstva', in T.Ia. Khabrieva and Iu.A. Tikhomirnov (eds) *Kontsepsi razvitiia rossiiskogo zakonodatelstva*, Moscow: Eksmo, 271–98.
Kibalnik, A. and Solomonenko, I. (2008) 'Ekstremistkoe khuliganstvo – nonsens ugolovnogo Zakona', *Zakonnost*, 4, 21–23.
Klebanov, L.P. (2006) 'Desiat let Ugolovnomu kodeksu Rossiiskoi Federatsii: Dostoinstva i nedostatki (nauchno-prakticheskaia konferentsiia)', *Gosudarstvo i pravo*, 9: 107–14.
Kon, I.S. (1997) 'Russia', in D.J. West and R. Green (eds) *Sociolegal Control of Homosexuality: A Multi-Nation Comparison*, New York: Plenum Press.
Kulikov, V. (2011) 'Svoboda zamedlenogo deistviia: Popravki v Ugolovnyi kodeks delaiut sistemu nakazanii bolee effektivnoi', *Rossiiskaia gazeta*, 8 June.
Lenta (2010) 'Miniust prelozhil otlozhit dekriminalizatsiia melkikh prestupleniia'. Online. Available http://lenta.ru/ews/2010/09/09/decrime/_Printed.htm (accessed 26 September 2011).
Lopashenko, N.A. (2009) *Ugolovnaia politika*, Moscow: Wolters Kluwer.
——(2010) 'Ugolovnaia politika Rossii v otnoshenii prestupleniia v sfere ekonomicheskoi deiatelnosti (analiz na osnove izmenenii ugolovnogo zakonodatelstva)', *Kriminologicheskii zhurnal Baikalskogo universiteta ekonomiki i prava*, 4(14): 36–44. Online. Available http://cj.isea.ru (accessed 26 September 2011).
Luneev, V.V. (2004) 'Tendentsii sovremennoi prestupnosti i borby s nei v Rossii', *Gosudarstvo i pravo*, 1: 5–18.
——(2007) *Epokha globalizatsii i prestupnost*, Moscow: Norma.
McCarthy, L. (2011) 'Trafficking (In)justice: Law Enforcement's Response to Human Trafficking in Russia', unpublished PhD thesis, University of Wisconsin.
Morshchakova, T. (2011) 'Podvesti chertu pod proshlym', *gazeta.ru*, 8 June.
Nagy, F. (2007) 'Transformation of Substantive Penal Law since the Political Transformation in Hungary', in V. Lamm (ed.) *Transformation in Hungarian Law (1989–2006)*, Budapest: Akademiai Kiado.
Nalogovye prestupleniia (2009) 'Vstupil v silu zakon o dekriminalizatsiia nalogovykh prestuplenii'. Online. Available http://prokuror.kaluga.ru/prok/ugolovnoe/VSTUPL_V_slu_zakon_O_Dekrim (accessed 26 September 2011).
Naumov, A.V. (1997) 'The New Russian Criminal Code as a Reflection of Ongoing Reforms', *Criminal Law Forum*, 8(2): 191–230.
——(2010) 'Istoriia rossiiskogo ugolovnogo zakonodatelstva ob otvetstvennosti za predprinimatelskuiu deiatelnost', in E. Novikova et al. (eds) *Kontseptsiia modernizatsiia ugolovnogo zakonodatelstva v ekonomicheskoi sfere*, Moscow: Liberalnaia missiia.
NEWScom.ru (2011) 'Medvedev soglasilsia vozglavit pravitelstvo i perechislil sem punktov svoei stragegii v dolzhnosti premera', 24 September 2011, in section: 'V Rossii'.

Nikitinskii, L. (2011) 'Gosudartsv "silovykh struktur" mozhet postroit tol'ko "rynochnuiu ekonomiki bez predprinimatelei". Predprinimateli sidiat na zonakh', *Novaia gazeta*, 24 April.

Noble, B. (2010) 'Decriminalizing Sodomy in the Former Soviet Union, 1991–2003', unpublished MPhil thesis, University of Oxford.

Novikova, E.V. et al. (2010) *Kontseptsiia modernizatsii ugolovnogo zakonodatelstva v ekonomicheskoi sfere*, Moscow: Fond 'Liberalnaia missiia'.

'Obrashchenie ekspertov' (2011) 'Ob amnistii predprinimateliam, privlechennym k ugolovnoi otvetstvenoosti', Obrashchenie ekspertov i obshchestvennosti k prezidentu RF, *Novaia gazeta*, 24 April.

Orlova, A.V. (2009) 'The Russian "War on Drugs" A Kinder, Gentler Approach?', *Problems of Post-Communism*, Jan–Feb: 23–34.

'O vnesenii' (2011) 'O vnesenii izmenenii v Ugolovnyi Kodeks i otdelnye zakonodatelnye akty Rossiiskoi Federatsii'. Federal'nyi zakon no. 420 ot 7 dekabria, *Rossiiskaia gazeta*, 16 December.

Peshkova, O.V. (2011) 'Ogranicheniia aresta predprinimatelei. Pervye rezultaty sudebnoi Praktiki', *Sud'ia*, May: 30–33.

Petrova, N. (2011) 'Prezident sudu ne UK', *Kommersant Dengi*, 13 June.

Popravki (2011) 'Popravki k vtoromu chteniiu zakonoproekta', No. 559740–45' i poiasnitelnaia zapiska. Unpublished documents.

Poslanie (2009) 'Poslanie prezidenta Federalnomu Sobraniiu Rossiikoi Federatsii ot 12 noiabria', Online. Available http://kremlin.ru/transcripts/5979 (accessed 26 September 2011).

Prava cheloveka v Rossii (2009) 'Proekt liberalizatsii UK: khorosho, no malo', Online. Available www.hro.org/node/5689 (accessed 26 September 2011).

Proekt Federalnyi zakon (2011) 'O vnesenii izmenenii v Ugolovnyi kodeks RF i otdelnye zakonodatelnye akty RF', *Rossiiskaia gazeta*, 8 June.

Radchenko, V.I. (2007) *Kommentarii k ugolovnomu kodeksu Rossiiskoi Federatsii*, St Petersburg: Piter Press.

——(2008) 'Obespechenie prav i interesov grazhdan pri osushchestvlenii ugolovnopravovoi politiki v Rossiiskoi Federatsii', Doklad Federalnoi palaty advokatov RF.

——(2009) 'Kak ispravit tiurmu. Chen otlichaetsia sisstema ispolneniia nakazaniia v bolshinstve stran ot nashei?', *Rossiiskaia gazeta*, September.

Radchenko, V.I. and Zhalinskii, A. (2011a) 'Ugolovnyi zakon: Bolshaia imitatsiia reformy', *Vedomosti*, 23 June.

——(2011b) 'Ugolovnyi zakon: politika izgnaniia Biznesa', *Vedomosti*, 24 June.

Radzinowicz, Sir L. and King, J. (1977) *The Growth of Crime: The International Experience*, New York: Basic Books.

Rodin, I. and Samarina, A. (2009) 'Ugolovnyi kodeks podvergnut liberalizatsii: Proshlogodnie prezidentskie porucheniia nakonets obretatiu formu zakonoproektov', *Nezavisimaia gazeta*, September 30.

Samarina, A. (2010) 'Miniust ne khochet liberalnykh pretsdentov', *Nezavisimaia gazeta*, 14 October. Online. Available www.ng.ru/printed/246455 (accessed 26 September 2011).

Samarina, A. and Rodin, I. (2010) 'Biznesu prikazano zhdat. Dekriminalizatsiia zakonodatelstva v oblasti ekonomicheskikh prestupleniia zaderzhivaetsia', *Nezavisimaia gazeta*, 9 October. Online. Available www.ng.ru/politics/2010–09–09/3_business.html (accessed 26 September 2011).

Shkel, T. (2011) 'Ubitoe destvo. Zakonoproekt o zashchite rebenka eshche do ego rozhdeniia vyzval goriachie spory', *Rossiiskaia gazeta*, 2 June.

Solomon, P.H., Jr. (1992) 'Reforming Criminal Law under Gorbachev', in D.D. Barry (ed.) *Toward the Rule of Law in Russia?* Armonk, NY: M.E. Sharpe.

——(2005) 'The Criminal Procedure Code of 2001: Will It Make Russian Justice More Fair?', in W.A. Pridemore (ed.) *Ruling Russia: Law, Crime, and Justice in a Changing Society*, Lanham, MA: Rowman and Littlefield.

——(2009) 'President Medvedev and the Courts: The Start of a New Era?', in J.L. Black and M. Johns (eds) *From Putin to Medvedev: Continuity or Change?* Manotick, Ontario: Penumbra Press.

——(2010) 'Sovershenstvovanie ugolovnogo zakonodatelstva v Rossiiskoi Federatsii: ekonomicheskie prestupleniia i gumanizatsiia', in E.V. Novikova et al. (eds) *Kontseptsiia modernizatsii ugolovnogo zakonodatelstva v ekonomicheskoi sfere*, Moscow: Fond Liberalnaia missiia.

SOVA Center (2011) SOVA center website. Online. Available www.sova-center.ru (accessed 26 September 2011).

Sudebnyi Department (2007) 'Otchet o rabote sudov pervoi instantsii po rassmotreniiu ugolovnykh del za 12 mesiatsov 2007'. Online. Available www.cdep.ru (accessed 26 September 2011) (otdel 'statistika').

——(2009) 'Operativnye statisticheskie svedeniia o rabote federalnykh sudov obshchei iurisdiktsii i mirovykh sudei za 9 mesiatsev 2009'. Online. Available www.cdep.ru (accessed 26 September 2011) (otdel 'statistik').

——(2010) 'Svodnye statisticheskie svedeniia o sostoianii sudimosti v Rossii za 2010 god', Table K3. Online. Available www.cdep.ru (accessed 26 September 2011) (otdel 'statistika').

Trunov, I. (2011) 'Ugolovnyi kodeks izdadut v miagkom pereplete', *Osobaia bukva*, 8 June. Online. Available www.specletter.com/pravosudie/2011-06–08/print/ (accessed 26 September 2011).

Volkov, V.V., Paneiakh, E.L. and Titaev, K.D. (2010a) 'Proizvolnaia aktivnost pravookhranitelnykh organov v sfere borby s ekonomicheskoi prestupnostiu. Analiz statistiki', St Petersburg: Institut problem pravoprimeneniia. Online. Available www.enforce.spb.ru (accessed 26 September 2011).

Volkov, V.V., Demitreva, A. and Primakov, V. (2010b) '*Zakonodatelnaia aktivnost, stabil'nos zakonodatelstva i kachestvo pravovoi sredy: sravnitelnyi Analiz post-sotsialisticheskikh stran'*, St Petersburg: Institut problem pravoprimeneniia. Online. Available www.enforce.spb.ru (accessed 26 September 2011).

Zabeida, A. (2009) 'V tiurmu iz kazino'. Online. Available www.gazeta-yurist.ru/prn_article.php?i=877 (accessed 26 September 2011).

Zakon (2006) 'O gosudarstvennom regulirovanii deiatel'nosti po organizatsii i provendeniiu azartnykh igr i o vnesenii izmenenii v nekotorye zakonodatelnykh aktov RF', Federalnyi zakon no. 244, 29 December.

7 Decriminalising sex between men in the former Soviet Union, 1991–2003

Conditionality and the Council of Europe[1]

Ben Noble

Between 1991 and 2003, most former[2] Soviet states decriminalised consensual sex between adult men.[3] Only Uzbekistan and Turkmenistan retain articles in their criminal codes that criminalise this form of sexual congress. The cluster of progressive reforms was surprising, not least because the morally sensitive changes were largely uncontested. Commenting on the possibility of decriminalisation, Igor Kon – the leading Russian academic on sexual minorities – wrote in 1993 (112): 'Even given a favourable outcome, the process is bound to be protracted, problematical and vastly different in the various regions and former republics'. This scenario, however, was not realised. The chapter will explore this group of decriminalisations, interrogating the existing view that legal reform was primarily the result of Council of Europe membership conditionality.

Introduction

Western influence is regularly invoked to explain progressive legal change in former Soviet states. This can be found in the existing literature on the decriminalisation of sex between men in the former Soviet Union (FSU): the Council of Europe (CoE) is often cited as the cause of this reform 'wave' – see, for example, Torra (1998: 77); Waaldijk (2000: 72); Sanders (2002: 17); and Štulhofer and Sandfort (2005: 13). When joining the CoE, post-Soviet states were required to sign the European Convention on Human Rights (ECHR) at the time of accession, and ratify it within a specified timeframe (Croft et al. 1999). In order to ratify the Convention, states entered a harmonisation process to bring their domestic legislation into conformity with the ECHR's substantive provisions, as well as its case law (Drzemczewski 1995). In the case of *Dudgeon v. UK* in 1981, the European Court of Human Rights (ECtHR) decided that the criminalisation of consensual, private, same-sex sexual intercourse contravened Article 8 of the ECHR.[4] In effect, this meant that all members and applicant states were required to remove laws criminalising sex between men. Put differently, decriminalisation was – in principle, at least[5] – a membership condition for the Council of Europe.

Most existing studies argue that CoE membership requirements were used to export a liberal, Western norm into what were seen as inimical domestic environments. The decriminalisation of sex between men in FSU states is chosen here, therefore, as a putative case of a 'wave' of reforms caused by a single international source – in this case, the CoE. The task of the chapter is to test this explanation by examining and comparing the actual processes of reform with those expected by such an explanation.[6] The research on which this chapter is based used process-tracing methods (see George and Bennett 2005: 6) to examine data collected on a field trip to the Council of Europe in September 2009, as well as the domestic dynamics of decriminalisation in former Soviet states. This methodology is in line with the 'policy-tracking approach' employed by Hughes et al. (2004b: 523) to examine EU conditionality.[7] Interviews were conducted with non-governmental organisation (NGO) officials, CoE officials, as well as legal and academic specialists on the region.[8] Documents consulted included texts of criminal codes, NGO reports, NGO newsletters, CoE reports on accession states, accession documents and media reporting.[9]

From the outset, the CoE membership conditionality argument is distinctly problematic. First, CoE membership conditionality cannot *prima facie* explain all decriminalisations in the former Soviet Union: Ukraine repealed its law criminalising sex between men well before its membership process began; and Kazakhstan, Kyrgyzstan and Tajikistan have never had a membership track open to them. Second, the account remains incomplete for the other FSU states. That is, in order to understand why these states decriminalised sex between men, it is not enough simply to point to an international organisation's (IO) membership requirements. As the literature on conditionality demonstrates, state compliance with IO conditions is far from a clear and uncontested process (see, for example, Killick et al. 1998; Checkel 2000; Jordan 2003; Hughes et al. 2004a, 2004b; Epstein 2008; Kochenov 2008; and Sasse 2008, 2009). Indeed, CoE pressure to decriminalise sex between men in the form of conditionality was met with sustained contestation in Romania, with exhortations from parliament that 'we want to join Europe, not Sodom' (see, for example, Long 1998; Stychin 2003; Nachescu 2005; Turescu and Stan 2005).[10] Third, the non-criminalisation of sex between men is not a distinctly Western norm. For example, the Soviet Russian criminal code promulgated in 1922 did not include a criminalising article, thus departing from the late Tsarist practice of criminalisation (Kon 1997); and many East European communist states decriminalised in the 1960s and 1970s (Tatchell 1992). Moreover, the pattern of compliance following *Dudgeon* was varied. Certain member states – Ireland and Cyprus, in particular – vehemently resisted what they saw to be a legal reform incompatible with their societies' morality (McLoughlin 1996).[11]

It will be argued that the decriminalisation of sex between men in FSU states was not a unitary, wholly Western-inspired 'wave'. More specifically, very little evidence can be marshalled to support the CoE membership conditionality explanation. A more nuanced picture of reform emerges by placing this cluster of legal changes in the longer narrative of Soviet laws regulating sexual practices, by revealing the patchiness of CoE pressure in this area and by tracing legislative reform dynamics in each state – a style of scholarship that is in line with Lacey's (2009: 942) call for 'historicising criminalisation'. This chapter will deal mainly with evidence relating to the CoE's activities, although summary sections on legal history and domestic reform processes are included.

History

The legal regulation of sex between men has a complex and varied history in FSU states. In Russia, for example, the legal status of this sexual practice alternated from Tsarist criminalisation to Bolshevik decriminalisation to Stalinist recriminalisation and back to post-Soviet decriminalisation (Kon 1997); certain other states, however, experienced consistent criminalisation (Healey 2001). The brief sketch of this history below will simply provide stage-setting points for the main section on the CoE.[12] This will involve making three points: first, that the legal regulation of sex between men varied temporally and geographically across states in the region; second, that societal sentiment towards sexual minorities in the late Soviet and early post-Soviet periods was not apparently conducive to progressive reform; and third, that it is possible to locate domestic ideational sources for reform in this area of criminal law.

Following the abrogation of the Tsarist criminal code in October 1917, an article criminalising sex between men was not included in the first Soviet Russian code of 1922 (Healey 1993: 31–32). Similarly, the criminal codes of the Ukrainian Soviet Socialist Republic (SSR), the Belorussian SSR and the Armenian section of the Transcaucasian Soviet Federative Socialist Republic did not criminalise this sexual practice. The criminal codes of all other Union republics, however, contained criminalising articles (De Jong 1982; Healey 2001). This institutional variation ended, however, on 7 March 1934, when sex between men was made a criminal offence across the Soviet Union – part of the wider Stalinist 'sexual thermidor' (Stites 1991: 376).[13]

Following criminalisation, the subject was removed from public debate (Kon 1997). Thus, as Essig (1999: 7) writes, 'homosexuality existed outside the public's view, glimpsed only fleetingly in a law that forbade it'. Indeed, the 'concept of homosexuality as a danger to the socialist state persisted' through the process of de-Stalinisation (Gessen 1994: 9). This 'discursive void' (Baer 2009: 44) was only broken during *glasnost'* (openness) in the late 1980s. However, early press articles argued that the decriminalisation of sex between men would lead to the spread of this 'infectious' 'perversion' (Tornow 1991). Indeed, this negative discourse was perpetuated and reinforced by the emergence of HIV/AIDS. High-profile medical experts – such as Academician Nikolai Burgasov (erstwhile Deputy Health Minister and Chief Hygiene Doctor of the USSR) – stated publicly that the virus did not pose a threat to the Soviet people, 'so far as homosexuality was a criminal offence' (Kon 1993: 95). An indication of societal attitudes towards the subject is captured by survey results from Russia conducted at the end of 1992, in which 'gay men' came second only to 'neo-fascists' as the most disliked group (Bahry et al. 1997). This would not seem to be the most propitious environment for progressive reform.

There were, however, domestic initiatives to decriminalise sex between men in the Soviet era. It is possible to trace reformist sentiment through, for example, a 1973 legal textbook, which noted the curious jurisprudential status of the offence,[14] and efforts by Professors Alexei Ignatov and Igor Kon to publish research on the topic as a means of urging reform (Gessen 1994; Kon 1997; Healey 2001). Although this progressive thought had little initial impact on official policy, *perestroika* (restructuring) provided a juncture for more liberal ideas. Thus, for example, Kon (1997: 228) notes that a 'draft of the revised Russian Criminal Code, prepared by a commission of lawyers in the mid-1980s, excluded' the article criminalising consensual sex between men in the Russian Soviet Federative Socialist Republic (RSFSR). This liberalising vein, moreover, was not restricted to the RSFSR. In 1990, a conference entitled 'Sexual Minorities and Society: the Changing Attitudes toward Homosexuality in 20th Century Europe' was hosted by the Institute of History of the Estonian Academy of Sciences. The meeting gathered both Soviet delegates and Western academics and activists[15] in what was framed as a sober scientific event to discuss various dimensions of sexuality; in practice, it served as an opportunity to discuss the possibility and necessity of removing laws criminalising sex between men (interview with Jeffrey Weeks, 2009).

Placing post-Soviet reform into a longer historical narrative – however brief its exposition – is vital. It displays historical experience of the non-criminalisation of sex between men in certain regions of the former Soviet Union well before the emergence of such a norm centred on ECHR case law. Furthermore, it is possible to appreciate both the difficulties of, and the possibilities for, reform in the late Soviet and early post-Soviet periods, thus setting the context for an analysis of putative international influence.

The Council of Europe and conditionality

The CoE membership conditionality explanation implies a particular temporal pattern of reform – that is, a distinctive sequential logic. In order for this explanation to be robust, the implied causal 'steps' (George and Bennett 2005: 207) between the putative cause – Council membership condition – and effect – the decriminalisation of sex between men – must be present in each case of reform. This central section will discuss whether the argument found in the existing literature is compatible with process-level evidence of the CoE's role in the decriminalisation of sex between men in the former Soviet Union.

The CoE did not grant automatic membership to post-communist states.[16] States interested in joining the Council were granted 'special guest status', facilitating basic institutional contact and reform advice (Manas 1996). As a formal pre-condition of membership – and in line with Article 3 of the organisation's statute (1949) – applicant states had to 'accept the principles of the rule of law and of the enjoyment by all persons within its jurisdiction of human rights and fundamental freedoms'. At the same time, the Council was conscious of the need to integrate post-communist states quickly for its own post-Cold War legitimacy and longevity (Croft et al. 1999). There was also an institutional belief held by many in the Council that an inclusive enlargement policy would help states reform as members of the organisation (Checkel 1999).[17]

This combination of exclusivity and inclusivity was problematic. On the one hand, the Council was expected – as Storey (1995: 137) puts it – to 'play the role of principal democratic auditor (or human rights "Bundesbank") of European states'.[18] Membership would, therefore, be an exclusive, respectable mark of levels (political, legal and judicial) already achieved. On the other hand, there was pressure for the Council to become an embodiment of pan-European unity and an active agent in reform (Simpson 2001). In this inclusive vision, the main criterion for membership became simply an aspiration to achieve liberal-democratic ideals (Tarschys 1995). This constituted, quite clearly, a jumble of roles and requirements, which resulted in a compromise: the Council would admit post-communist states quickly but with conditions attached to their membership.

The CoE's variant of conditionality was peculiar. Unlike the European Union's (EU) *ex ante* form of conditionality, the CoE included considerable elements of *ex post* conditionality.[19] As Vachudova (2005: 133) notes, the Council 'often settled for only a commitment to change domestic policies in the *future*'. Compliance with accession commitments would then be monitored by both the Parliamentary Assembly of the Council of Europe (PACE) and the Committee of Ministers (Croft et al. 1999). Clearly, this form of conditionality was dictated by the two competing views on the organisation's enlargement noted above.[20]

The Council was also particular in its use of 'tailored' conditions. In other words, it applied different conditions for different aspirant states (Meron and Sloan 1996). These differences were determined by the findings of rapporteurs from PACE sent to investigate conditions in applicant states, as well as the results of 'eminent jurists' reports'. Overall, the trend was for more stringent conditions to apply to later joining states (Storey 1995).

There is no automatic link between conditionality and compliance. Hughes et al.. (2004a), for example, warn against assuming the (positive) causal effects of conditionality on state behaviour. This is particularly apparent for an ostensibly 'weak institution' (Sasse 2011: 171) such as the Council of Europe, with limited mechanisms for sanctioning non-compliance. And yet, Schimmelfennig et al. (2006: 7) are wrong to argue that the CoE was limited to socialisation strategies other than conditionality, without the high material benefits of institutions such as the EU and the North Atlantic Treaty Organization (NATO). As Kelley (2004) demonstrates, the Council was successful in bringing about change using conditionality in certain circumstances. For example, Kelley concludes that 'unrelenting' (2004: 444) CoE conditionality in Latvia was successful in amending citizenship legislation. This insight reinforces the need to pay close attention to the specific processes of conditionality – in particular, the 'politics of conditionality' (Sasse 2008: 842; see also Kochenov 2008). With this very focus, however, it is clear that compliance with the norm created by *Dudgeon* would be problematic as the judgment was contested by a number of existing Council member states. This lack of 'taken-for-grantedness' (Epstein 2008: 15) diminished the authority with which the Council could impose conditions for membership.

Hughes et al. (2004b: 526) distinguish between 'formal' and 'informal' EU conditionality. Whereas the former relates to the black letter of conditions, the latter 'includes the operational pressures and recommendations applied by actors'. Thus, we might say that formal conditions are *animated* by informal conditionality. In the legal harmonisation process associated with ECHR ratification, it is possible that Council officials highlighted or emphasised particular areas for reform in their interactions with officials from 'special guest status' states. Similarly, Checkel (2000) – writing about Council efforts in Ukraine to abolish the death penalty – describes the 'conditionality-plus-dialogue approach'. In essence, this combines conditionality with other socialisation techniques, such as persuasion, social learning and social influence. Vachudova (2005: 285, note 74) terms this 'soft conditionality'. For Kelley (2004: 449), this mix was the norm: 'institutions never applied conditionality without also relying on softer efforts'. Checkel (2000) writes of CoE attempts to 'convince Ukrainian elites that abolishment [sic] of capital punishment was the appropriate thing to do as a democratising, rule-of-law polity'. Peshkopia and Imami (2008) corroborate the use of this mixed strategy, using the case of Albania. They note, furthermore, that the Council attempted to socialise the elites of accession states, while insulating this reform process – particularly for morally sensitive pieces of legislation – from the public.

If CoE membership conditionality was responsible for the decriminalisation of sex between men in this group of states, then we would expect to see a particular pattern of compliance: either states would decriminalise while holding 'special guest status' – therefore subject to pressure from PACE rapporteurs and helped by legal experts through the *Demosthenes-bis*[21] programme (Manas 1996); or, for states that had not decriminalised before gaining membership, we would expect decriminalisation to be made an accession commitment, with subsequent compliance. Table 7.1 presents the relevant data for this first stage of analysis.

As noted above, four states fit neither pattern: Kazakhstan, Kyrgyzstan, Tajikistan and Ukraine. Six states fit the first pattern variant – decriminalisation during 'special guest status': Azerbaijan, Belarus,[22] Estonia, Latvia, Moldova and Russia. Of course, noting a pattern match is not the same as finding a causal relationship. In order to evaluate the latter, we need to drill down to a different level of data: evidence of the Council's activities around the issue of decriminalisation in accession states. The three remaining states –

Table 7.1 Soviet criminal code articles, start years of CoE 'special guest status', years of the decriminalisation of sex between men and accession years for CoE member states (arranged by decriminalisation year)

State	*Soviet article*	*CoE guest*	*Decriminalise*	*CoE member*
Ukraine	122	1992	1991	1995
Latvia	124	1991	1992	1995
Estonia	118	1991	1992	1993
Lithuania[1]	122	1991	1993	1993
Russia	121	1992	1993	1996
Belarus	119	1992	1994	X
Moldova[2]	106	1993	1995	1995
Kazakhstan	104	X	1998	X
Kyrgyzstan	112	X	1998	X
Tajikistan	125	X	1998	X
Georgia	121	1996	2000	1999
Azerbaijan	113	1996	2000	2001
Armenia	116	1996	2003	2001
Uzbekistan	100	X	X	X
Turkmenistan	126	X	X	X

Sources: EURO-Letter (various); Ottosson (2008); Council of Europe reports and accession documents (various). Online. Available http://assembly.coe.int/ASP/Search/PACEWebItemSearchDoc_E.asp (accessed 21 November 2011). Decriminalisation took the form of amendments to Soviet-era codes in Belarus, Estonia, Latvia, Lithuania, Moldova, Russia and Ukraine; decriminalisation in Armenia, Azerbaijan, Georgia, Kazakhstan, Kyrgyzstan and Tajikistan occurred with the introduction of new post-Soviet codes.

Notes: 1 More detail on timings is required to make clear the temporal pattern: Lithuania became a member of the Council of Europe on 14 May 1993, and decriminalised sex between men on 11 June 1993.

2 As for Lithuania, more detail on timings is required: Moldova decriminalised sex between men on 15 June 1995, and became a member of the Council of Europe on 13 July 1995.

Armenia, Georgia and Lithuania – are candidates for the second pattern variant, but assessing this requires information on the content of accession agreements. The following section will examine this more fine-grained evidence of the Council's efforts, drawing on archival sources and the accounts of officials involved with accession processes.

On 1 October 1981, PACE adopted Recommendation 924, 'On discrimination against homosexuals'. *Inter alia*, this called on CoE member states to remove laws criminalising sex between men, in line with – although pre-dating – the ECtHR's judgement in *Dudgeon v. UK*. This constituted a declaratory political precedent for the Assembly's position on the legal regulation of sex between men. Quite clearly, the statement was made with reference to existing members. With later enlargement to post-communist space, however, PACE's position became ambiguous. Should it require decriminalisation *before* accession or simply exert pressure when states became members? An initiative advocating the former approach can be seen in

Written Declaration 227 (18 February 1993), 'On homosexual rights in the new democracies'. This document suggested that attention to the legal status of sex between men should be included in accession reform considerations. Torra (1998) cites this as a clear sign of Council pressure. However, Torra fails to note that the document was not adopted by PACE but, rather, signed by only 11 members of the Assembly. As such, although non-criminalisation technically formed part of the ECHR *acquis*, political support for emphasising decriminalisation as an accession condition was weak. Indeed, further research reveals that the motivation for Written Declaration 227 came from an NGO – the International Lesbian and Gay Association (ILGA) – which lobbied an Austrian parliamentarian, Mrs Graenitz, to submit the document for members of the Assembly to sign (EURO-Letter 7 1992).[23]

By the end of the 1990s, political will in this area had increased significantly. In a meeting of the Sub-Committee on Human Rights of the Committee on Legal Affairs and Human Rights (CLAHR) in Paris on 14 October 1999, members discussed the situation of sexual minorities in CoE member states. The situation in 'special guest states' was also discussed. The event provided a wealth of information on continued discrimination, and displayed a renewed consensus on advocating the removal of discriminating legal provisions. Similar points were made by Mr Csaba Tabajdi – rapporteur for CLAHR – in his report, 'Situation of lesbians and gays in Council of Europe member states', presented to PACE on 6 June 2000. This formed the basis for a debate in the Assembly on 30 June, and the adoption on 26 September of Recommendation 1474 (2000). *Inter alia*, this called on member states to 'remove all legislative provisions rendering homosexual acts between consenting adults liable to criminal prosecution' (part 11 iii b), and 'to release with immediate effect anyone imprisoned for sexual acts between consenting homosexual adults' (part 11 iii c).

Recommendation 1474 (2000) is interesting for another reason. The document notes: 'Under the accession procedure for new member states, the Assembly ensures that, as a *prerequisite for membership*, homosexual acts between consenting adults are no longer classified as a criminal offence' (part 4).[24] This equates to *ex ante* conditionality. It is, furthermore, important to stress that this is an apparent statement on existing procedures, rather than a recommendation for future practice.[25] And yet, we have already noted PACE's ambiguous position on the place of decriminalisation in accession. It is clear by looking at accession documents, in fact, that this characterisation of decriminalisation conditionality is at best misleading, at worst false.

Following a state's application to join the CoE, the Committee of Ministers is mandated by Statutory Resolution 51 (30 A) to seek the advice of PACE in the form of an official 'Opinion'. We would expect to find evidence of Council pressure on states to decriminalise sex between men in these documents. There are, however, few references to such efforts. None is present in the documents relating to the accession of Estonia, Georgia, Latvia, Lithuania, Russia and Ukraine.[26] This is particularly puzzling for Georgia and

Lithuania, as sex between men remained a criminal offence at the time of the states' accession to the CoE. Decriminalisation was clearly, therefore, not a prerequisite for membership; neither was it an explicit accession commitment. This is made even more puzzling given the fact that a decriminalisation commitment was attached to Romania's accession in 1993. Why was such a commitment not extended to states in a similar position? Peter Schieder – Honorary President of PACE – revealed in a speech that a focus on decriminalising sex between men often fell victim to intra-Assembly politics and was, therefore, not always included in accession agreements (Schieder 2009). This, again, highlights the importance of paying attention to the politics of conditionality.

The first reference to efforts to decriminalise sex between men in a post-Soviet state can be found in the CLAHR opinion on Moldova's application, written by Mr Columberg and Mr Jeszensky (15 June 1995). They note:

> We have received a letter from a human rights group fighting for the rights of homosexuals, which pointed out that the amended Soviet Criminal Code still penalises homosexual relationships between consenting adults (in November 1994). The Moldova authorities have assured us that this provision is not implemented, and that the new draft Criminal Code decriminalises such relationships. We expect that no amendment will be introduced to the new draft Code on this point. This we consider covered in the commitment to adopt a new Criminal Code in conformity with Council of Europe standards.

A decriminalisation condition was, therefore, not included in the Assembly's 'Opinion' (No. 188) on Moldova's application for membership (adopted by PACE on 27 June 1995). Wider research reveals that the letter mentioned was sent by Alexandra Duda on behalf of ILGA-Europe (EURO-Letter 32 1995).

The second reference is found in the CLAHR opinion on Azerbaijan's application, written by Mr Georges Clerfayt (presented on 27 June 2000). Noting the continued presence of an article criminalising sex between men in the state's criminal code, the rapporteur recommended adding an accession commitment of decriminalisation to the state's accession document (see Amendment E). However, such a reference to decriminalising sex between men was not included in PACE's 'Opinion' (No. 222). This was due, it seems, to the fact that a new criminal code had already been adopted on 30 December 1999, which did not criminalise consensual sex between men; it was to come into force on 1 September 2000.

The only other references relate to Armenia's accession. The CLAHR opinion, written by rapporteur Mr Michael Spindelegger, notes in Section 34 that sex between men remained a criminal offence at the time (6 June 2000). Furthermore, the Ministry of the Interior is reported as stating that in 1999 four men were charged for consensual sex and were awaiting trial. As such, Spindelegger recommended that decriminalisation be made an explicit accession commitment. PACE's 'Opinion' (No. 221) on Armenia's application includes the following obligation: 'to adopt, within one year of its accession, the second (specific) part of the Criminal Code, thus abolishing *de jure* the death penalty and decriminalising consensual homosexual relationships between adults' (part 13 iii a).

Armenia did not comply. A report by the Committee on the Honouring of Obligations and Commitments by Member States of the Council of Europe, written by Mrs Irena Belohorska and Mr Jerzy Jaskiernia (presented to PACE on 13 September 2002), found that, although the new draft criminal code decriminalised sex between men in line with its accession commitment, the code had not yet been adopted (see Section 76). The rapporteurs also noted that, since 1994, 48 people had been convicted under Article 116, with 15 prosecuted in 1999 and six in 2000 (see Section 77). PACE's Resolution 1304 (26 September 2002) on the 'Honouring of obligations and commitments by Armenia', therefore, called on the Armenian government to adopt the new criminal code as soon as possible, thereby decriminalising sex between men. This change was confirmed in the same committee's report of 12 January 2004, written by rapporteurs Mr René André and Mr Jerzy Jaskiernia (see Section G, paragraphs 220–22).

Information provided by Council officials in interviews mirrors this picture of patchy attention. Some reported that the decriminalisation of sex between men was never discussed. Daniele Cangemi – head of the Human Rights Law and Policy Division – stated that nothing specific was mentioned in the accession of FSU states, due in part to the unconsolidated nature of the ECHR's case law. In other words, the issue was not pressed given the emergent norm's continued contestation. Guy de Vel – former Director General of Legal Affairs – reported that the legal regulation of sex between men was not part of the reform assistance given by his department; and yet this is precisely the section of the Council that we would expect to be active. Finally, Georges Clerfayt – the CLAHR rapporteur for Azerbaijan's accession – stated that decriminalisation was 'never raised and discussed' with officials from Azerbaijan, despite his proposal for a decriminalisation commitment noted above.

Other officials, however, argued that decriminalisation was discussed with some acceding FSU states. A former CLAHR official recalled that the issue was raised with certain states, in particular Romania and Moldova. Indeed, at the 1999 Paris meeting of the Sub-Committee on Human Rights referred to above, the Chair – Mr Jaskiernia – remarked that the sub-committee 'had always taken a special interest in the situation of homosexuals, particularly when new member states joined the Organisation'.[27] Dennis van der Veur – an adviser in the Office of the Commissioner for Human Rights – noted the increased confidence of the Council in pressing the issue with FSU states as enlargement progressed. This was confirmed by Catherine Maffucci-Hugel – former Co-Secretary of the Committee on Legal Affairs and Human Rights of the Parliamentary Assembly – and a senior official in the Directorate of Democracy and Political Affairs.

What explains this mix of views? It could be that certain officials were unaware of relevant activities, or that they have since forgotten. Either way, both interpretations are consistent with the fact that the decriminalisation of sex between men was, at most, a low-profile issue in the Council's enlargement process. This can be contrasted with the high visibility accorded to the abolition of the death penalty (see Checkel 2000; Peshkopia and Imami 2008; Saari 2008) and minority rights (Kelley 2004; Sasse 2008). Indeed, an anecdotal piece of evidence uncovered in an interview with Nigel Warner – ILGA-Europe's CoE adviser – supports this view. After presenting a report to PACE, Terry Davis – the then Political Affairs Committee rapporteur for Georgia's accession – was approached by Warner and asked why a decriminalisation commitment was not included in Georgia's accession document, to which Davis replied, 'I'm sorry: I forgot'.

This evidence is surprising. The CoE is widely regarded as the cause of the 'wave' of decriminalisations of sex between men in post-Soviet space through the use of membership conditionality; yet, there is remarkably little evidence from Strasbourg – of both formal and informal conditionality – to support this view. In addition, there is no evidence that the Council took part in wider socialising efforts around decriminalising sex between men in its assistance programmes with FSU states.[28] Socialisation around sexual minorities by the CoE more broadly has only recently begun (see, for example, the March 2010 report by Mr Andreas Gross for CLAHR, 'Discrimination on the basis of sexual orientation and gender identity').

The influence of the CoE was much less powerful, more complex and distinctly messier than suggested by the membership conditionality model. However, other means of Council influence can be posited: for example, what Haggard et al. (1993: 182) call 'anticipatory adaptation' – 'a country's unilateral adoption of a set of norms associated with membership in an organisation prior to its actually being accorded full status in that organisation, or even receiving guarantees of entry' – or what Vachudova (2005: 65) terms 'passive leverage'.[29] The worry is, however, that – without sufficient data – these arguments automatically assume international influence as the source of change. Exploring the domestic dynamics of reform is, therefore, the next necessary step. The following section summarises this information.

Domestic processes of reform

The plausibility of process-tracing analysis depends on detail (Checkel 2005: 4). As such, this short summary can only provide a cursory overview of domestic processes of reform.[30] Despite these limitations, process-level evidence paints a clear and largely uniform picture of decriminalisation: quiet, elite-led reform, largely insulated from public discussion and emergent civil society activity, as part of wider institutional liberalisation following the collapse of the Soviet Union.[31] The problems of negative politicisation seen in Romania were, on the whole, absent from decriminalisations in FSU states.

And yet, the causes of this cluster of legal reforms varied across post-Soviet space. The 15 FSU states can be placed into four groups: first, those in which the decriminalisation of sex between men was largely a function of domestic elite initiative (Estonia, Latvia, Russia and Ukraine); second, those in which international influence – the Council of Europe, in some cases – tipped the balance of domestic interests in the favour of progressive reform (Armenia, Azerbaijan, Belarus, Georgia, Lithuania and Moldova);[32] third, those Central Asian states for which the Model Criminal Code of the Inter-Parliamentary Assembly of the Commonwealth of Independent States (IPA-CIS) provided the influential model for reform (Kazakhstan, Kyrgyzstan and Tajikistan);[33] and finally, the two states that have not decriminalised sex between men (Turkmenistan and Uzbekistan).

Previous scholarship on this topic has tended to lump post-Soviet states together. However, the research that this section summarises demonstrates the heterogeneity of processes involved in decriminalising sex between men; this, in turn, underlines the need to disaggregate the concept of post-Soviet space. For example, in Ukraine – the first state to decriminalise – reform was motivated by the *Rada*'s (parliament) Committee on Health Issues' belief that decriminalising this form of sexual activity was crucial to combating the emergent HIV/AIDS epidemic (Nash Mir 2004: 4). Thus, an epidemiological argument prevailed over historically inculcated notions of legal moralism. Russian decriminalisation – considered by Štulhofer and Sandfort (2005: 10) to be the '[p]aradigmatic case' of external reform pressure – was primarily the result of domestic reform initiatives.[34] Armenia's experience comes closest to the pattern expected from formal CoE membership conditionality, albeit with a notable delay between membership and decriminalisation. Such variation should not be surprising, however, given the historical differences noted in the history section of this chapter and the different paths taken in the transition from Soviet regimes.

Conclusions

The conditionality model might seem like an appealing explanatory framework at first sight. It presents a simple story: ECHR case law prohibits the criminalisation of consensual sex between men; most post-Soviet states decriminalised this activity around the same time as many of them joined the CoE; therefore – so the story goes – this 'wave' of reforms was caused by Council membership conditionality. Sanders (2002: 17), for example, writes: 'During the 1990s the Council of Europe's [membership] requirements were responsible for the almost total repeal of offending criminal laws in eastern Europe'. However, this chapter has shown the story to be deeply flawed. Existing works often ignore the domestic dynamics of reform, as well as the various legal and ideational heritages of post-Soviet states, and the varying political weight attached by the CoE to this area in accession processes. This is not to deny the Council's influence completely. Rather, the chapter has challenged the extent and nature of the CoE's influence as described in existing literature.

It is naïve to presume that liberal reforms are the result of Western influence. To be sure, the collapse of communism instigated an unparalleled period of legal interconnectivity between East and West (see, for example, Ajani 1995). Moreover, the 'critical juncture'[35] experienced by Soviet criminal law certainly allowed an increased opportunity for international influence, whether in the form of 'linkage' or 'leverage' (Way and Levitsky 2007). Yet, reform models were not only to be found abroad: jurists could sometimes draw on domestic precedent, as well as domestic and regional reformist sentiment.[36] By placing this group of reforms in the context of a longer-term narrative of policy development (Pierson 2005) – albeit in a very short version in this chapter – it is possible to appreciate the complexities and possibilities of progressive change. It appears that, without this historical context, previous scholarship has mistakenly emphasised the role of exogenous reform models and sources. As such, the findings underline the advantages gained from 'historicising criminalisation' (Lacey 2009: 942).

The chapter's findings also relate to the wider scholarship on the diffusion of criminal law policies. As Dubber and Farmer (2007: 5) write: 'Systems of criminal law do not develop in isolation from each other but are embedded in power relations between different states or between states and their colonies'. Indeed, Grattet et al. (1998) move a step further, suggesting that 'criminalization is best viewed as a process of institutionalization that involves the diffusion of legal forms and practices across polities comprising an interstate system'. Although it is necessary to acknowledge the growing international interdependence of criminal law – that is, of moving 'beyond domestic law' (see the concluding chapter of this collected edition) – there is a danger of jumping to conclusions. It is vital, in other words, to distinguish between policy convergence and policy interdependence. As Pravda (2001: 27) warns, it can be easy 'to mistake policy confluence for policy influence'. This chapter has demonstrated the importance of paying close attention to process-level evidence, in order to distinguish between hypotheses concerning the aetiology of criminal law reform.

The above analysis relates to formal legal reforms. However, the phenomena of criminalisation and decriminalisation are clearly much more complex than the simple letter of the law. Lacey (2009: 959–60) reminds us that they are 'complex social institution[s]', including both formal and substantive dimensions. This is certainly apparent in post-Soviet states. Regarding Kyrgyzstan, for instance, Robert Oostvogels notes that '[n]o measures were taken to spread awareness among the general population' that sex between men had been decriminalised (Human Rights Watch 2008: 30). As a result, Vladimir Tyupin (referring to the situation in Tajikistan) reports that many members of society – including gay men themselves – 'do not know that homosexuality is legal'.[37] Furthermore, regarding Belarus, Lalo and Schitov (2005: 188–89) claim that convictions for sex between men 'in some instances … may also refer to consensual homosexual intercourse', using data provided by the Ministry of Justice for the period 1996–2000.

Decriminalisation has been analysed far less frequently than criminalisation (see, for example, Jenness 2004: 149). As Brown (2007) demonstrates for the American 'overcriminalisation' literature, instances and processes of decriminalisation have largely been ignored by scholars, to the clear detriment of analytical precision. Although this chapter has focused on one particular dimension of this process, it highlights both the possibilities and the pitfalls of emerging scholarship on the international dimensions of decriminalisation.

Notes

1 This chapter is based on research for the author's MPhil thesis in Russian and East European Studies, University of Oxford, 2010. The author would like to thank Harold Carter, Paul Chaisty, Kay Goodall, Carol Leonard, Margaret Malloch, Gwen Sasse and Peter Solomon for their many helpful comments and suggestions. Parts of the chapter were written during the author's tenure of an Alfa Fellowship in Moscow; he gratefully acknowledges the Alfa Fellowship Program's generous support.
2 Ukraine was the only state to decriminalise before the formal dissolution of the Union of Soviet Socialist Republics (USSR).
3 The Russian term for this activity, *muzhelozhstvo*, is often translated as 'sodomy' or 'pederasty', and defined as 'sexual intercourse of a man with a man'. Non-consensual, or aggravated, sex between men remained criminalised, as well as sex with minors.
4 *Dudgeon v. United Kingdom* (1981) 4 E.H.R.R. 149. This judgment was affirmed in *Norris v. Ireland* (1988) 13 E.H.R.R. 186 and *Modinos v. Cyprus* (1993) 16 E.H.R.R. 485.
5 As will be demonstrated below, however, there is a significant difference between a technical condition of membership and a condition that is clear, determinate and politically visible during accession processes.
6 See also, for example, Gerring (2007), Hall (2008) and Capoccia and Ziblatt (2010) on the key role of analysing causal mechanisms for analytical leverage in causal inference.
7 This method is congruent with an ontological understanding of conditionality as a complex process rather than a 'clear-cut phenomenon' (Sasse 2009: 17). Kelley's (2004: 426) work also demonstrates the gains made from analysing particular areas of policy, rather than simply 'broad democratic trends', as seen, for example, in Schimmelfennig (2007).
8 Individuals were selected by a combination of chain-referral (snowball) sampling (Tansey 2007) and reputational and positional sampling.
9 For more details on the methodology, research design and data used in this research, see Noble (2010).
10 The Romanian case of vociferous contestation accords with expectations that cultural dissonance, or a value 'mis-match', will hamper norm diffusion – see, for example, Strang and Meyer (1993) and Checkel (1999). According to Stychin (2003: 122), this cultural barrier in Romania was only overcome as a result of subsequent EU conditionality.
11 As Epstein (2008) notes, we would imagine this continued contestation by Council member states to weaken the credibility of the norm centred around *Dudgeon*, thereby reducing the CoE's authority to push for compliance in accession states.
12 For richly detailed examinations of this history, see in particular Engelstein (1995) and Healey (2001). See also Smirnov (2011) and Chapter 2 of Noble (2010); see Tatchell (1992) for short histories of East European states and the emergence of sexual minority social movements towards the end of the communist era.

13 This criminalisation applied to all new territories on incorporation into the Union. The Baltic states' histories regarding the legal regulation of sex between men has received less scholarly attention. The available information is, therefore, patchy. According to Lavrikovs (EURO-Letter 43 1996), all three states decriminalised in the inter-war period, with recriminalisation on their forced inclusion into the USSR in 1940. This account of inter-war decriminalisation is supported by Veispak (1991: 108), but only for Estonia. Further research is required.

14 *Kurs sovetskogo ugolovnogo prava: chast' osobennaya* (Leningrad: Leningrad State University Press). Quoted in Gessen (1994: 9–10).

15 Professor Jeffrey Weeks – a leading Western sociologist and delegate at the conference – noted participants from Estonia, Latvia, Lithuania and Russia, as well as nationals from Austria, Britain, Denmark, Finland, Germany, the Netherlands, Sweden and the United States.

16 This can be contrasted with the Conference on Security and Cooperation in Europe (CSCE) (later the Organization for Security and Cooperation in Europe (OSCE)), which carried out the most 'inclusive' post-communist enlargement.

17 This strategy can be contrasted with the EU's 'exclusive' approach to enlargement: use the 'carrot' of membership to pressure compliance with EU conditions by keeping applicants 'out of the club'.

18 Similarly, Schimmelfennig et al. (2006: 41) write that the CoE 'likes to portray itself as "Europe's democratic conscience"'.

19 Killick et al. (1998) name this latter 'modality' of conditionality 'residual conditions'.

20 Despite being the clearest list of conditions, these accession commitments were in many respects associated with the least leverage, as satisfying them was expected after membership had been granted (see Killick et al. 1998).

21 This was the CoE programme of reform assistance extended to 'special guest status' states from the FSU.

22 Belarus' 'special guest status' was suspended by PACE in January 1997.

23 As the research on which this chapter is based makes clear, the activities of the NGO ILGA – and, more specifically, ILGA-Europe from 1996 – were crucial in providing information for the CoE on the legal status of sexual minorities in post-Soviet states (as well as further afield), thereby maintaining the visibility of the politically contested norm established around the ECHR by *Dudgeon v. UK*; they also lobbied the Council for an explicit inclusion of non-criminalisation as a condition of CoE membership.

24 Emphasis added.

25 Fellmeth (2008: 822) is mistaken, therefore, in arguing that PACE announced in 2000 'a policy of accepting for membership only those states that had abolished criminal prohibitions on homosexual intercourse'. Rather, point 4 of Recommendation 1474 is an incorrect characterisation of existing Council policy regarding the place of the decriminalisation of sex between men in accession procedures, as shown, for example, by the earlier accession of Georgia and the later accession of Armenia.

26 We would not, clearly, expect to find a reference in Ukraine's accession materials, given its early decriminalisation.

27 However, the constancy suggested by this remark is contradicted somewhat by the language, for example, in the CLAHR opinion on Moldova's application for membership cited above. Here, it seems that their attention was brought to the law criminalising sex between men not by the sub-committee, but by an NGO: ILGA-Europe.

28 See Drzemczewski (1993, 1995) for an overview of Council assistance programmes early in enlargement.

29 In a slight variation, Way and Levitsky (2007: 53) distinguish between 'linkage' and 'leverage', with the former referring to the 'myriad networks of interdependence' between 'Western democratic communities' and other states.

30 For more details, see Chapter 4 of Noble (2010), with a particularly detailed section on the Russian reform process.
31 This insulated reform process helps to explain a more general finding by Adamczyk and Pitt (2009) that there is no statistically significant relationship between public attitudes and the legal regulation of sex between men on a global level.
32 The precise details of the decriminalisation processes for these states require further investigation.
33 On the wider role of the IPA-CIS's Model Criminal Code as an influential document for reform in post-Soviet states, see Klebanov (2006) and Luneev (2005: 199–279). For the IPA-CIS's Model Civil Code's influence, see Korableva (2003).
34 Despite Kon's (1997: 229) assertion that Russia decriminalised as a result of 'strong pressure from Western public opinion and in order to obtain a place in the Council of Europe', no evidence is provided to support this claim. See also Smirnov (2011: 154) for a similarly unsupported claim about the influence of the Council. Moreover, Healey (2001: 249) is wrong to assert that this decriminalisation was the result of a presidential decree (*ukaz*): the RSFSR criminal code was amended by a federal law, signed by President Yeltsin on 29 April 1993.
35 See Capoccia and Kelemen (2007) for a discussion of this concept within the context of historical institutionalism.
36 See, also, the literature on the reintroduction of jury trials in Russia for another case of disputed legal aetiology: for example, Thaman (1995); Pashin (2001); Bowring (2003); and De Muniz (2004). See Markovits (2004), however, for a critique.
37 Quoted in IRIN (2004).

References

Adamczyk, A. and Pitt, C. (2009) 'Shaping Attitudes About Homosexuality: The Role of Religion and Cultural Context', *Social Science Research*, 38(2): 338–51.

Ajani, G. (1995) 'By Chance and Prestige: Legal Transplants in Russia and Eastern Europe', *The American Journal of Comparative Law*, 43(1): 93–117.

Baer, B. (2009) *Other Russias: Homosexuality and the Crisis of Post-Soviet Identity*, Basingstoke: Palgrave Macmillan.

Bahry, D., Boaz, C. and Gordon, S. (1997) 'Tolerance, Transition, and Support for Civil Liberties in Russia', *Comparative Political Studies*, 30(4): 484–510.

Bowring, B. (2003) 'Rejected Organs? The Efficacy of Legal Transplantation and the Ends of Human Rights in the Russian Federation', in E. Örücü (ed.) *Judicial Comparativism in Human Rights Cases*, London: UKNCCL, BIICL.

Brown, D. (2007) 'Democracy and Decriminalization', *Texas Law Review*, 86(2): 223–75.

Cangemi, D. (2009) Head of the Human Rights Law and Policy Division, Council of Europe. Transcript of a research interview carried out for Noble (2010) on 17 September 2009.

Capoccia, G. and Kelemen, D. (2007) 'The Study of Critical Junctures: Theory, Narrative, and Counterfactuals in Historical Institutionalism', *World Politics*, 59(3): 341–69.

Capoccia, G. and Ziblatt, D. (2010) 'The Historical Turn in Democratization Studies: A New Research Agenda for Europe and Beyond', *Comparative Political Studies*, 43 (8–9): 931–68.

Checkel, J. (1999) 'Norms, Institutions, and National Identity in Contemporary Europe', *International Studies Quarterly*, 43(1): 83–114.

——(2000) 'Compliance and Conditionality', *ARENA Working Paper*, WP 00/18.

——(2005) 'It's the Process Stupid! Process Tracing in the Study of European and International Politics', *ARENA Working Paper*, WP 05/26.

CLAHR Doc. 7325 (1995) 'Opinion on the Application of Moldova for Membership of the Council of Europe'. Online. Available http://assembly.coe.int/main.asp?Link=/documents/workingdocs/doc95/edoc7325.htm (accessed 21 November 2011).

CLAHR Doc. 8756 (2000) 'Opinion on Armenia's Application for Membership of the Council of Europe'. Online. Available http://assembly.coe.int//main.asp?link=http://assembly.coe.int/Documents/WorkingDocs/doc00/EDOC8756.HTM (accessed 21 November 2011).

CLAHR Doc. 8757 (2000) 'Opinion on Azerbaijan's Application for Membership of the Council of Europe'. Online. Available http://assembly.coe.int//main.asp?link=http://assembly.coe.int/Documents/WorkingDocs/doc00/EDOC8757.HTM (accessed 21 November 2011).

CLAHR Report (2000) 'Situation of Lesbians and Gays in Council of Europe Member States'. Online. Available http://assembly.coe.int//main.asp?link=http://assembly.coe.int/Documents/WorkingDocs/doc00/edoc8755.htm (accessed 21 November 2011).

——(2010) 'Discrimination on the Basis of Sexual Orientation and Gender Identity'. Online. Available http://assembly.coe.int/Main.asp?link=/Documents/WorkingDocs/Doc10/EDOC12185.htm (accessed 21 November 2011).

CLAHR Sub-Committee on Human Rights (2000) Meeting minutes from 14 October, 'Situation of lesbians and gays in Council of Europe member states' (copy on file with the author).

Clerfayt, G. (2009) CLAHR Rapporteur for Azerbaijan. Transcript of a research interview carried out for Noble (2010) on 16 December 2009, and a follow-up interview on 20 December 2011.

Committee on the Honouring of Obligations and Commitments by Member States of the Council of Europe Doc. 9542 (2002) 'Honouring of Obligations and Commitments by Armenia'. Online. Available http://assembly.coe.int//Main.asp?link=http://assembly.coe.int/Documents/WorkingDocs/doc02/EDOC9542.htm (accessed 21 November 2011).

Committee on the Honouring of Obligations and Commitments by Member States of the Council of Europe Doc. 10027 (2004) 'Honouring of Obligations and Commitments by Armenia'. Online. Available http://assembly.coe.int//Main.asp?link=http://assembly.coe.int/Documents/WorkingDocs/doc04/EDOC10027.htm (accessed 21 November 2011).

Croft, S., Redmond, J., Wyn Rees, G. and Webber, M. (1999) *The Enlargement of Europe*, Manchester: Manchester University Press.

De Jong, B. (1982) '"An Intolerable Kind of Moral Degeneration": Homosexuality in the Soviet Union', *Review of Socialist Law*, 4: 341–57.

De Muniz, P. (2004) 'Judicial Reform in Russia: Russia Looks to the Past to Create a New Adversarial System of Criminal Justice', *Willamette Journal of International Law and Dispute Resolution*, 11: 81–122.

De Vel, G. (2009) Former Director General of Legal Affairs, Council of Europe. Transcript of a research interview carried out for Noble (2010) on 4 June 2009.

Drzemczewski, A. (1993) 'The Council of Europe's Co-operation and Assistance Programmes with Central and Eastern European Countries in the Human Rights Field: 1990 to September 1993', *Human Rights Law Journal*, 14.

——(1995) 'Ensuring Compatibility of Domestic Law with the European Convention on Human Rights Prior to Ratification: The Hungarian Model', *Human Rights Law Journal*, 16.

Dubber, M. and Farmer, L. (2007) 'Introduction: Regarding Criminal Law Historically', in M. Dubber and L. Farmer (eds) *Modern Histories of Crime and Punishment*, Stanford, CA: Stanford University Press.

Dudgeon v. United Kingdom (1981) 4 E.H.R.R. 149. Cited here from the judgment of the Court (Plenary), 22 October. Online. Available http://cmiskp.echr.coe.int/tkp197/view.asp?action=html&documentId=695350&portal=hbkm&source=externalbydocnumber&table=F69A27FD8FB86142BF01C1166DEA398649 (accessed 21 November 2011).

Engelstein, L. (1995) 'Soviet Policy Toward Male Homosexuality: Its Origins and Historical Roots', *Journal of Homosexuality*, 29(2): 155–78.

Epstein, R. (2008) *In Pursuit of Liberalism: International Institutions in Postcommunist Europe*, Baltimore, MD: The Johns Hopkins University Press.

Essig, L. (1999) *Queer in Russia: A Story of Sex, Self, and the Other*, Durham, NC: Duke University Press.

EURO-Letter 7 (1992) July. Online. Available www.ilga-europe.org/europe/publications/euro_letter (accessed 21 November 2011).

EURO-Letter 32 (1995) March. Online. Available www.ilga-europe.org/europe/publications/euro_letter (accessed 21 November 2011).

EURO-Letter 43 (1996) August. Online. Available www.ilga-europe.org/europe/publications/euro_letter (accessed 21 November 2011).

Fellmeth, A. (2008) 'State Regulation of Sexuality in International Human Rights Law and Theory', *William and Mary Law Review*, 50: 797–936.

Former CLAHR official, Council of Europe (2009) Transcript of a research interview carried out for Noble (2010) on 16 September 2009.

George, A. and Bennett, A. (2005) *Case Studies and Theory Development in the Social Sciences*, Cambridge, MA and London: MIT Press.

Gerring, J. (2007) *Case Study Research: Principles and Practices*, New York: Cambridge University Press.

Gessen, M. (1994) *The Rights of Lesbians and Gay Men in the Russian Federation*, San Francisco, CA: IGLHRC.

Grattet, R., Jenness, V. and Curry, T. (1998) 'The Homogenization and Differentiation of Hate Crime Laws in the United States, 1978 to 1995: Innovation and Diffusion in the Criminalization of Bigotry', *American Sociological Review*, 63(2): 286–307.

Haggard, S., Levy, M., Moravcsik, A. and Nikolaidis, K. (1993) 'Integrating the Two Halves of Europe: Theories of Interests, Bargaining, and Institutions', in R. Keohane, J. Nye and S. Hoffmann (eds) *After the Cold War: International Institutions and State Strategies in Europe, 1989–1991*, London and Cambridge, MA: Harvard University Press.

Hall, P. (2008) 'Systematic Process Analysis: When and How to Use it', *European Political Science*, 7(3): 304–17.

Healey, D. (1993) 'The Russian Revolution and the Decriminalisation of Homosexuality', *Revolutionary Russia*, 6(1): 26–54.

——(2001) *Homosexual Desire in Revolutionary Russia: The Regulation of Sexual and Gender Dissent*, Chicago, IL and London: The University of Chicago Press.

Hughes, J., Sasse, G. and Gordon, C. (2004a) *Europeanization and Regionalization in the EU's Enlargement to Central and Eastern Europe: The Myth of Conditionality*, Basingstoke: Palgrave Macmillan.
——(2004b) 'Conditionality and Compliance in the EU's Eastward Enlargement: Regional Policy and the Reform of Sub-national Government', *Journal of Common Market Studies*, 42(3): 523–51.
Human Rights Watch (2008) *These Everyday Humiliations: Violence against Lesbians, Bisexual Women, and Transgender Men in Kyrgyzstan*, New York: Human Rights Watch.
IRIN (2004) 'Tajikistan: Gay Rights Face Uphill Struggle'. Online. Available www.irinnews.org/report.aspx?reportid=24445 (accessed 21 November 2011).
Jenness, V. (2004) 'Explaining Criminalization: From Demography and Status Politics to Globalization and Modernization', *Annual Review of Sociology*, 30: 141–71.
Jordan, P. (2003) 'Does Membership Have Its Privileges? Entrance into the Council of Europe and Compliance with Human Rights Norms', *Human Rights Quarterly*, 25: 660–88.
Kelley, J. (2004) 'International Actors on the Domestic Scene: Membership Conditionality and Socialization by International Institutions', *International Organization*, 58: 425–57.
Killick, T. with Gunatilaka, R. and Marr, A. (1998) *Aid and the Political Economy of Policy Change*, London: Routledge.
Klebanov, L. (2006) 'Desyat' let ugolovnomu kodeksu Rossiiskoi Federatsii: dostoinstva i nedostatki', *Gosudarstvo i Pravo*, 9: 107–14.
Kochenov, D. (2008) *EU Enlargement and the Failure of Conditionality: Pre-Accession Conditionality in the Fields of Democracy and the Rule of Law*, Alphen aan den Rijn: Kluwer Law International.
Kon, I. (1993) 'Sexual Minorities', in I. Kon and J. Riordan (eds) *Sex and Russian Society*, Bloomington and Indianapolis, IN: Indiana University Press.
——(1997) 'Russia', in D. West and R. Green (eds) *Sociolegal Control of Homosexuality: A Multi-Nation Comparison*, New York and London: Plenum Press.
Korableva, M. (2003) 'A Comparative Study of the Protection of Civil Rights: The Civil Codes of CIS Countries', *Review of Central and East European Law*, 28(2): 167–82.
Lacey, N. (2009) 'Historicising Criminalisation: Conceptual and Empirical Issues', *Modern Law Review*, 72: 936–61.
Lalo, A. and Schitov, N. (2005) 'Sexualities in Belarus: Some Major Patterns of Sexual Behaviour and Their Cultural Background', in A. Štulhofer and T. Sandfort (eds) *Sexuality and Gender in Postcommunist Eastern Europe and Russia*, Binghamton, NY: The Haworth Press.
Long, S. (Human Rights Watch and the International Gay and Lesbian Human Rights Commission) (1998) *Public Scandals: Sexual Orientation and Criminal Law in Romania: A Report*, London and New York: Human Rights Watch.
Luneev, V. (2005) *Prestupnost' XX veka: mirovye, regionalnye i Rossiiskie tendentsii*, Moscow: Walters Kluwer.
Maffucci-Hugel, C. (2009) Former Co-Secretary of the Committee on Legal Affairs and Human Rights of the Parliamentary Assembly of the Council of Europe. Transcript of a research interview carried out for Noble (2010) in the Palais d'Europe on 18 September 2009.

Manas, J. (1996) 'The Council of Europe's Democracy Ideal and the Challenge of Ethno-National Strife', in A. Chayes and A. Chayes (eds) *Preventing Conflict in the Post-Communist World: Mobilizing International and Regional Organizations*, Washington, DC: Brookings Institution.

Markovits, I. (2004) 'Exporting Law Reform – But Will It Travel?', *Cornell International Law Journal*, 37: 95–114.

McLoughlin, M. (1996) 'Crystal or Glass? A Review of *Dudgeon v. United Kingdom* on the Fifteenth Anniversary of the Decision', *Murdoch University Electronic Journal of Law*, 3(4).

Meron, T. and Sloan, J. (1996) 'Democracy, Rule of Law and Admission to the Council of Europe', *Israel Yearbook on Human Rights*, 26.

Modinos v. Cyprus (1993) 16 E.H.R.R. 485. Cited here from the judgment of the Court (Chamber), 22 April. Online. Available http://cmiskp.echr.coe.int/tkp197/view.asp?item=1&portal=hbkm&action=html&highlight=modinos&sessionid=52854353&skin=hudoc-en (accessed 21 November 2011).

Nachescu, V. (2005) 'Hierarchies of Difference: National Identity, Gay and Lesbian Rights, and the Church in Postcommunist Romania', in A. Štulhofer and T. Sandfort (eds) *Sexuality and Gender in Postcommunist Eastern Europe and Russia*, Binghamton, NY: The Haworth Press.

Nash Mir (2004) *Ukrainian Gay Men and Lesbians at the Threshold of the Millennium*, Kiev: Nash Mir.

Newton, S. (2003) 'Transplantation and Transition: Legality and Legitimacy in the Kazakhstani Legislative Process', in D. Galligan and M. Kurkchiyan (eds) *Law and Informal Practices: The Post-Communist Experience*, Oxford; New York: Oxford University Press.

Noble, B. (2010) *Decriminalising Sodomy in the Former Soviet Union, 1991–2003*, unpublished MPhil Russian and East European Studies thesis, University of Oxford.

Norris v. Ireland (1988) 13 E.H.R.R. 186. Cited here from the judgment of the Court (Plenary), 26 October. Online. Available http://cmiskp.echr.coe.int/tkp197/view.asp?item=1&portal=hbkm&action=html&highlight=norris&sessionid=52854353&skin=hudoc-en (accessed 21 November 2011).

Ottosson, D. (2008) *State-Sponsored Homophobia: A World Survey of Laws Prohibiting Same Sex Activity between Consenting Adults*. ILGA. Online. Available http://ilga.org/Statehomophobia/ILGA_State_Sponsored_Homophobia_2008.pdf (accessed 21 November 2011).

PACE Opinion No. 188 (1995) 'Application by Moldova for Membership of the Council of Europe'. Online. Available http://assembly.coe.int/main.asp?Link=/documents/adoptedtext/ta95/eopi188.htm (accessed 21 November 2011).

PACE Opinion No. 221 (2000) 'Armenia's Application for Membership of the Council of Europe'. Online. Available http://assembly.coe.int/main.asp?Link=/documents/adoptedtext/ta00/eopi221.htm (accessed 21 November 2011).

PACE Opinion No. 222 (2000) 'Azerbaijan's Application for Membership of the Council of Europe'. Online. Available http://assembly.coe.int/main.asp?Link=/documents/adoptedtext/ta00/eopi222.htm (accessed 21 November 2011).

PACE Resolution 1304 (2002) 'Honouring of Obligations and Commitments by Armenia'. Online. Available http://assembly.coe.int/Main.asp?link=/Documents/AdoptedText/ta02/ERES1304.htm (accessed 21 November 2011).

Pashin, S. (2001) 'The Reasons for Reintroducing Trial by Jury in Russia', *Revue internationale de droit pénal*, 72(1): 253–57.

Peshkopia, R. and Imami, A. (2008) 'Between Elite Compliance and State Socialization: The Abolition of the Death Penalty in Eastern Europe', *The International Journal of Human Rights*, 13(3): 353–72.

Pierson, P. (2005) 'The Study of Policy Development', *Journal of Policy History*, 17(1): 34–51.

Pravda, A. (2001) 'Introduction', in J. Zielonka and A. Pravda (eds) *Democratic Consolidation in Eastern Europe: International and Transnational Factors*, Oxford; New York, NY: Oxford University Press.

Recommendation 924 (1981) 'On Discrimination against Homosexuals', adopted 1 October. Online. Available http://assembly.coe.int/main.asp?Link=/documents/adopted text/ta81/erec924.htm (accessed 21 November 2011).

Recommendation 1474 (2000) 'Situation of Lesbians and Gays in Council of Europe Member States', adopted 26 September. Online. Available http://assembly.coe.int/main.asp?Link=/documents/adoptedtext/ta00/erec1474.htm (accessed 21 November 2011).

Saari, S. (2008) 'Russia's Creeping Challenge to European Norms: European Promotion of Abolition of the Death Penalty in Russia', in T. Hopf (ed.) *Russia's European Choice*, Basingstoke; New York: Palgrave Macmillan.

Sanders, D. (2002) 'Human Rights and Sexual Orientation in International Law', *International Journal of Public Administration*, 25(1): 13–44.

Sasse, G. (2008) 'The Politics of EU Conditionality: The Norm of Minority Protection during and beyond EU Accession', *Journal of European Public Policy*, 15(6): 842–60.

——(2009) 'Tracing the Construction and Effects of EU Conditionality', in B. Rechel (ed.) *Minority Rights in Central and Eastern Europe*, Abingdon; New York: Routledge.

——(2011) 'The Council of Europe as a Norm Entrepreneur: The Political Strengths of a Weak International Institution', in N. Walker, J. Shaw and S. Tierney (eds) *Europe's Constitutional Mosaic*, Oxford and Portland, OR: Hart.

Schieder, P. (2009) Speech made at the conference, 'The Global Arc of Justice', California State University, Los Angeles, 14 March 2009.

Schimmelfennig, F. (2007) 'European Regional Organizations, Political Conditionality, and Democratic Transformation in Eastern Europe', *East European Politics and Societies*, 21(1): 126–41.

Schimmelfennig, F., Engert, S. and Knobel, H. (2006) *International Socialization in Europe: European Organizations, Political Conditionality, and Democratic Change*, Basingstoke: Palgrave Macmillan.

Senior official in the Directorate of Democracy and Political Affairs, Council of Europe (2009) Transcript of a research interview carried out for Noble (2010) in the Palais d'Europe on 21 September 2009.

Simpson, A. (2001) *Human Rights and the End of Empire: Britain and the Genesis of the European Convention*, Oxford: Oxford University Press.

Smirnov, A.M. (2011) *Istoriya gosudarstvennogo presledovaniya i prestupnosti v otnoshenii lits s seksual'nymi inversiyami v zarubezhnykh stranakh i Rossii*, Moscow: Iurlitinform.

Statute of the Council of Europe (1949) Online. Available http://conventions.coe.int/Treaty/en/Treaties/html/001.htm (accessed 21 November 2011).

Stites, R. (1991) *The Women's Liberation Movement in Russia: Feminism, Nihilism, and Bolshevism, 1860–1930*, Princeton, NJ: Princeton University Press.

Storey, H. (1995) 'Human Rights and the New Europe: Experience and Experiment', *Political Studies*, 43: 131–51.

Strang, D. and Meyer, J. (1993) 'Institutional Conditions for Diffusion', *Theory and Society*, 22: 487–511.

Štulhofer, A. and Sandfort, T. (2005) 'Introduction: Sexuality and Gender in Times of Transition', in A. Štulhofer and T. Sandfort (eds) *Sexuality and Gender in Post-communist Eastern Europe and Russia*, Binghamton, NY: The Haworth Press.

Stychin, C. (2003) '"We Want to Join Europe, not Sodom": Sexuality and European Union Accession in Romania', in C. Stychin (ed.) *Governing Sexuality: The Changing Politics of Citizenship and Law Reform*, Oxford: Hart.

Tansey, O. (2007) 'Process Tracing and Elite Interviewing: A Case for Non-probability Sampling', *Political Science and Politics*, 40(4): 765–72.

Tarschys, D. (1995) 'The Council of Europe: The Challenge of Enlargement', *The World Today*, 51(4).

Tatchell, P. (1992) *Europe in the Pink: Lesbian and Gay Equality in the New Europe*, London: GMP Publishers.

Thaman, S. (1995) 'The Resurrection of Trial by Jury in Russia', *Stanford Journal of International Law*, 31(1): 61–274.

Tornow, S. (1991) 'Homosexuality and Politics in Soviet Russia', in T. Veispak and U. Parikas (eds) *Sexual Minorities and Society: The Changing Attitudes toward Homosexuality in 20th Century Europe*, Tallinn: Eesti Teaduste Akadeemia Ajaloo Instituut.

Torra, M. (1998) 'Gay Rights After the Iron Curtain', *The Fletcher Forum of World Affairs*, 22(2): 73–87.

Turescu, L. and Stan, L. (2005) 'Religion, Politics and Sexuality in Romania', *Europe-Asia Studies*, 57(2): 291–310.

Vachudova, M. (2005) *Europe Undivided: Democracy, Leverage and Integration after Communism*, New York: Oxford University Press.

Van der Veur, D. (2009) Adviser in the Office of the Commissioner for Human Rights, Council of Europe. Transcript of a research interview carried out for Noble (2010) in the Palais d'Europe on 16 September 2009.

Veispak, T. (1991) 'Homosexuality in Estonia in the 20th Century: Ideological and Juridical Aspects', in T. Veispak and U. Parikas (eds) *Sexual Minorities and Society: The Changing Attitudes toward Homosexuality in 20th Century Europe*, Tallinn: Eesti Teaduste Akadeemia Ajaloo Instituut.

Waaldijk, K. (2000) 'Civil Developments: Patterns of Reform in the Legal Position of Same-Sex Partners in Europe', *Canadian Journal of Family Law*, 17: 62–88.

Warner, N. (2009) ILGA-Europe Council of Europe adviser. Transcript of a research interview carried out for Noble (2010) on 4 August 2009.

Way, L., and Levitsky, S. (2007) 'Linkage, Leverage, and the Post-Communist Divide', *East European Politics and Societies*, 21(1): 48–66.

Weeks, J. (2009) Professor at London South Bank University. Transcript of a research interview carried out for Noble (2010) in London on 9 September 2009.

Written Declaration 227 (1993) 'On Homosexual Rights in the New Democracies', signed on 18 February. Online. Available http://assembly.coe.int/Mainf.asp?link=/Documents/WorkingDocs/Doc93/EDOC6779.htm (accessed 21 November 2011).

Part III

Policing, justice and transformation

8 Reforming the Ukrainian police

The challenges of understanding and addressing violence

Yulia Chistyakova

Introduction

The liberal democratic ideals of 'rights'-regarding police bound by the 'rule of law' emerged in the 1990s as a model for the former communist police systems. This took place while past violence and abuses associated with authoritarian methods of policing were brought into the spotlight. However, the realities of transition – deepening social divisions and inequalities, and the escalation of conflict and lethal violence (Karstedt 2003) – seemed to evoke once again repressive methods of policing and crime control and tended to displace democracy in political agendas (Bayley 1997; Mawby 2001; Los 2003; Favarel-Garrigues and Le Huerou 2004; Karstedt and Lafree 2006; Pino and Wiatrowski 2006). An additional challenge appeared to be the lack of public trust in 'compromised' justice institutions inherited from autocratic regimes (Karstedt and Lafree 2006).

Twenty years on, Ukraine continues to struggle with the coercive legacies of Soviet policing. More worryingly, some research suggests that the use of torture has become a systematic practice (Amnesty International 2005; Rushchenko 2005a, 2005b; Karpacheva 2011). This poses a number of questions, such as the extent to which Soviet legacies continue to play a role in contemporary police practices and whether there is perhaps a new demand for violent policing. What role do legislative reforms play in instilling in the Ukrainian police a culture of respect for individual rights?

This chapter will review legislative and institutional reforms of the past 20 years that aimed to address police torture and illegal violence, and it will discuss the limitations of adopted measures and barriers to reform rooted in existing practices and institutions of policing. The chapter will argue that, unless effective political accountability mechanisms are in place, criminalisation of torture and abuse of power have limited capacity to effect change.

The emergence of the problem of illegal violence and pressures to adopt policy changes

During its first decade of independence, Ukraine adopted several legislative instruments expressing its aspiration to make human rights and the rule of law the guiding principles of the new state. The new constitution adopted in June 1996 declared Ukraine a sovereign and democratic state based on the rule of law and guaranteed its citizens a number of rights and freedoms.[1] In 1995, Ukraine signed the European Convention for the Protection of Human Rights and Fundamental Freedoms and, in 1996, it signed the European Convention for the Prevention of Torture and Inhuman or Degrading Treatment or Punishment. Protection of human rights and freedoms was also seen, at least in legislative terms, as the priority of the police. The new 'Law on the Police' adopted in 1991 stated that 'the police should protect the rights, freedoms, life and health of citizens'. These legislative initiatives arguably put pressure on the Ukrainian state to implement certain human rights standards in criminal justice and law enforcement (Foglesong and Solomon 2001; Canton 2006).

The human rights non-governmental organisations (NGOs) that began to emerge during the 1990s drew attention to legislative practice and to inconsistencies between the legislation inherited from the Soviet system and Ukraine's new international obligations (Martynenko 2010). Educational initiatives from human rights groups were set up to examine what it meant for Ukraine to be a member of the Council of Europe and how human rights could be protected by the new state. One of these initiatives was to abolish the death penalty.[2] Educational programmes were developed to teach law enforcement personnel human rights principles, the rule of law and international instruments for the prevention of torture and cruelty. Human rights NGOs also began to offer legal assistance to the victims of violations of human rights by the police. According to the leader of the Kharkiv group, they helped hundreds of people to win their cases in court (Kharkiv Human Rights Group n.d.).

Although the law enforcement bodies were often willing to participate in the educational programmes of human rights NGOs, their reaction to the initiatives was at best reserved, and communication of their personnel with the NGOs was closely monitored to prevent any information or criticism from emerging. Strained relations with the non-governmental sector were to some extent the legacy of the hostile attitude of the Soviet regime to human rights dissidents (Zakharov 2010). In addition, media attention to violations of human rights by the police was seen by Ministry of Internal Affairs (MIA) officials as an attempt to discredit and misrepresent their work (korrespondent.net 2008).

Although statistical information related to violations among law enforcement personnel remained largely inaccessible even for police leaders, critiques of the law enforcement practices began to emerge from various sources. Academics working for the MIA played a key role in this process. They began to openly publish research on topics previously closed to the public. In 1996, publication of a research paper on the 'professional degradation' of police officers was met with resentment and ostracism on the part of the leadership of the ministry (Medvedev 1996). Human rights activism led to regular media attention on the problem of torture, cruelty and other crimes perpetrated by police officers (violence, drug dealing, extortion and collusion with criminal groups). International human rights organisations such as Amnesty International published regular reports about violations of human rights by the police. In 2003, the Kharkiv Human Rights Group established a series of publications 'Against Torture', in which they discussed international human rights standards and decisions of the European Court (Kharkiv Human Rights Group n.d.). Human rights groups also initiated the creation of several independent internet news sites.

International and local experts and human rights groups argued for the removal of restrictions on media freedom and demanded greater transparency from the law enforcement bodies. The MIA found itself under increased pressure to open to the public by publishing information about its activities and establishing channels of communication. At the end of the 1990s, the MIA created a website where they began to publish news and press releases (Ministry of Internal Affairs of Ukraine n.d.). The 'Programme of Partnership between the Police and the Public', adopted in 1999, required the MIA to inform the public about its activity through the mass media. At the same time, the ministry saw closer relations with the media as an opportunity to improve its image and reputation in the eyes of the public. This has led in practice to the creation of several TV programmes, columns in newspapers, telephone 'hot lines' and regular issues of 'reports of the police to the Ukrainian people'. In 1998, Kharkiv University of Internal Affairs published, for the first time, a review of the statistics of crimes committed by employees of the MIA (Martynenko 2010). In 1999, the first doctorate was awarded by the Academy of the MIA for research on crime committed by police officers (Shalgunova 1999). By the mid-2000s, research and debate on crime committed by police personnel broadened significantly and created an incentive for closer collaboration between the MIA and NGOs in the area of human rights. In 2003, researchers from the MIA took part in a campaign against torture initiated by the Kharkiv Human Rights Group, which has resulted in a series of sociological studies and seminars for police officers. For example, in 2009, researchers at the Kharkiv Institute of Social Research conducted a nationwide survey of torture and cruelty in the activities of internal affairs agencies. Nearly half the respondents (49 per cent) said that the practice of torture and cruelty was widespread in the work of the Ukrainian police (Kobzin et al. 2010).

In addition to the activities of human rights organisations and academic research, the perceived need to comply with European standards in the area of policing was another factor behind the recognition of torture as a problem. Ratification of several international human rights documents led to changes in national laws, and Ukraine adopted several initiatives as part of its collaboration with the Council of Europe.

The following section provides a brief review of legislative and institutional changes adopted in the last 20 years that address the problem of police torture and illegal violence in Ukraine. Many of these operate by criminalisation.

Legislative and institutional reforms

Article 127, which criminalises torture, was added to the Ukrainian Criminal Code in 2001. The definition of torture in the first version of Article 127 was criticised by Amnesty International for its failure to recognise 'torture by public officials' and 'psychological torture' (Amnesty International 2005). The article was subsequently modified in 2005 adding 'torture by employees of law enforcement bodies' so that it expressly criminalised such conduct when committed by law enforcement officials and introduced a stricter punishment – 10–15 years' imprisonment. Police officers can also be prosecuted for exceeding authority or official powers under Article 365 of the Criminal Code of Ukraine (a significantly less serious offence). The legal recognition of 'torture by law enforcement employees' is no doubt significant. The text of the article is now arguably in line with the definition of torture in the Convention against Torture (Amnesty International 2005). However, the big question is of course the implementation of the law and the extent to which it is able to act as a deterrent; the next section will look at some of the reasons why this might be problematic.

In addition, several legislative and normative instruments were adopted to establish procedural safeguards to protect the rights of people detained by the militia. In 2000, the MIA developed a programme of reform of special police facilities (temporary detention cells, reception centres) and adopted several normative instruments aimed to prevent torture and other forms of violence in police detention centres. The 'Law on advocacy' (1993) for the first time allowed a lawyer to take part in the criminal procedure from the moment of detention of a suspect, and gave the right to the accused to refuse to give evidence before talking to their lawyer. In 1994, Ukraine adopted the 'Law on the compensation of harm caused to citizens by unlawful actions of investigating bodies, prosecution and court'. In 2005, additionally, Article 5 of the 'Law on the Police' defined the rights of the detained to see a lawyer and their right to compensation for material and emotional harm caused by unlawful acts of police officers.

Several institutions were established to provide independent monitoring of police conduct. Perhaps the most significant of these developments was the creation of Mobile Groups. In 2004, as part of collaboration with the Council of Europe, and in compliance with the 'Law on democratic civilian control over military and law enforcement bodies', Ukraine began an experiment to create Mobile Groups for monitoring human rights standards in police custody in the eastern regions. In 2005, such groups were set up in every region. The groups made regular visits to police stations and detention facilities to monitor conditions of detention and identify and analyse evidence of violations of human rights by police officers (Ministry of Internal Affairs of Ukraine 2004). Their reports were then sent to the MIA. In 2008, the MIA expanded the powers of the groups, enabling them to make sudden visits to police divisions, including night-time visits.

In 2005, as part of its policy on greater transparency and accountability, the MIA signed an edict on the establishment of regional public councils on human rights. The councils have the status of a consultative–advisory body that works with the ministry to implement human rights standards and carry out civilian control of its activities. The councils consider complaints from individuals and organisations on violations of human rights and freedoms, and have a right to conduct civilian investigations of violations of human rights by police officers. In October 2009, for the first time, the councils carried out public hearings on human rights in the activity of internal affairs agencies that included the theme of torture and cruelty (Martynenko 2010).

To coordinate human rights monitoring, in 2004, the MIA introduced the post of Adviser to the Minister of the Interior on Human Rights and Gender Issues. The adviser was subordinated to the minister and conducted analysis of the extent to which human rights legislation was being observed, including its implementation and operation. She also established contacts with the Human Rights Ombudsman of Ukraine. In 2008, the post was abolished, and a Human Rights Monitoring Centre was set up in the ministry. Its main mission was to create a system of monitoring of human rights standards in accordance with international standards of law enforcement (Alekseeva 2009). Forty-one per cent of the employees of the centre were human rights activists (Martynenko 2010). The focus of the work of the centre was to monitor practices of detention, pre-trial investigation, public order maintenance and work with the public (Alekseeva 2009). Torture and cruelty were to become a separate statistical category. It was also envisaged that video cameras would be installed in police divisions, and responsiveness to public complaints would be improved (Martynenko 2010).

Thus, in the last two decades, a series of legislative changes and institutional reforms were adopted to tackle the problem of torture in police detention. It would seem the reforms were a big step forward in terms of establishing legal safeguards of individual rights and independent oversight and control. However, as recent research cited earlier suggests, the problem of torture persisted. The following sections will look at the limitations of the adopted measures and barriers to change. It will be shown that the legal provisions and systems for monitoring police conduct are not sufficient to deter the misuse of power. I begin with the existing system of measuring performance and then look at the impact of the lack of transparency, unwillingness of the prosecution to open criminal investigations and gaps in the procedures of detention and investigation.

Barriers to and limitations of adopted measures

The 'fight against crime' and performance indicators

Although the 'Law on the Police' states that 'the police should protect the rights, freedoms, life and health of citizens', a widespread belief is that crime control remains the main task of the MIA (Martynenko 2010). There are certainly grounds for such views as clear-up rates remain the main criteria for assessment of police performance. Success is evaluated in terms of the increase or decrease in clear-up rates compared with previous periods. The main task therefore is to gain information leading to the clearing up of a crime as quickly as possible using the most effective methods at the investigating officer's disposal. Scarcity of technical means and investigative skills mean that the use of torture is often the easiest and fastest way to receive needed information or to obtain a confession. The system of measuring performance is often seen as one of the reasons for the systematic use of torture, unlawful detention of citizens and abuses of power (Shepeleva 2005; Ministry of Internal Affairs of Ukraine 2007; Kobzin et al. 2010). A police officer who is able to provide good statistics can count on his bosses turning a blind eye to his misdeeds and violations of legislation (Novikova 2005). Research suggests that every second case of battery in district police divisions is committed by investigators with the aim of obtaining confessions (Karpacheva 2003; Yarmish 2005). The number of cleared-up crimes remains the criterion for the career progression of investigators, and they continue to resort to cruelty with respect to detainees and suspects in order to achieve better clear-up rates (Martynenko 2010).

The lack of transparency

Amnesty International criticised legislative changes that were meant to increase the transparency and openness of the police and ensure the observance of human rights (Amnesty International 2005: 28). Although the MIA showed some willingness to collaborate with human rights organisations and made attempts to demonstrate greater openness to the public, it continued to refuse to disclose information about prosecutions, convictions and complaints against their employees about torture and ill-treatment (Amnesty International 2005). Despite the creation of institutions with a remit to monitor human rights, the MIA continued to effectively hold the full monopoly on information related to its activities and saw the maintenance of the regime of secrecy a condition of effective pursuance of its organisational objectives. While such attitudes prevailed, it was unlikely that the police as an institution would become more open to public scrutiny.

Despite the expansion of the network of NGOs over the last 20 years, their oversight of MIA activities is in many ways limited. Their role is mainly consultative, which means they can give advice and make recommendations but cannot demand any action from the MIA. Even though NGOs, media representatives, public bodies such as the Human Rights Ombudsman or members of the public may request information from the MIA, there is no guarantee they will be provided with such information. The MIA does not have a system for monitoring public opinion and has not developed effective ways of engagement with the non-governmental sector (Martynenko 2010).

Practices of detention and interrogation

In post-Soviet Ukraine, judges tend to rely heavily on the use of pre-trial detention[3] (Foglesong and Solomon 2001; Amnesty International 2005; Solomon 2008) and on confessional evidence (Amnesty International 2005). Pre-trial detention is imposed on anyone alleged to have committed property or violent crimes and is used as a tool to exert psychological and physical pressure on suspects to admit their guilt (Solomon 2008). This is explained by the specifics of criminal procedure in Ukraine. The 'operative' officers view the detention of a suspect as an effective start in the process of solving crime. They try to obtain evidence of guilt 'at any price'. Methods of pressuring the suspects during the so-called 'preliminary investigation', including beatings and torture, are reportedly widespread, and the victims of ill-treatment face great difficulties when seeking justice (Amnesty International 2005). Even if judges later dismiss such evidence, it would not have any impact upon the operative officers: they have achieved the desired result (Rushchenko 2005a: 60; Kobzin et al. 2010). The European Committee for the Prevention of Torture also draws attention to the misuse of the Administrative Code to bring people into police custody for questioning about criminal offences, and the fact that judges often failed to react to allegations of ill-treatment (Amnesty International 2008).

Invisibility of torture

Low visibility of torture is related to the existing practice of delayed registration of a suspect (Amnesty International 2005; Yarmish 2005; Kobzin et al. 2010). Registration of a detainee (completion of a protocol of detention) means that they acquire certain rights. According to the Code of Criminal Procedure of Ukraine, no later than three hours after detention, the detainee must be placed in a temporary detention cell and undergo a physical examination. Within 72 hours, the detainee should be brought before the judge who makes a decision on further detention or release. These norms are frequently violated in practice. Police officers see these procedural rules as an obstacle to achieving results in their work with the suspect. A way to avoid these procedures is to delay the formal registration of the detainee, sometimes for hours or even days. This period, when the detainee has no formal status ('on paper' they do not exist), is used to exert psychological and physical pressure in order to 'convince' the person to confess. Detainees are held not in temporary detention units but in police units (in contravention of the law). Rushchenko (2005b) argues that the delay in registration strips the detainee of a formal status and rights and provides the investigating officers with almost unlimited power over the suspect. The very fact of falling into this 'gap of uncertainty' proves for some so psychologically disabling that it is often sufficient to make the detainee confess. However, if this is not enough and investigators have to resort to physical coercion or torture, the facts are very difficult to prove later because detention has not been documented and there is no evidence of the facts of interrogation. The absence of video cameras in police stations makes it easier to maintain the invisibility of torture.

Violation of detainees' rights

Although there are several legal provisions that define the rights of detainees, it is up to the police officers who detain them to make sure that they can exercise these rights. Among the rights is access to a lawyer and medical assistance. Police officers are required to inform the detainee of their right to a lawyer during questioning but, in practice, this right is frequently denied (Amnesty International 2005). There are several ways in which this right can be denied, including for instance failing to inform detainees of their right or delaying the registration of their arrest. Similarly, to undergo medical examination to confirm the fact of battery or torture, the victim is required to obtain an authorising document from the police. This creates another obstacle on the way to investigating cases of torture (TCH.ua 2010). Amnesty International also points out that it is difficult for victims to lodge complaints and to get them investigated promptly, independently and impartially (Amnesty International 2005).

Official denial – institutional causes of illegal violence denied

There are several ways in which criminal justice officials deny the facts of illegal violence. Materials containing evidence and allegations of torture are sent to the Prosecutor's office for consideration, but the Prosecutor rarely opens criminal investigations (Amnesty International 2010). According to a recently published report commissioned by the Council of Europe, 'few police officers are ever called to account for their unlawful behaviour; even fewer are ever convicted' (Murdoch 2010). In 2010, the Prosecutor's office received 7,000 complaints about violations of human rights by police officers, but only a few criminal cases were opened. In the overwhelming majority of cases, the Prosecutor's office refused to open a case because of the lack of evidence that a crime had been committed (Yakubovich 2011).

Second, when evidence of illegal violence is difficult to deny and a decision is made to open an investigation, the actions of perpetrators are defined not as 'torture' but as 'exceeding authority and official powers' or 'intentional infliction of grievous bodily harm' (Amnesty International 2005; finzah.com.ua 2011a, 2011b). In 2010, the majority (70 per cent) of prosecutions were for 'exceeding authority' (Amnesty International 2010). These offences carry significantly lesser punishment than torture (Sydorenko 2010).

Third, high-profile cases of torture are typically presented as cases of individual deviance, lack of skills or professional degeneration. A policy of selective punitiveness targets officers who were not careful enough, or unlucky to 'get caught'. In the words of a police officer:

> … their philosophy is: 'if you'll be caught in this, we will not save you, it will be your problem. Yes, we know that you provide cover to those salesmen, and that you have gipsy families selling drugs, but if the prosecution office is going on at you, or there is a scandal, a high-profile case, then this is your problem – we will punish you, sack you'. And they know that these are 'the rules of the game'.
>
> IR (2006) cited in Chistyakova (2009: 207)

As the quote suggests, the informal rules enable police officials to distance themselves from responsibility for any wrongdoing by their subordinates that comes under the spotlight and at the same time keeps rank-and-file officers fully dependent on their superiors.

Taken together, performance requirements and practices of detention and interrogation are such that the use of coercive methods and torture in police custody is likely, despite legislative provisions that criminalise such acts. A combination of the performance measurement system, low transparency, invisibility of torture and official denial work in concert to generate demands for coercion, enable coercive practices and conceal the institutional origins of violence. However, a review of institutional requirements and practices of policing reveals only some mechanisms of illegal violence. The following two sections consider police violence as part of a broader socio-economic and political context.

Coercion and violence for sale

The growing market in post-Soviet states created a demand for violence (Favarel-Garrigues and Le Huerou 2004) and gave rise to a new phenomenon of 'violent entrepreneurship' (Volkov 2002). Research in Ukraine suggests that torture and coercion are often used by police officers, not only in the fulfilment of their professional duties, but also as a method of extortion (Yarmish 2005; Kobzin et al. 2010). Such small-scale rent-seeking is often a means of survival for the rank-and-file officers: in a study of police corruption, respondents reported that their limited monthly salaries were the primary motivation for their supplemental economic activities and the motivation for their willingness to participate in misconduct and corruption (Wilson et al. 2007: 73). The author's research based on several in-depth interviews with police officers in Kharkiv, Ukraine, in 2006 revealed that extortion provides a source of regular income not only for rank-and-file officers but also for their superiors. Police officers are required to collect a certain amount of 'rent' from their beats; this rent goes to the 'upper levels' (Chistyakova 2009). It is also argued that low pay makes rank-and-file officers dependent on their superiors and in a sense powerless (TCH.ua 2011; Yakubovich 2011).

Although the majority of cases of extortion known from criminological research represent so-called 'small-scale' corruption, it can be argued that there is at least a possibility that police are involved in the provision of 'services' to criminal groups and businesses, although no reliable data exist to support such claims (Foglesong and Solomon 2001: 70). In a study of police engagement in 'economic activities' in Russia, researchers commented that the typical attitude they observed was 'we have epaulets, guns and business ideas – let's take on the market' (Wilson et al. 2007), clearly suggesting that some form of coercion (even if not direct physical force) plays a key role in these business endeavours. The 'hybrid' nature of policing in Ukraine, where private security companies maintain close relations with local police and the State Protection Service of the MIA, also provides commercial services to private clients and creates ample opportunities for the provision of coercive services both legally and illegally (Caparini and Marenin 2005; Born et al. 2006). Commentators have suggested that established links bring together various agencies representing state and non-state actors, most notably organised crime, private security and former state security and law enforcement employees – a 'criminal–political nexus' (Shelley 1999; Los 2003).

Violence as an instrument of political repression

Although it is recognised that the use of the police for political ends (to suppress particular groups) is a phenomenon not limited to authoritarian regimes and one which can frequently take place in societies such as the US and UK, there are perhaps significant differences between societies in the extent to which this pattern represents typical police conduct (Gerber and Mendelson 2008). In the years of independence, Ukraine experienced several waves of democratisation followed by returns to authoritarian methods of government, and many commentators point to the role of the police and security forces in these processes. Levitsky and Way (2002), for instance, suggest that, during the presidency of Kuchma (1994–2005), which they characterise as a period of 'competitive authoritarianism', the law enforcement institutions played a key role in extensive surveillance and coercion to control opposition, as well as to monitor and encourage loyalty and obedience from subordinates and allies (Levitsky and Way 2002; Way and Levitsky 2006). Stories about police harassment of journalists, ethnic minority and other groups, suppression of opposition and public protests, torture and brutality regularly appeared in the media (Prava Ludyny 2003).

In 2000, President Kuchma and Interior Minister Kravchenko were implicated in the murder of a journalist known for his critical commentary on the president and the 'oligarchs'. The Head of the Security Service and the Interior Minister were dismissed and, in 2008, three senior police officers were charged with the abduction and murder (*Kyiv Post* 2009). Recordings, reportedly made in the office of the Ukrainian President Kuchma and released in 2001, suggested that the MIA and secret services were involved in blackmail to pressure local elites to falsify election results (Darden 2002). Another commentator suggests that Ukrainian opposition faced one of the greatest degrees of state-backed violence in the second wave of democratisation in 2004 (Kuzio 2010). He identifies several state-backed violent strategies used in the 2004 elections: inciting regional and interethnic conflict, assassinations, violence against the opposition, counter-revolution and use of the security forces.

Whether or not the use of police violence for political ends represents a dominant tendency in Ukrainian policing is a debatable question that requires further research. However, there is little doubt that police and security forces and their coercive capabilities have frequently been used by political leaders in ways that are non-transparent and often illegal. It would appear that this represents part of a general pattern of the dominance of informal control over the use of violence by the authorities in Ukraine.

Structural violence

The use of police violence as a repressive instrument is also demonstrated by its bias against disadvantaged groups. A study by Rushchenko (2005b: 72) suggests that certain categories of people, such as those with low social status, the underage, homeless and those who have had problems with the law in the past, are the most likely victims of police brutality and most likely to suffer torture. A recent study of drug users in Ukraine found that this group frequently faced police harassment and discrimination (Mimiaga et al. 2010). Powerlessness, prejudices held by the police about certain categories of people as more likely to be guilty of crime and the knowledge that the vulnerability of these groups makes it easier to extract confessions and makes complaints less likely seem to provide plausible explanations for such findings. This interpretation is supported by the findings from a similar study of police violence in Russia, which indicated that low social status exposes individuals to police abuses; the latter 'may feel they have greater impunity to brutalise lower status individuals' (Gerber and Mendelson 2008: 22).

Weak civil society

Perhaps the greatest challenge in overcoming the tendency of police to rely on abuse and coercion is the fact that the perpetrators face little resistance and can often act with impunity. The need for the development of civil democratic control of law enforcement bodies to ensure their respect for people's rights and freedoms has been officially recognised in the Concept Paper for Reforming the Ministry of Internal Affairs (Ministry of Internal Affairs of Ukraine 2007). However, as Goldsmith (2005) argues, the common problem post-authoritarian societies face is weak civil society. These societies are 'poorly organised and positioned to seek greater information and influence over policing' (Goldsmith 2005: 463). Although the non-governmental sector in Ukraine today is larger and more integrated than 20 years ago (Martynenko 2010) and its representatives have more experience, still only a relatively small percentage of the population are involved in civic activities. In addition, NGOs often lack financial independence and transparency. State funding is primarily available to those organisations whose activities are prioritised by the state, whereas private voluntary donations have been, until recently, virtually non-existent in Ukraine (Zakharov 2004). The process of offering tenders for government-financed projects lacks transparency and accessibility (Stewart 2009), and only those NGOs with connections in the government are able to receive such grants (Marat 2008). Besides, there is little willingness to fund human rights advocacy and monitoring activities (Zakharov 2004). As a result, NGO activists pursue short-term benefits over long-term development (Henderson 2002; Wedel 2005) and are often 'found to be lacking democratic internal structures and transparent financial reporting' (Stewart 2009: 7).

Goldsmith (2005) adds that 'people are too scared in many instances to stand up publicly to police abuses or inaction'. Similarly, Smith (2009: 254), who analyses police complaints in the UK, notes that people often do not complain because hierarchies of credibility used by the police can disarm and discredit complainants. This observation can be applied to the situation of 'loss of status and rights' by detainees in police custody in Ukraine (Rushchenko 2005b). Smith also suggests that complaining is a political act – and the power of the MIA remains a great challenge for Ukrainian human rights activists.

In addition, perhaps paradoxically, post-Soviet societies combine distrust of the state and law enforcement institutions with the approval of coercive methods of control. On the one hand, the level of trust and confidence in the police is low (Beck 2005; Beck and Robertson 2009); on the other hand, when coercion or even torture are applied to 'real criminals', such methods are often met with public approval (Novikova 2005; Shepeleva 2005). The common view is that it is impossible to fight crime without breaking the law (especially without violating the rights of suspects). Police officers who rely on coercive methods in their work expect that the public 'will understand'. In the words of one police officer convicted for battery of a suspect, 'if a police officer does everything to make the criminal confess, uses any means available in good faith, how can you call this abuse? [T]he public is happy to watch police officers beat up a hooligan' (Shepeleva 2005: 41).

Torture: problems of definition

Finally, the definition of what constitutes torture or illegal violence is also part of the problem. 'At the heart of any discussion of the use of force by police officers are some difficult definitional issues', admit Stenning et al.. (2009: 99). Researchers agree that it may be difficult or even impossible to distinguish between legitimate and non-legitimate, or reasonable and excessive use of force (Reiss 1974; Westmarland 2001; Sanders and Young 2003; Stenning et al. 2009). A further difficulty arises in identifying different degrees of abuse: 'it is not always possible to draw a clear line between the type of abuse that amounts to torture, and that which amounts to other forms of ill-treatment' (Amnesty International 2005).

Although physical torture in the process of interrogation in Ukraine remains a major problem that continues to attract the attention of media and non-governmental groups, focusing exclusively on physical torture might mean that less visible forms of coercion remain out of sight. Ukrainian criminologists point out the need for a broader interpretation and definition of illegal violence. The extent of illegal police violence they have analysed includes murder, violation of the right to personal inviolability, illegal detention and arrest, being illegally taken to a police station and searched, inhumane conditions of detention, cruel treatment of the detained, torture or rape (Rushchenko 2005a: 29). It is argued that, in Ukrainian law, there are no clear criteria for setting apart torture and cruel, inhumane and degrading treatment (Rushchenko 2005a: 23), and that it is important to distinguish between physical and psychological violence (Rushchenko 2005a: 28).

Conclusions

This chapter has provided an overview of how the problem of police violence has been addressed in Ukraine and why the reforms have been difficult. Coercion and torture appear to represent an established police practice in Ukraine. The 'culture of impunity' (Amnesty International 2010) has its roots in the Soviet system. Law enforcement institutions continue to guide police conduct through informal and non-transparent command and control rather than the framework of the law. As noted by Darden (2002), the police behaviour that is sanctioned is not necessarily the behaviour that is required of them by law. A range of decisions can be made on a discretionary basis and informal expectations must be met, but not necessarily by compliance with laws. In Ukraine, clear-up rates are a powerful incentive (Beck 2005), and non-compliance with this requirement has more certain and immediate consequences for police officers than non-compliance with the requirements of the law. In this sense, violent and coercive methods used by Ukrainian law enforcers can be described as 'violence in pursuance of state goals which violate human rights … ' (Green 2010: 239).

The systematic practice of cruelty and torture cannot be explained only by cultural legacies, lack of skills or individual deviance. These practices are a response to a demand for violence generated by institutions of policing and the wider socio-economic and political context. Police continue to be used to extract rents, suppress public protest and political opposition or to secure compliance of political opponents or allies. Low visibility of illegal violence, gaps in legislation, impunity of perpetrators and institutional denial mean that criminalisation has little effect in deterring such practices. The weakness of civil society also contributes to a perpetuation of impunity. Perhaps not unexpectedly, deprived and marginal groups are the primary targets of coercive methods (Rushchenko 2005a).

This is not to suggest that the legislation that defines torture and responsibility for such acts is insignificant. The fact that torture perpetrated by law enforcement officers is now recognised in Ukrainian law as a criminal offence undoubtedly represents a progressive development. It creates the possibility for victims to defend their rights through the law; it begins to open illegal practices to public scrutiny through the development of institutes for monitoring police practice; and, perhaps most importantly, it enables critical discourse about illegal violence and torture that begins to challenge existing institutional frameworks and ways of thinking about policing.

These observations can be applied to other post-Soviet states. In neighbouring Russia, police violence and torture is no less of a problem (see, for example, Chistyakova and Robertson forthcoming 2012). Like Ukraine, Russia has adopted legal instruments restricting police use of force and prohibiting torture. Other regions of the former Soviet Union have been undertaking reforms of their police forces, with variable success (Lewis 2011). There is little doubt that criminalisation of police violence in post-Soviet societies is symbolically and normatively significant. It signals a departure from the totalitarian past and recognition that the state's monopoly over legitimate use of coercive violent power can be misused by those to whom this power is delegated. However, the adoption of legal instruments that criminalise police violence does not automatically translate into changes in everyday police conduct. Informal non-transparent rules and practices of policing remain more powerful regulators of police behaviour than the law. At the same time, the law can be used selectively against certain individuals rather than being applied equally to all.

This suggests that theorisation of processes of criminalisation with regard to the police in post-Soviet societies should involve an understanding of the ways in which informal rules and practices of policing mediate the implementation and operation of the legal instruments that criminalise violence. It is also important to identify strategies used by various actors (including authorities, the police themselves and private actors) involved in the definition of demand for, provision and use of violence.

This chapter has also highlighted the role of domestic and international actors in promoting criminalisation of police violence. The human rights discourse plays a key role in defining the problem of illegal violence, creating knowledge about it and identifying legal means to address it. Civil society groups are beginning to pursue and develop strategies whereby police are held to account through various means both within and outside the legal domain. However, there is still lack of broad public dialogue and of robust institutions of public authority. Existing stereotypes and ways of thinking about policing and public order remain perhaps the key obstacle to more accountable policing.

This should remind us of the importance of seeing police violence and its criminalisation not simply as a matter of legal definition but as a site of ongoing political and discursive struggles over the definition and redefinition of legitimate use and misuse of power. The meaning and use of police powers is contingent, to paraphrase Lyons (2002), on the struggles to control resources for the power to say what is legitimate and illegitimate use of police coercive powers. Such perspectives enable a broader scope for analysis of police malpractice and can illuminate political contexts within which it emerges, as well as connections between coercion and seemingly less coercive but powerful methods of control.

Notes

1 The document was based on principles stipulated in a number of international legal instruments such as the Universal Declaration of Human Rights (1948), the European Convention on Human Rights and Fundamental Freedoms (1950), the International Covenant on Civil and Political Rights (1966), The Charter of Paris for a New Europe (1990) and the constitutional experiences of a number of countries.
2 The death penalty was abolished in Ukraine in 2000.
3 A similar situation with pre-trial detention in Russia is noted by Piacentini (2004: 48).

References

Alekseeva, L. (2009) *Rol pomoschnika po pravam cheloveka v ministrerstve vnutrennykh del ukrainy*, UMDPL Association. Online. Available http://umdpl.info/index.php?id=1254162452 (accessed 11 August 2011).

Amnesty International (2005) *Ukraine, Time for Action: Torture and Ill-treatment in Police Detention*. Online. Available www.amnesty.org/en/library/info/EUR50/004/2005 (accessed 21 October 2009).

——(2008) *Ukraine – Amnesty International Report 2008*. Online. Available www.amnesty.org/en/region/ukraine/report-2008 (accessed 07 December 2011).

——(2010) *Ukraine – Amnesty International Report 2010*. Online. Available www.amnesty.org/en/region/ukraine/report-2010 (accessed 11 August 2011).

Bayley, D.H. (1997) 'Who are we Kidding? On Developing Democracy through Public Reform', in National Institute of Justice (ed.) *Policing in Emerging Democracies: Workshop Papers and Highlights*, Washington, DC: National Institute of Justice.

Beck, A. (2005) 'Reflections on Policing in Post Soviet Ukraine: A Case Study of Continuity', *The Journal of Power Institutions in Post-Soviet Societies*, Issue 2. Online. Available www.pipss.org/index330.html (accessed 20 October 2009).

Beck, A. and Robertson, A. (2009) 'The Challenges to Developing Democratic Policing in Post Soviet Societies: The Russian Experience', *Police Practice and Research: An International Journal*, 10(1): 285–93.

Born, H., Caparini, M. and Cole, E. (2006) *Regulating Private Security in Europe: Status and Prospects*, Draft report, Geneva Centre for the Democratic Control of Armed Forces (DCAF).

Canton, R. (2006) 'Penal Policy Transfer: A Case Study from Ukraine', *Howard Journal of Criminal Justice*, 45(5): 502–20.

Caparini, M. and Marenin, O. (2005) 'Crime, Insecurity and Police Reform in Post-Socialist CEE', *The Journal of Power Institutions in Post-Soviet Societies*, Issue 2. Online. Available www.pipss.org/index330.html (accessed 20 October 2009).

Chistyakova, Y. (2009) *Revisiting Community Policing in Ukraine: Lessons for Police Reform*, unpublished thesis, Milton Keynes: Open University.

Chistyakova, Y. and Robertson, A. (forthcoming, 2012) 'YouTube Cops and Power without Limits: Police Violence in 21st Century Russia', *Journal of Power Institutions in Post-Soviet Societies.*

Darden, K. (2002) *Graft and Governance: Corruption as an Informal Mechanism of State Control*, New Haven, CT: Yale University Working Paper.

Favarel-Garrigues, G. and Le Huerou, A. (2004) 'State and the Multilateralization of Policing in post-Soviet Russia', *Policing and Society*, 14(1): 13–30.

finzah.com.ua (2011a) *ot nasiliya v militsii umiraet vse bolshe ludej*. Online. Available http://finzah.com.ua/113/news/4131.html (accessed 11 August 2011).

——(2011b) *zaderzhan serzhant militsii izbivshii do smerty nevinnogo kharkovchanina*. Online. Available http://finzah.com.ua/113/news/4182.html (accessed 11 August 2011).

Foglesong, S. and Solomon, P.H. (2001) *Crime, Criminal Justice and Criminology in Post-Soviet Ukraine*, National Institute of Justice, Washington: Office of Justice Programs.

fraza.ua (2011) *pravozaschitnik: kazhdye 40 sekund v Ukraine proischdit akt nezakonnogo nasiliya v militsii*. Online. Available www.fraza.ua/news/02.08.11/121275.html (accessed 11 August 2011).

Gerber, T. and Mendelson, S. (2008) 'Public Experiences of Police Violence and Corruption in Contemporary Russia: a Case of Predatory Policing?', *Law & Society Review*, 42(1): 1–44.

Goldsmith, A. (2005) 'Police Reform and the Problem of Trust', *Theoretical Criminology*, 9(4): 443–70.

Green, P. (2010) 'The State, Terrorism and Crimes Against Humanity', in J. Muncie, D. Talbot and R. Walters (eds) *Crime, Local and Global*, Milton Keynes: Willan.

Henderson, S.L. (2002) 'Selling Civil Society, Western Aid and the Nongovernmental Organisational Sector in Russia', *Comparative Political Studies*, 35(2): 139–67.

Karpacheva, N. (2003) *Stan dotrimaniya ta zakhistu prav I svobod ludini d Ukraini*, Kiev: Verkhovna Rada.

——(2011) *Bez kardinalnyk shagov po preodoleniyu nasiliya Ukraina podvergnetsya tretiemy pilotnomu resheniyu evrosuda po pravam cheloveka*, Kyiv: Press Service of the Human Rights Ombudsman of Ukraine.

Karstedt, S. (2003) 'Legacies of a Culture of Inequality: The Janus Face of Crime in Post-Communist Countries', *Crime, Law and Social Change*, 40: 295–320.

Karstedt, S. and Lafree, G. (2006) 'Democracy, Crime and Justice', *The Annals of the American Academy of Political and Social Science*, 605(1): 6–23.

Kharkiv Human Rights Group (n.d.) *A Brief Introduction to the Kharkiv Human Rights Protection Group*. Online. Available www.khpg.org/en/index.php?r=2.1 (accessed 11 August 2011).

Kobzin, D., Chernousov, A. and Martynenko, O. (2010) *Monitoring nezakonnogo nasilstva v organakh vnutrishnikh sprav ukrainy*, Kharkiv: Prava Ludiny.

korrespondent.net (2008) Mvd: rassledovaniya kanala 1+1 napravleny na diskreditatsiyu militsii. Online. Available http://korrespondent.net/ukraine/events/652272-mvd-rassledovaniya-kanala-11-napravleny-na-diskreditaciyu-milicii (accessed 11 August 2011).

Kuzio, T. (2010) 'State-led Violence in Ukraine's 2004 Elections and Orange Revolution', *Communist and Post-Communist Studies*, 43: 383–95.

Kyiv Post (2009) 'Key Suspect in Gongadze Murder arrested; Pukach allegedly Strangled Journalist, but who gave the Order?', *Kyiv Post*, 22 July.

Levitsky, S. and Way, L. (2002) 'The Rise of Competitive Authoritarianism', *Journal of Democracy*, 13(2): 51–65.

Lewis, D. (2011) *Reassessing the Role of OSCE Police Assistance Programming in Central Asia*, Open Society Foundations, Occasional Paper Series No. 4. Online.

Available www.soros.org/initiatives/cep/articles_publications/publications/occasional-paper-4-20110411/OPS-No-4-04-11-2011.pdf (accessed 30 September 2011).

Los, M. (2003) 'Crime in Transition: The Post-Communist State, Markets and Crime', *Crime, Law and Social Change*, 40: 145–69.

Lyons, W. (2002) *The Politics of Community Policing: Rearranging the Power to Punish*, Michigan: University of Michigan Press.

Marat, E. (2008) 'March and After: What has Changed? What has Stayed the Same?', *Central Asian Survey*, 27(3–4): 229–40.

Martynenko, O. (2010) *MVD Ukrainy i Nepravitelstvennye Organizatsii – Istoriya Vzaimootnoshenii v Oblasti Prav Cheloveka*. Online. Available http://helsinki.org.ua/ru/index.php?id=1287491515 (accessed 7 December 2010).

Mawby, R. (2001) 'The Impact of Transition: A Comparison of Post-Communist Societies with Earlier "Societies in Transition"', in A. Kadar (ed.) *Police in Transition*, Budapest: CEU Press.

Medvedev, V.S. (1996) *Problemy professionalnoy deformatsii sotrudnikov organov vnutrennikh del, teoretitchestkie i prikladnye aspekty* (in Ukrainian), Kiev: Kiev Academy of the Ministry of Internal Affairs.

Mimiaga, M., Safren, S. and Dvoryak, S. (2010) '"We Fear the Police, and the Police Fear us": Structural and Individual Barriers and Facilitators to HIV Medication Adherence among Injection Drug Users in Kiev, Ukraine', *AIDS Care*, 22(11): 1305–13.

Ministry of Internal Affairs of Ukraine (n.d.) *Official website*. Online. Available http://mvs.gov.ua/mvs/control (accessed 11 August 2011).

——(2004) *Pro zatverzhennya timchasovogo polozheniya pro mobilni grupy z monitoringu dotrimaniya konstitutsionnykh prav I svobod gromadyan u diyalnosti organyv vnutrishnykh sprav*. Edict No. 286, 17 March.

——(2007) *Concept Paper for Reforming the System of the Ministry of Internal Affairs*, Kiev: Ministry of Internal Affairs of Ukraine.

Murdoch, J. (2010) *'Ukraine: Combating Impunity – the Effective Investigation of Allegations of Ill-treatment inflicted by the Police'*, Council of Europe, April.

Novikova, A. (2005) 'Portrety ryadovykh militsionerov v soveremennoy pravookhranitelnoy systeme', *Neprikosnovenny Zapas*, 42(44). Online. Available http://magazines.russ.ru/nz/2005/42/ru16.html (accessed 27 October 2009).

Piacentini, L. (2004) *Surviving Russian Prisons: Punishment, Politics and Economy in Transition*, Cullompton: Willan Publishing.

Pino, N.W. and Wiatrowski, M.D. (2006) 'The Principles of Democratic Policing', in N.W. Pino and M.D. Wiatrowski (eds) *Democratic Policing in Transitional and Developing Countries*, Aldershot: Ashgate.

Prava Ludyny (2003) 'Special Squads of Militia are trained to disperse the Meetings of Opposition', *Prava Ludyny*. Online. Available www.khpg.org/en/index.php?id=1071486129 (accessed 27 October 2009).

Reiss, A.J. (1974) 'Police Brutality – Answers to Key Questions', in L. Rainwater (ed.) *Deviance and Liberty*, Chicago: Aldine Publishing.

Rushchenko, I. (2005a) 'Nezakonne zatrimannya i negumanne utrimannya gromadyan pid chas diznannya, dosudovogo sledstva i uv'yaznennya', in V. Sobolev (ed.) *Protivozakonne nasil'stvo v organakh vnytrishnikh sprav, sotsiologichny ta istoriko-pravovii analiz*, Kharkiv: National University of Internal Affairs.

——(2005b) 'Bez statusa ili "v yame neopredelennosti". K probleme nezakonnogo nasiliya v organakh militsii po dannym Ukrainskich issledovanii', *Neprikosnovennyj*

Zapas, 42(4). Online. Available http://magazines.russ.ru/nz/2005/42/ru16.html (accessed 27 October 2009).

Sanders, A. and Young, R. (2003) 'Police Powers', in T. Newburn (ed.) *Handbook of Policing*, Cullompton: Willan.

Shalgunova, S. (1999) *Ugolovno-pravovye i kriminologitcheskie mery preduprezhdenyua vzyatochnichestva sredi sotrudnikov organov vnutrennykh del*, Kiev: Kiev Academy of Internal Affairs.

Shelley, L. (1999) 'Post-Socialist Policing: Limitations on Institutional Change', in R. Mawby (ed.) *Policing Across the World, Issues for the Twenty First Century*, London: UCL Press.

Shepeleva, O. (2005) 'Proizvol v rabote militsii: tipichnye praktiki', in O. Shepeleva and A. Novikova (eds) *Reforma pravookharnitelnykh organov: preodolenie proizvola*, Collection of papers, Centre for Assistance to Research on the Problems of Civil Society, Moscow: Demos.

Smith, G. (2009) 'Why Don't More People Complain Against the Police?', *European Journal of Criminology*, 6(3): 249–66.

Solomon, P.H. (2008) *Criminal Justice and its Reform in Post-Soviet Ukraine*, unpublished manuscript.

Stenning, P., Birkbeck, C. and Adang, O. (2009) 'Researching the Use of Force: The Background to the International Project', *Crime, Law and Social Change*, 52: 95–110.

Stewart, S. (2009) 'NGO Development in Ukraine since the Orange Revolution', in Juliane Besters-Dilger (ed.) *Ukraine on its Way to Europe, Interim Results of the Orange Revolution*, Frankfurt am Main: Peter Lang Verlag.

Sydorenko, S. (2010) 'When Victims Collude with Torturers', *Transitions Online*. Online. Available www.tol.org/client/article/21777-when-victims-collude-with-torturers.html (accessed 11 August 2011).

TCH.ua (2010) *Eksperty schitayut chto prichinoy pytok v militsii yavlyaetsya neobespechenie prav na etape zaderzhaniya*. Online. Available http://ru.tsn.ua/ukrayina/nazvany-prichiny-pytok-v-ukrainskoy-milicii.html (accessed 11 August 2011).

——(2011) *Pravozaschitniki v militsii uchastilis sluchai nezakonnogo nasiliya*. Online. Available http://ru.tsn.ua/ukrayina/pravozaschitniki-v-milicii-uchastilis-sluchai-nezakonnogo-nasiliya.html (accessed 11 August 2011).

Volkov, V. (2002) Violent Entrepreneurs: The Use of Force in the Making of Russian Capitalism, Ithaca, NY: Cornell University Press.

Way, L. and Levitsky, S. (2006) 'The Dynamics of Autocratic Coercion after the Cold War', *Communist and Post-Communist Studies*, 39: 387–410.

Wedel, J. (2005) 'U.S. Foreign Aid and Foreign Policy: Building Strong Relationships by Doing it Right!', *International Studies Perspectives*, 6: 35–50.

Westmarland, L. (2001) 'Blowing the Whistle on Police Violence: Gender, Ethnography and Ethics', *British Journal of Criminology*, 41: 523–35.

Wilson, D., Kolennikova, O., Kosals, L., Ryvkina, R. and Simagin, Yu. (2007) 'The "Economic Activities" of Russian Police', *International Journal of Police Science and Management*, 10(1): 65–75.

Yakubovich, T. (2011) *Dlya soblyudeniya prav cheloveka militsioneram ne chvataet deneg*. Online. Available http://ru.radioera.com.ua/eranews/?idArticle=34172 (accessed 11 August 2011).

Yarmish, A. (ed.) (2005) *Unlawful Violence in Law Enforcement Agencies: Sociological, Legal and Historical Analysis*, Kharkiv: Kharkiv University of Internal Affairs.

Zakharov, E. (2004) 'Human Rights NGOs in Ukraine and their Relations with the Authorities, Human Rights in Ukraine', Information Website of the Kharkiv Human Rights Protection Group. Online. Available www.khpg.org/en/index.php?id=1084787939 (accessed 23 July 2010).

——(2010) 'Prava cheloveka v Ukraine', *Glavnoe.* Online. Available http://glavnoe.ua/articles/a3223 (accessed 11 August 2011).

9 Police reform and building justice in Russia

Problems and prospects

Annette Robertson

This chapter presents an overview of the role of police reform in building justice in Russia. Since becoming an independent state in 1991, the Russian Federation has sought to reform various component parts of its criminal justice system, including the police, or the militia (*Militsiya* in Russian) as it was still named until very recently. Many of the reforms envisaged for the militia were ambitious and appeared – on paper at least – to propose the development of democratic policing structures and organisations, where the priority would be to serve the public rather than the state (Beck and Robertson 2009a). Concomitantly, the expectation was that the militia would be compelled by existing legislation (specifically related to the militia/police, their role in public office and, more generally the Russian Criminal Code) to adhere to, as well as uphold, the rule of law. However, the implementation of reforms has been inconsistent and increasingly suggestive of a 'one step forward and two steps back' process, whereby some of the more positive proposed developments have been hampered or eroded by inertia, a lack of political will and an apparent tendency to retreat to past practices and ideologies (Beck and Robertson 2005). Most significantly, perhaps, during the last few years, attention has increasingly been focused on militia abuse of their powers, that is criminal and deviant acts committed while both on and off duty, the seriousness of which eventually resulted in calls for reform. The focus of this chapter will be on the latest wave of reform that resulted in the coming into force of the new 'Law on the Police' in March 2011, and the key problems that still present obstacles in terms of the police making a meaningful and lasting contribution to the building of justice in Russia. These include police brutality, police corruption and a continued lack of independent oversight of the police. In conclusion, it is suggested that, although the police undoubtedly have a key role to play in the building of justice, the hit-and-miss results of police reform to date, as well as early indicators and assessments of the new law and its implementation, may indicate another missed opportunity for the development of genuine democratic policing and, consequently, for the police making a lasting contribution to the building of justice in the Russian Federation. This will doubtless continue to be the case until police power 'without limits' is subjugated to the rule of law.

The role of the police in building justice

The police have a crucial role to play in the building of justice in any country. Although their role can be constructed in different ways, and for different purposes (see, for example, Hinton and Newburn 2009), as the frontline service that acts, in a sense, as the gatekeeper to the larger criminal justice system, it is the government agency that the public is most likely to come into contact with – in one form or another – on a day-to-day basis. It is therefore vital that the public have confidence and trust in the police in the performance of their day-to-day activities; in other words, that the police have legitimacy in the eyes of the public (Bayley 2001).

However, in 'transition countries', or 'developing democracies', the police have a larger role to play beyond the standard functions of crime prevention and maintenance of social order: namely, they are intrinsic to the promotion and maintenance of the new legal structures and processes that are required for the kind of democratic reform envisaged in such transitions. Police reform therefore 'has an important role to play in the process of democratic transition' (Gerber and Mendelson 2008: 3). In the Russian Federation, this role has continued to be undermined, to a great extent, by many problems associated with how the police perceive and perform their standard functions, but also by structural issues, such as corruption, that affect not just the police, but the whole of Russian society, as well as an apparent inability to shake off the legacy of the Soviet era. It is fundamentally undermined, however, by a significant growth in the abuse of police power (see below).

A brief history of police reform in Russia

Throughout the Soviet period, the police (formally designated the militia after the 1917 Russian Revolution) acted as the strong hand of the state (Conquest 1968; Shelley 1996), a function which, to a great extent, lingers to the present day (Galeotti 2011). In terms of organisation, the Soviet militia was 'a highly militarised, centralised and bureaucratised organisation, governed by decree rather than rule of law' (Beck and Robertson 2009b: 149): characteristics that again appear to have withstood the test of time and continue to define, to some extent, the current law enforcement agencies in Russia – in spite of 20 years of reform (Beck and Robertson 2009a: 63).

The various changes and reforms that have been attempted since 1991, when the first post-Soviet Law on the Militia was introduced in the newly independent Russia, have been well documented elsewhere (see, for example, Timoshenko 1997; Gilinskiy 2000; Favarel-Garrigues and Le Huerou 2004; Robertson 2004; Solomon 2005; Beck and Robertson 2005, 2009a, 2009c), and have touched upon many issues including the legal status of the police, organisational structures and policies, operational policies and work patterns, and supervision and control (see Robertson 2004). On paper at least, the 1991 Law on the Militia appeared to encompass many of the key principles required for the development of democratic policing in Russia, which was initially an encouraging symbol of a break with the country's Soviet past. Unfortunately, the reforms failed to have any lasting success in terms of developing more democratic policing structures in Russia, for many reasons, as documented elsewhere (e.g. Robertson 2004; Solomon 2005; Beck and Robertson 2009a), including a continued lack of professionalism, legitimacy and accountability and, ultimately, a failure to adhere to the rule of law – and not to be consistently or justly punished for this; all of which continue to have a negative impact on the ability of the police to build justice in Russia. Not surprisingly, then, when asked towards the end of 2007 whether the police needed to be reformed, 74 per cent of respondents to a national survey agreed, 16 per cent did not know and only 10 per cent disagreed (Public Verdict 2010). When further asked what they considered should be the aims of police reform, the response selected most often was 'To improve the quality and effectiveness of the police in its everyday activity' (56 per cent), followed by 'To stop corruption and other violations by the police' (38 per cent) and 'To focus police work on protecting the interests and rights of the public and not the bureaucracy' (32 per cent) (Public Verdict 2010), which indicates the key problems the public associate with the police.

Police–public relationships

One of the key aims of recent police reform has been to try to address what is generally recognised as being a very poor relationship between the police and the public by adopting a more public-oriented approach. For many years, public opinion polls have consistently reported that the police are the public body considered the least trusted, most corrupt and most likely to be bribed by the public. The public's overwhelmingly negative view of the police is doubtless the result of Russian law enforcement's abysmal service reputation (indeed, they are more likely to be regarded as a force rather than as a service), but also a much reported predisposition for brutality and corruption, as detailed later in the chapter.

Successive reforms and publicity campaigns have been aimed at 'turning the face of the police towards the public' (Beck and Robertson 2005) with few positive results. When asked to describe a modern police officer in a 2006 survey, more than half of respondents (54 per cent) provided a negative image, including 'law-breaker', 'bribe-taker', 'thief', 'uniformed gangster', 'rude', 'evil', 'unscrupulous' and 'dishonest' (Public Opinion Foundation 2006).

In recent years, the negative public image of the police has been strengthened further by an apparent upsurge in police deviancy and criminality – as reflected in media reports. For example, in March 2009, a police officer chopped off the hand of a junior officer with an axe in a Moscow police station; in April 2009, an off-duty police officer opened fire in a Moscow supermarket, killing three people and injuring six more; in July 2009, a police investigator was charged with aiding and abetting the shooting of two holidaymakers in the Chelyabinsk Region (including providing a gun); and in August 2009, a traffic cop ran over a woman, hid her body and then proceeded to investigate the crime himself (*Moscow Times*, various reports, 2009).

It is perhaps therefore not surprising that the public continue to distrust the police and show little confidence in their abilities to provide a public service: when asked in a recent survey what needed to be done to improve the work of the police in Russia, the highest ranked response was 'make the punishment for professional misconduct/crime more severe' (Public Verdict 2010). This suggests that the public do not currently believe that legislation sufficiently punishes the police when they are found guilty of an offence. Research suggests, however, that it is not so much the lack of severity that is an issue: serious crime committed by a police officer is tried under the Russian Criminal Code, whereby committing an offence in uniform is considered a 'circumstance that aggravates punishment' (The Russian Criminal Code, Article 63 (m)).

The Ministry of Internal Affairs (MVD) is well aware of the public's negative views of its officers and has taken some steps to try to boost police popularity by improving their professionalism, including issuing a revised code of conduct in March 2009, which stipulated how officers should behave in both public and private, for example, prohibiting them from engaging in a range of inappropriate activities, from swearing and smoking in public to associating with criminals, offering or accepting bribes and even adultery. In June 2009, the MVD announced that its officers were to wear name badges and that patrol cars and traffic patrol cars (the traffic police are seen as the most corrupt) were to be equipped with video cameras, measures that were seen as having an anti-corruption function. As a result of the criminal and deviant acts mentioned above (especially the Moscow supermarket shooting), in July 2009, tougher oversight was announced for the police, including annual psychological testing for all police officers permitted to carry firearms; lie-detector tests for police candidates; and senior officials being held personally responsible for police leadership appointments. In March 2010, a nationwide public relations campaign was launched by the MVD again to try to improve the police's reputation (Bratersky 2010).

These 'softer' rules and guidelines have been accompanied by 'harder' legal regulations, including, for example, an amendment to the Law on the Militia passed in July 2010 that prohibited anyone with a criminal record from serving in the police. The new law also set harsher punishments for police officers found guilty of committing a crime, including longer sentences for police officers than civilians who had committed similar crimes could expect (*RIA Novosti* 2010). Indeed, it has been reported in the press that the president is calling for police officers found guilty of torture to receive twice the punishment of others convicted of this crime (RT 2010b).

Although all these steps potentially have merit, as with other such measures implemented over recent years, even those that have a legislative basis (that is those that criminalise certain behaviours) will prove meaningless unless they are effectively enforced.

The 2011 police reform

The new Law on the Police (*Zakon 'o politsii'*) came into force in the Russian Federation on 1 March 2011, replacing the Law on the Militia (*Zakon 'o militsii'*), the legislative tool that had regulated – at least on paper – the functions and operation of the Russian militia for 20 years. The development of the new Law on the Police is worthy of note as, for the first time since 1993 (when a public discussion was held on the draft Russian Constitution), the preliminary draft of the Law on the Police was published on a dedicated website for public discussion, which was ongoing between 7 August and 15 September 2010. According to the MVD, the draft stimulated much public interest, and the site attracted more than 20,000 comments on all the bill's articles. Consequently, amendments were made to the original draft and the revised version was then approved by the State Duma on 28 January 2011 and the Federation Council on 2 February 2011 before being signed off by President Medvedev on 7 February 2011 and finally becoming law on 1 March. According to the MVD, the adoption of the Law on the Police heralded a new era in the history of Russian internal affairs bodies, and guaranteed the further progress of Russian law enforcement agencies on the path to modernisation (MVD website: www.mvd.ru/).

The MVD claims that the new law will improve police performance, because their powers, duties and responsibilities are detailed for them meticulously. However, critics have argued that the law is not as clear as it could be in some sections (in relation to police powers) and that, given that police personnel simply ignored the old law when it suited them, why should or would they suddenly adhere to the new one? This point will be returned to at the end of the chapter. Before moving on to review the key provisions introduced under the 2011 law, there are two significant changes not envisaged by the law, but part of the wider police reform process worthy of mention: these are a change to the name of the Russian law enforcement body and a move towards greater centralisation.

Change of name

With the introduction of the new law on 1 March 2011, the Russian police force's name was changed from the militia ('*militsiya*'), as it had been known since the Russian Revolution (see above), to the more internationally recognised and universal name for law enforcement bodies – the police ('*politsiya*'). Although this could be construed as a superficial change, it is – at least symbolically – significant in terms of highlighting a break from the Soviet legacy, especially when taken into account alongside the other changes envisaged by the law, as detailed below. However, there is a possibility that this change – however symbolic – may end up being of superficial significance because it has not, for example, been accompanied by any change in the structure of the police, which will retain its military-style ranking system that defines police personnel from rank-and-file 'police officer' all the way up to police general (Article 26.1) and brings concomitant rewards and bonuses in terms of remuneration.[1]

Whether this change in name will result in improvements to the quality of the service provided by the Russian police forces remains to be seen. There is a sense that this could be a case of 'old wine in new bottles' with the danger being that the new police will bear a striking resemblance to the old militia, albeit with new uniforms and insignia, in much the same way that the Soviet militia ended up very similar to the Tsarist police force it was supposed to replace (Galeotti 2011). A major concern, therefore, is that the new police, albeit greatly reduced in numbers (see below), will continue to behave in the same way as the old, particularly with respect to their generally relaxed attitude towards their work and – more particularly – towards corruption and violence (both discussed later in the chapter).

Increased centralisation

Given that, for many years, the Russian government has advocated the progressive decentralisation of the MVD, as befits a more democratic policing system (Beck and Robertson 2005), it appears a bit of a *volte face* that the new wave of reforms strengthens, rather than weakens, the centralised nature of the police. This is facilitated by the federal budget assuming the total cost for all policing throughout the Russian Federation, whereas previously there was scope for local police forces to be partly or indeed wholly funded by their local authorities. Although this may appear puzzling from both a financial and a reform perspective, it may make good sense when the peculiarities of Russia's regional power dynamics are taken into consideration. For example, first, the additional costs associated with the federal budget assuming full responsibility for policing will simply be clawed back by making associated cuts to the subsidies paid each year by central government to the regions. In this way, for no real additional financial burden, the federal government is able to bring all policing in the country under its control, which is important from an operational perspective. Second, it is also important from a political (power base) point of view: a further benefit of the new funding arrangement is that it removes an important power mechanism previously discernible at the local level, whereby the local authorities, sometimes (if not often or always) working closely with local businesses and possibly criminal organisations, were able to use the local police that they funded to their own ends, which were not always legal or in the interests of central government.

As can be seen, therefore, an apparently retrograde move may bring positive outcomes – in this case, the removal of a key mechanism that allowed a certain type of collusion and corruption to flourish at both the local and the regional level. Again, only time will tell if this strategy is successful in countering such seemingly invincible networks of local actors perceived to be working to further their own interests.

Key new provisions of the Law on the Police

Although the new Law on the Police is the end result of consultation about the role, scope and powers of the Russian police, it is perhaps best considered as the first, rather than the final, major step in the reform of the Ministry of Internal Affairs. In this respect, it is important to note that other phases of reform are envisaged, for example the reform of the nationwide police training and education system and changes to the way police performance is measured. According to President Medvedev, 'this law was worked out on my initiative and is just the first step in reforming the country's Interior Ministry' (RT 2011). Some of the key provisions of the new law are reviewed below, namely changes to police functions, the core tasks of the police and changes to their powers, including restrictions on the use of force.

Changes to police functions

Successive police reform measures in Russia have progressively attempted to modify their functions, mainly by ridding the Russian police of some of their less universally recognised (as policing) roles and responsibilities. In this respect, the new Law on the Police is no exception and specifies the roles and functions Russian law enforcement agencies are to lose before 1 January 2012. According to Article 54.1, these include:

- the expulsion of foreign national and stateless people from the Russian Federation;
- the organisation of medical detoxification work (drunk tanks);
- the carrying out of technical checks on vehicles and car parts;
- escorting individuals who have been arrested and placed on remand to and from holding facilities;
- investigating debtors.

As with the loss of other functions and responsibilities, part of the rationale behind these changes is that it should free up the police to focus on their core tasks, which in accordance with Article 2.1 are:

- to protect individuals, society and the state from criminal encroachments;
- to prevent and reduce crime and administrative violations;
- to detect and clear up crimes and conduct enquiries for criminal cases;
- to investigate individuals;
- to process administrative violations and enact administrative sanctions;
- to maintain public order;
- to provide for safety on the roads;
- to ensure that Russian legislation is observed on the sale of weapons;
- to ensure that Russian legislation is observed on private detective (investigations) and security activity;
- to guard property and premises on a contract basis;

- to offer state protection for victims, witnesses and other participants of criminal cases, judges, prosecutors, investigators, other officers of the law enforcement and control agencies, and other protected individuals.

Changes to police powers

Several key changes have been made in the new law that should, in theory, protect members of the public from the unjustified violations of their rights by the police. For example, under Article 14 of the new law, the police are not allowed to hold suspects for more than 48 hours, when they must be presented to court for a detainment hearing or released. The police are also now required to inform people they detain for any reason of their rights (similar to reading a suspect their rights in the UK or the 'Miranda' warning in the US), which was not previously the case. This includes the right to legal assistance, to translation services, to contact a close relative or friend to inform them of their detainment, and the right to refuse to answer questions (Article 14.3).

Under Article 5, 'Observing and respecting the human rights and liberties of citizens', the police are now also required to identify themselves in all dealings with members of the public, by stating their position, rank, surname, showing their police ID and then informing them of the reason for the contact (Article 5.4). This appears to formalise the requirement previously mentioned that police personnel wear name badges so as to enable members of the public to take a note of their names if necessary. According to Section 5 of the same article, where the member of the public initiates the contact, the police are obliged to listen attentively, take corresponding measures in accordance with their powers or find out which body can facilitate a resolution to the stated problem (Article 5.5).

As with the previous Law on the Militia, the new Law on the Police emphasises the importance of police impartiality, by prohibiting them from joining political parties, or supporting financially and participating in the activities of political parties (Article 7.2), and stipulating that they must fulfil their duties regardless of gender, ethnicity, nationality, place of residence, religion, convictions, membership of public association or other circumstances (Article 7.1).

Under the new law, more demanding requirements are made of police personnel in respect of what is considered to be proper conduct: for example, they are now obliged to report to their superior officer any conflict of interest that may arise in carrying out their duties, and also to take steps to prevent such conflicts of interest from occurring in the first place (Article 27.1.13). More generally, police personnel are prohibited – both on and off duty – from doing anything that could discredit their honour and/or raise doubts about their impartiality or result in a loss of their authority (Article 7.4).

New prohibitions on the police use of force

New restrictions have also been introduced on the use of force: for example, the police are prohibited from hitting people with their truncheons on the head, neck, collar bone area, stomach, genitals or heart area (Article 22.2.1), ominously suggesting that this is currently practised. It is interesting to note that this provision counteracts the prime minister's comments made in 2010 that demonstrators who refused to act on police instructions could reasonably expect to be hit on the head with a truncheon (RT 2010a). Such advice from Putin would now be tantamount to encouraging the police to break the new law.

The police are not allowed to use special force on women who show signs of being pregnant, people who appear disabled and the underage, except under special circumstances (Article 22.1.1). They are also not permitted to use force to stop unlawful assemblies, meetings, demonstrations, marches and pickets of a non-violent nature if they pose no threat to public order, transportation, communication links or organisations (Article 22.1.2). It will be interesting to see to what extent this latter point influences the police response when faced with such circumstances, as they have often used force in the past, such as against non-violent public displays of opposition against the government. In fact, although Russia is a signatory to the European Convention on Human Rights, which guarantees freedom of assembly, requests for permission to demonstrate are often turned down and protesters subsequently beaten and arrested. This has happened not only to political protesters, but also to economic and social activists.[2]

What is most significant in respect of the prohibitions outlined above is that, in limiting police powers, the new law also recognises the conditions upon which the police can be challenged by any member of the public who, individually or as part of a group, is subject to more force than the law allows. This leads us on to a discussion of one of the key problems associated with police reform: police misconduct.

Police misconduct

Police misconduct is a serious problem in Russia that ultimately has the result of undermining democracy (Gerber and Mendelson 2008: 3). Although it occurs on many levels and takes many forms, for the purposes of this chapter, two key issues will be considered, namely police corruption and police brutality.

Police corruption

Although corruption is endemic in Russian society, and therefore not just a problem associated with law enforcement agencies, the Russian police is the public agency that regularly tops corruption charts published in the country. For example, of the 1,300 Russians sentenced for accepting bribes in 2008, 31 per cent worked for the Ministry of Internal Affairs (i.e. the police) compared with 20 per cent in healthcare, 12 per cent teachers and 9 per cent local authority workers (Russian Supreme Court statistics, cited in RT 2009). However, it is interesting to note that most of the corruption cases dealt with by the judicial system involve relatively low sums of money: for example, 81 per cent of these cases involved bribes of no more than 30,000 roubles or around US$1000 (RT 2009). These overall prosecution numbers are suspiciously low, and cannot be taken as an indication of the real level of corruption/bribe-taking that occurs in the country, nor the huge sums of money that can be involved: they are likely to represent the very tip of the corruption iceberg.

The new Law on the Police includes some provisions aimed at preventing corruption by police personnel. In accordance with Article 27.10, police personnel are now obliged to provide information not just about their own income, property and 'obligations of a material character', but also those of their spouses or underage children – and the results are published openly on the MVD's website (www.mvd.ru/). It is not clear, however, to what extent this is reliable or indeed valid.

In spite of such measures, according to Galeotti (2009), attempts to deal with corruption continue to have limited effect. Partly, this is the result of a lack of enforcement, but also more generally the result of corruption being not so much an individual or professional problem, but rather a structural one that affects all of Russian society. Although President Medvedev has made it his key mission to tackle the country's corruption problem, for this to be effective, efforts must be deployed simultaneously across the public and private sectors, and towards changing the mindset of the Russian population who are an intrinsic part of the corruption equation.

Police brutality

Police brutality, or 'the law of the fist' ('*kulachnoe pravo*'; Galeotti 2011), is another serious issue that continues to blight the reputation of the Russian police. Abuses of power in the treatment of suspects are well documented (Human Rights Watch 1999, 2011; Amnesty International 2011), and a significant proportion of the complaints made to the Russian Human Rights Ombudsman relate to police violence (Coalson 2004; Ekho Moskvy Radio 2005). Given the lack of justice received from their own state, Russian citizens have turned increasingly to the European Court of Human Rights to seek justice (*Nezavisimaya Gazeta* 2004). Clearly, the Russian police's record in terms of observing and respecting the rights of its citizens is extremely poor: a recent report suggests that as many as one in every 25 people in Russia is tortured, beaten or harassed by law enforcement officers each year (O'Flynn 2009).

The new Law on the Police seeks to address this problem by introducing some new restrictions on the use of force by police (as outlined above) and banning the use of 'torture, violence or other treatment that is demeaning to human dignity. Officers are obliged to stop action which deliberately inflicts pain or physical or moral suffering' (Article 5.3). Officers are also prohibited from hitting a suspect repeatedly on the same part of the body. Human rights organisations have criticised the inclusion of the word 'torture' in the new law, as torture is a crime, and banning it in the law could be construed as giving it some legitimacy (RT 2010b). It is suggested, however, that this further criminalisation of traditional (albeit informal) policing methods will not prove useful in preventing such violence on the part of the police, unless it is accompanied by other wide-ranging reforms to police education and training – including in ethics and human rights – and to the way police performance is measured.

As regards the latter point, although in no way an attempt to absolve any police officer who engages in brutality and torture, it is important to note that such acts may be encouraged by a police performance system that has long relied only on quantitative indicators rather than on the more usual mixture of quantitative and qualitative indices of service now favoured in many police services around the world. For example, it is argued by Gerber and Mendelson (2008: 36) that 'the primary structural basis for violence appears to be pressure from higher authorities to obtain "confessions by torturing suspects"'. In a similar vein, between 40 per cent and 60 per cent of prison inmates claim to have been tortured before their cases came to court (Public Verdict 2010). See also the discussion of similar institutional incentives for the resort to police torture in Yulia Chistyakova's chapter on Ukraine in this volume.

The new Law on the Police addresses this problem, to some extent, by encouraging the measurement of police performance using not just performance indicators such as detection and clear-up rates, service data, but also public assessment of the work of the police by, for example, the use of public satisfaction surveys (see below for more detail).

Other key problems

Too many c(r)ooks ...

For many years, the MVD claimed to be suffering from a shortage of personnel, caused in part by high turnover as officers left the force for more lucrative jobs, including the provision of private security services (Beck and Robertson 2009a). It appears, however, that these so-called 'shortages' were in fact an artefact of the Soviet system, whereby there was no objective measure of how many officers were required to police society; rather, the aim was to maintain previous personnel levels for various strategic reasons.

Although it has been suggested that Russia is one of the most heavily policed countries in the world (and paradoxically one of the most lawless; Galeotti 2011), finding official sources of data to corroborate such claims proves difficult. Using a process of extrapolation based on the most recent population data (143 million according to 2010 Russian Census figures) and an estimated total MDV staff figure of 1.4 million, we end up with a current estimated police–public ratio (per 100,000 of the population) of around 979 for Russia, compared with, for example, 317 in Scotland, 263 in England and Wales, 493 in Northern Ireland and 227 in the US (UNODC website), as summarised in Table 9.1.[3]

Table 9.1 Number of police officers per 100,000 of the population

Country	*Number of police officers per 100,000 people*
Russia	979
Northern Ireland	493
Scotland	317
England and Wales	263
USA	227

Source: Adapted from UNODC website figures, apart from the Russian figure, which is based on the author's calculations.

Although methods for collecting and counting such data differ across countries in relation to what agencies are included and measures used (for example, actual people or budget posts), the figures cited above suggest that Russia's police personnel far exceed the worldwide median of 300 police officers per 100,000 (UN 2010).

Depending on the perspective adopted, Russia's very high ratio of police to population could help to explain their comparatively low levels of recorded crime, or could alternatively raise questions about the veracity of their recording techniques (see Tables 9.2 and 9.3).

The figures in Tables 9.2 and 9.3 show that the overall and per capita crime rates recorded in Russia are far lower than the selected countries' figures provided for comparison. Although it could be argued that Russia's lower crime rates are a result of the high ratio of police personnel to population, it is more likely to be the case that a high percentage of crimes experienced are either not reported to the police by victims or, if reported, are not recorded by the police, again at least partly as a result of the police's performance indicators being focused on meeting clear-up targets, as mentioned earlier (Favarel-Garrigues and Le Huerou 2004).

The MVD has now also recognised that its personnel levels are high and is seeking to reduce numbers significantly: a key mechanism of the current reform is to reduce total police personnel by 20 per cent by the end of 2011. This is to be implemented by a process of *attestatsiya* or re-accreditation, whereby every serving member of personnel (including the Minister of Internal Affairs) will be compelled to reapply for their job and undergo testing. Article 54.3–5 details this special re-accreditation, to be conducted within a period specified by the Russian president. Those employees who do not undergo re-accreditation will be made redundant in accordance with existing MVD service regulations, whereas those who are successfully re-accredited will continue as police personnel under the provisions laid down in the new law. The aim is to reduce the number of unprofessional, incompetent and corrupt police officers in the ministry.

Although this may appear a progressive move on the part of the MVD, critics are already arguing that it will not have the desired effect of weeding out the less-committed, -qualified or -professional staff because the re-accreditation will be implemented by the upper echelons of the police hierarchy, allowing

Table 9.2 Recorded crime per 1,000 of the population

Country	*Crimes recorded by the police per 1,000 people*
Russia	20.58
Northern Ireland	85.55 (UK total)
Scotland	
England and Wales	
USA	80.06

Source: Adapted from UNODC website figures.

Table 9.3 Total number of recorded crimes and population statistics for selected countries

Country	*Total number of crimes recorded by the police*	*Population*
Russia	2,628,800 (2010)	141,900,000
Northern Ireland	105,040 (2010/11)	1,800,000
Scotland	901,763 (2009/10)	5,200,000
England and Wales	4,200,000 (2010/11)	55,000,000
USA	Not available	Not available

Source: Adapted from Russian MVD website figures; Scottish Government (2010); Home Office (2011); Police Service of Northern Ireland (2011).
Note: The figure for Scotland includes 338,028 crimes (considered more serious) and 563,753 offences (considered less serious).

for professional patronage – a form of corruption – to continue. Anecdotal evidence of corruption as a result of this 're-accreditation' mechanism being implemented has already been reported in the media, where it has been claimed that senior officers have been demanding 'kickbacks from their subordinates' to ensure they are reappointed (Galeotti 2011).

As well as the re-accreditation of all existing MVD personnel mentioned above, the law makes other provisions for improving the quality of MVD staff through new recruitment mechanisms. For example, Article 35.4 specifies new selection procedures for job candidates including psychological checks as well as alcohol, drug and other toxic substance dependency testing. The psychological checks are doubtless at least partly the result of concerns about officers being involved in serious offences such as the Moscow supermarket shooting in April 2008, and alcohol dependency testing is perhaps related to claims that around 20 per cent of the current police force is suffering from alcoholism (Public Verdict 2010).

Salary increases

Alongside the 20 per cent cut in personnel, the salaries for remaining staff are to be increased threefold. This is intended to put a stop to any 'need' for rank-and-file and other officers to rely on bribes to supplement what are both essentially and relatively (compared with other state employee and private sector salaries) very low basic incomes. It is interesting to note that a similar initiative was implemented in 2003, when salaries for all police officers were doubled overnight but, unfortunately, this does not appear to have had any long-term impact on bribe-taking or more serious corruption within the police, which now appear to be worse than in 2003. Perhaps this new initiative, coupled with a more active corruption prevention policy (involving much harsher punishments for those found guilty of such professional misconduct), will have a more positive effect.

In this respect, it has been mooted by Russian commentators that every police officer found to have committed such professional misconduct should be summarily dismissed from the police, both to demonstrate the government's commitment to stamping out corruption in the police force, and as a means of reducing overall numbers (Public Verdict 2010). Although there is promise in preventive measures, such as new applicant screening, re-accreditation and increased salaries, a deeper reconceptualisation of what amounts to corrupt practices appears to be absent from this framework. Rather than explicitly criminalise specific practices, the aim appears to be to deter them: a strategy that has not met with great success in the past.

Public oversight of the police

A final issue worthy of note is the development of public oversight of the police. The new law contains a section on 'Public trust and support', which stipulates, among other things, that 'public opinion is one of the key criteria in the official evaluation of police activity' (Article 9.6) and provides for the creation of 'public councils' (Article 9.7), with a range of aims, including 'implementing public control of police activity' (Article 9.7.5).[4]

In terms of assessing police work, it is clear that President Medvedev is eager to implement genuine public oversight and, to this end, he has issued a separate decree 'On issues concerning the assessment of the work of Russia's Interior Ministry Agencies'. Doubtless this is seen as an additional weapon in the fight against police corruption and improving relations between the police and public. However, it is interesting to note in this respect that, when asked what needed to be done to improve the work of the police, the public were more likely to answer: 'Strengthen control over police work by government bodies, city and local council and the Prosecutor's Office' (30 per cent chose this response) than: 'Strengthen public control over police work, including taking into account public opinions, involving the public in tackling crime and social order problems in their local areas; being directly accountable to the public' (22 per cent) (Public Verdict 2010). Punitive supervision thus seems a more popular solution than public supervision. As similar initiatives introduced over the last 10 years have failed to have any meaningful impact on police–public relations or police deviancy and corruption, it remains to be seen whether this time the results will be different. Again, criminal punishment seems to be eschewed in favour of a worthwhile initiative that may not, however, have the power to tackle the structural problems.

Conclusions

Given all the problems outlined above, what are the prospects for the police making a meaningful contribution to the building of justice in Russia? Clearly, the police have the most important role to play of all government agencies in upholding the rule of law, but they must also be subject to this themselves. Only time will tell if the new requirements placed on the police in relation to ensuring citizens' human rights and civil liberties are respected have the desired effect. Likewise, it will take time for an assessment to be made on whether the new prohibitions that the law places on police powers, including the use of violence, are adhered to and, if not, whether appropriate legal sanctions are subsequently applied. All the relevant legislation for this to happen is already in place. Further criminalisation is not required; rather, existing rules, regulations and law relating to various types of police abuse of power, including corruption and brutality and torture, need to be properly enforced. As long as police personnel understand that they can break the law with relative impunity, they will continue to do so.

Unfortunately, the hit and (largely) miss results of previous reform measures suggest that what at first looks promising on paper is not always easily translated into practice. According to early indicators, even some of the more novel reform measures, such as the re-accreditation process, already appear to be coming unstuck as a result of the mechanisms involved, which lend themselves to continued patronage and thus abuse. Many of the other provisions may also be subject to legal interpretation, which could potentially undermine the restrictions and requirements placed on the use of police powers – to the detriment of the Russian public. As such, it could be argued that the new law could become another missed opportunity for the development of genuine democratic policing and consequently for the police making a lasting contribution to the building of justice in the Russian Federation. However, perhaps a more optimistic assessment would view the introduction of the new law not as a panacea, but as the beginning of a longer-term and more effective police reform than in the past. In this respect, the recentralisation of the police could be – paradoxically – a step in the right direction of bringing them more under the control of not just the government, but of the law. Ultimately, this is what will prove effective in terms of the police being in a position to contribute to building justice: not just implementing the new Law on the Police, but making sure the police themselves abide by its provisions and, where they do not, that they are subject to the full force of relevant legislation.

Notes

1 The ranking system has five categories: (1) rank and file (police officer); (2) junior officers (junior sergeant; sergeant; senior sergeant; sergeant major; warrant officer; senior warrant officer; (3) middle-ranking officers (junior lieutenant; lieutenant; senior lieutenant; captain); (4) senior ranks (police major; colonel; lieutenant-colonel; colonel); (5) most senior ranks (major-general; lieutenant-general; colonel-general; police general) (Article 26.1 of the Law on the Police, 2011).

2 For example, in December 2008, a Dissenters' March was banned in Moscow and protesters were arrested. The following February, a Moscow police chief tried to get six students from the Higher School of Economics expelled for taking part in the 'unauthorised' December march. In March 2009, a Russian opposition activist was detained by police and forcibly hospitalised in a mental institution in St Petersburg, where he was held for two weeks before being released. In May 2009, many demonstrators, including a veteran British gay activist, Peter Tatchell, were arrested when Moscow police violently broke up a rally after the mayor of Moscow had banned it, having described Gay Pride parades as 'satanic'.

3 Data available from www.unodc.org/unodc/en/data-and-analysis/crimedata.html (accessed 21 July 2011).

4 Article 50 on 'Public control of police activity' covers in more detail the various ways in which oversight of the police should be enacted, including through the Federal Public Chamber, the Public Investigations Committee and Public Councils. Oversight over all police activity is also effected through the courts (Article 51) and the Prosecutor's Office. Complaints about individual officers who have violated the rights and legal interests of a member of the public, state or municipal body, public association, religious or other organisation may be made to senior police officers, the Prosecutor's Office or directly to the courts (Article 53).

References

Amnesty International (2011) *Russian Federation Annual Report*. Online. Available www.amnesty.org/en/region/russia/report-2011 (accessed 28 July 2011).

Bayley, D. (2001) *Democratizing the Police Abroad: What To Do and How To Do It*, Washington, DC: Department of Justice.

Beck, A. and Robertson, A. (2005) 'Policing in Post-Soviet Russia', in W. Pridemore (ed.) *Law, Crime, and Justice in Transitional Russia*, Lanham, MD: Rowan and Littlefield, 247–60.

——(2009a) 'Policing in the New Russia', in M.S. Hinton and T. Newburn (eds) *Policing Developing Democracies*, London: Routledge, 50–72.

——(2009b) 'Russia', in A. Wakefield and J. Fleming (eds) *The Sage Dictionary of Policing*, London: Sage, 149–50.

——(2009c) 'The Challenges to Developing Democratic Policing in Post-Soviet Societies: the Russian Experience', *Police Practice and Research*, 10(4): 285–93.

Bratersky, A. (2010) 'Police Roll Out Plan to Improve Reputation', *Moscow Times*, 18 March 2010.

Coalson, R. (2004) 'Analysis: Russia's Ombudsman Speaks Out', Radio Free Europe/ Radio Liberty. Online. Available www.rferl.org/featuresarticle/2004/06 (accessed 25 September 2007).

Conquest, R. (1968) *The Soviet Police System*, London: The Bodley Head.

Ekho Moskvy Radio (2005) 'Interview with Russia's Human Rights' Ombudsman, Vladimir Lukin'. Online. Available www.eng.yabloko.ru/Publ/2004/radio/040213_ekho.html (accessed 25 September 2007).

Favarel-Garrigues, G. and Le Huerou, A. (2004) 'State and the Multilateralization of Policing in Post-Soviet Russia', *Policing & Society*, 14(1), 13–30.

Galeotti, M. (2009) Three Reasons Why Russia's Police Remain Unreformed, RFERL, 6 September 2009.

——(2011) 'Medvedev's Law on Police: A Quiet Revolution?', *Open Democracy*. Online. Available http://cma.opendemocracy.net/od-russia/mark-galeotti/medvedev%E2%80%99s-law-on-police-quiet-revolution (accessed 21 July 2011).

Gerber, T.P. and Mendelson, S.E. (2008) 'Public Experiences of Police Violence and Corruption in Contemporary Russia: A Case Study of Predatory Policing?', *Law & Society Review*, 42(1): 1–44.

Gilinskiy, Y. (2000) 'Challenges of Policing Democracies: The Russian Experience', in D. Das and O. Marenin (eds) *Challenges of Policing Democracies: A World Perspective*, Amsterdam: Gordon and Breach Publishers, 173–94.

Hinton, M. and Newburn, T. (eds) (2009) *Policing Developing Democracies*, London: Routledge.

Home Office (2011) *Statistical News Release: Crime in England and Wales 2010/11*, London: Home Office.

Human Rights Watch (1999) *Confessions at any Cost: Police Torture in Russia*, New York: Human Rights Watch.

——(2011) *World Report 2011: Russia*. Online. Available www.hrw.org/en/world-report-2011/russia (accessed 28 July 11).

Moscow Times (2009) 'Traffic Cop Runs Over Woman, Hides Body, Investigates Self', *Moscow Times*, 25 August 2009.

Nezavisimaya Gazeta (2004) 'Lukin becomes a Dissident', *Nezavisimaya Gazeta*, 17 June.

O'Flynn, K. (2009) 'Police Crime Wave Sparks Talk of Reform in Russia', Radio Free Europe online. Online. Available www.rferl.org/content/Russia_Police_Crime_Wave_Sparks_Talk_of_Reform/1764434.html (accessed 21 July 2011).

Police Service of Northern Ireland (2011) *Police Recorded Crime in Northern Ireland 1998/99 to 2010/11*, Belfast: Police Service of Northern Ireland.

Public Opinion Foundation (2006) Online. Available www.fom.ru/ (accessed 21 July 2011).

Public Verdict (2010) *Police Reform: Public Evaluation and Expectations: The Results of Sociological Research and Expert Commentaries*, Moscow: 'Public Verdict' Fund. (Translated from original Russian text: Fond 'Obshchestvennii verdikt' (2010) *Reforma militsiya: otsenki i ozhidaniya grazhdan: resultaty sotsiologicheskikh issledovanii i kommentarii ekspertov*, Moscow: Fond 'Obshchestvennii verdikt').

RIA Novosti (2010) 'Former Criminals banned from Russian Police Force', *RIA Novosti*, 14 July 2010.

Robertson, A. (2004) 'Police Reform in Russia', in M. Caparini and O. Marenin (eds) *Transforming Police in Central and Eastern Europe*, Munster: Lit Verlag.

RT (2009) 'Police Top's Russia's Corruption Chart', published 28 January 2009. Online. Available http://rt.com/news/police-tops-russia-s-corruption-chart/ (accessed 20 July 2011).

——(2010a) 'Putin on Banned Protests: No Permission – Get Hit on the Head', 2 September 2010. Online. Available http://rt.com/politics/official-word/putin-interview-kommersant-opposition/ (accessed 21 July 2011).

——(2010b) 'People's Trust in the Police Dropped Twenty-fold in 20 Years', published 21 September 2010. Online. Available http://rt.com/politics/shkhagoshev-police-reform-law/ (accessed 10 October 2011).

——(2011) 'Russian Police Changing Image as Medvedev signs New Law', published 7 February 2011. Online. Available http://rt.com/news/russia-police-law-signed/ (accessed 21 July 2011).

Scottish Government (2010) *Recorded Crime in Scotland 2009–10*, Statistical Bulletin Crime and Justice Series, 7 September, Edinburgh: Scottish Government. Online. Available www.scotland.gov.uk/Resource/Doc/323661/0104236.pdf (accessed 12 December 2011).

Shelley, L. (1996) *Policing Soviet Society: The Evolution of State Control*, London: Routledge.

Solomon, P.H. (2005) 'The Reform of Policing in the Russian Federation', *Australian and New Zealand Journal of Criminology*, 38(2): 230–41.

Timoshenko, S. (1997) 'Prospects for Reform of the Russian Militia', *Policing and Society*, 8: 117–24.

UN (2010) *Twelfth United Nations Congress on Crime Prevention and Criminal Justice, Salvador, Brazil, 12–19 April 2010*, New York: UN.

Part IV

Some concluding thoughts

10 Beyond domestic law

Themes and prospects

Kay Goodall, Margaret Malloch and Bill Munro

This book has provided a range of analyses that highlight the challenges and complexities of defining and comprehending processes of transition as manifested through economic, political and constitutional change. The very identity of a transition state and what it means to be 'post-transition' has been interrogated in the preceding chapters. To various degrees, this book has highlighted the significance of understanding these contexts as whole systems, with each element of the state impacting on others. However, examination of the processes of criminalisation serves to highlight the complex and often unpredictable ways in which the law is operationalised in societies undergoing transitional change. The attention given to these different aspects of transition (economic, political and constitutional) provides particular lenses through which the processes of transition can be understood. Although there may be a presumption that these systemic factors always drive changes in criminal law, the reality is that some influences are stochastic or peripheral. In this concluding chapter, we identify the themes that have emerged from the book, consolidate the key debates and consider future prospects.

Civil society and legitimacy

The relationship between legality and legitimacy is emphasised in Weber's (1978) assertion that a legal system that is logically coherent and free from internal contradictions is necessary for the legitimation of modern societies. Legitimacy can be understood in Weber's terms as relating to the legal form of political authority: that is the belief or public perception of the *legality* of the exercise of political power. Kimmo Nuotio, in this volume, highlights this connection between law, legitimacy and power when he writes that criminal law constitutes a structure as well as a social practice: it also reflects political circumstances and state ideologies. Therefore, it is important when examining what happens to criminal laws in processes of transition that not only are we alert to the fact that history and tradition impose many limitations on reform and change, but that the political imperatives and actions of national states are also influenced by external political and economic factors. Agendas are increasingly set at international and transnational levels, not only in the former East but also in the West. Nuotio also emphasises the unconscious processes of cultural adaptation and adjustment to the development of legal and political culture and how the needs and values of late modern society are reflected in what is and what is not to be criminalised. In this way, criminal law can be understood not only as a mechanism for socialisation and integration, but also as a mechanism of civil society, as part of the institutionalisation of society's ideas, customs and morals.

However, criminal law can also be an important technique in depoliticising political processes, and it is often harnessed to broader social aims beyond the control of crime, such as the individualisation and criminalisation of social problems in the newly emerging economies. Here, criminal law plays a symbolic role in the realm of security and attainment of social trust, and in turn plays a key role in people's perception (or social representation) of justice, i.e. of what is just. Although distrust and cynicism have been labelled as 'the predictable legacy of communist rule', Peršak, in her study on Slovenia, argues that there is a contrast between trust in justice on the books and trust in the judicial application of criminal law as justice in action. Despite the steady decline of social trust in the application of (criminal) laws, i.e. distrust in courts – and in those entrusted with the delivering of justice – the legitimacy of the criminal law and its powers seems to persist, albeit in the form of a popular punitivism. In this case, 'justness' appears to be related to retribution.

The above discussion of criminalisation is located in the context of a general rule-of-law discourse and conventional criminality. However, Arunas Juska and Charles Woolfson concentrate on the absence of criminalisation of entrepreneurial practices during the period of privatisation of state property in the early 1990s and how this affected trust and social solidarity between individuals, the state and the wider polity. In their chapter, questions of legitimacy and trust are related not to the application of the law but to its suspension in relation to what were generally perceived as economic crimes.

The 1990s saw the implementation of privatisation and land reforms that were characterised by the lax enforcement of regulations that were underdeveloped and contradictory. It was a process that saw the rise of a new capitalist class, a new species of 'robber baron' – the Russian oligarch and *krysha*. It was a period characterised by widespread corruption and semi-criminal and criminal deals (see also the chapter by Munro in this volume).

Organised theft, the stripping of business assets, insider-dealing and nepotism produced a largely 'criminalistic', but not, as yet, 'criminalised', entrepreneurial class. The suspension of criminal law in this case was a mechanism by which an elite was able to impose new definitions of property to their greater advantage. The absence of criminalisation of those perceived to be stealing public property was accompanied by the rapid pauperisation of large segments of the population, and signalled a profound transformation in public trust in the institutions of the state and society.

Arato (2000) argued that it was important to separate civil society from the economic imperatives of capitalism because it was necessary to emphasise its universalising ethical implications and its status as a relatively autonomous community. However, during the process of privatisation, the Russian state had not only undermined social solidarity by ignoring the collective interests of the people and the basic principles of social justice; by prioritising a rapid systemic transformation to capitalism, it neglected the structural and institutional basis for the political consensus-building necessary for civil society to flourish. *Prichvatization* therefore was not only an internally motivated set of processes but, as Munro argues, it was also externally driven, albeit unintentionally, by Western diplomacy.

Although an ideal civil society provides a combination of values and institutions to generate the capacity for a democratic culture, real civil society as it has developed in many Eastern European countries is not only fragmentary but, as we have seen, it provides the dynamic for the suppression of social solidarity and the institutions necessary for democratic integration. Whether criminal law and institutional reform can impose inhibitions upon the actions of the new elite, their protectors and the police remains to be seen. Annette Robertson and Yulia Chistyakova examine this question in relation to police reform in Russia and the Ukraine and consider questions of legitimacy and the civil sphere.

Robertson argues that, in 'transition countries', the police have an important role to play beyond crime prevention and the maintenance of social order, intrinsic to the promotion and maintenance of the new legal structures and the processes that are required for democratic reform. Her chapter focuses on militia abuse of their powers and examines the grey area between arbitrary extra-legal power and the rule of law. Earlier reforms that attempted to break with the country's Soviet past failed to have any lasting success in terms of developing more democratic policing structures in Russia. Reasons for this included lack of professionalism, an absence of legitimacy and accountability and, most significantly, a failure to adhere to the rule of law. Public opinion polls have consistently reported that the police are considered the least trusted and most corrupt public body in Russian society. This negative public image of the police has been strengthened further by media-reported incidents of police deviancy and criminality.

Similarly, Chistyakova reports a lack of public trust in the police and justice institutions in the Ukraine. She examines in her chapter the extent to which Soviet legacies continue to play a role in contemporary police practices, including torture, and whether there is perhaps a new demand for violent policing. Here, the growing market created a demand for violence, in that torture and coercion are often used by police officers as a method of extortion and not only in the fulfilment of their professional duties.

Chistyakova argues that one of the central problems that post-communist societies face is a weak civil society. For a democratic political culture, a strong civil society is necessary to underpin the promotion and maintenance of democratic structures and processes. In the case of the Ukraine, civil society is too poorly organised and positioned to seek influence over policing.

As we have seen elsewhere in East Central Europe, civil society and the state were viewed as two social forces in opposition and, although state funding is primarily available to those organisations whose activities are prioritised by the state, the non-governmental and voluntary sector in Ukraine is unsupported.

Transition and processes of criminalisation

Individual states are touched by a number of spheres of influence, both internal and external. Large global or state-wide organisations can set agendas for individual states, such as, for example, NATO, the EU, the IMF and the World Bank. As the chapters in this book have illustrated, surrounding states can impact on the form that transition may take: economic power can determine priorities for compliance or allegiance (previously the USA's, more currently China's). A closer examination of the actual processes of reform, however, can serve to illustrate the problematic assumption that liberal reforms are the result of 'Western' and/or 'democratic' influence (Held 1993). Processes of both criminalisation and decriminalisation require an understanding of the state in transition and the distinction between 'policy convergence and policy interdependence' (see the chapter by Noble in this volume). In this respect, attention to process-level evidence is crucial. In relation to law, Teitel (2000: 6) notes that 'in dynamic periods of political flux, legal responses generate a *sui generis* paradigm of transformative law'.

In some of the examples provided in this book, criminalisation has resulted from requirements on the basis of international obligations and the need to harmonise laws as part of EU accession. Ben Noble discussed the lack of clarity concerning the Council of Europe in requiring legislative change in potential accession states prior to membership and the ambiguity surrounding the commitment of individual states to make changes as part of a 'democratising' process subsequent to membership. In relation to the decriminalisation of sex between men, it appears to have been afforded a low priority in discussion around accession, despite being an important issue for certain lobbying groups (i.e. LGBT rights). The influence of feminist and victims' rights movements has also resulted in different forms of security governance in other contexts.

Distinct groups of states, therefore, appear to have embraced reform in different ways (external and/or internal). There has been a shift to criminalise behaviour causing 'offence' rather than 'harm' (Peršak), but there has been less emphasis on sexuality or sexual identity as offensive (as Noble has highlighted). This is emblematic of the emphasis given to the protection of legal interest rather than legal moralism (see Nuotio's chapter; also Peter Solomon's mention of the growing influence of the Russian Orthodox Church and its increased reflection on 'moral values' in law). Yet, although there have been shifts in the law to accompany social and political liberalisation, new controls have emerged associated with the regulation of a capitalist or market economy.

In this respect, 'historicisation' is of importance (see the chapter by Noble in this volume; also Teitel 2000; Stan 2008), particularly as states attempt to break with the legislative past (through new Criminal Codes) and, at the same time, attempt to resemble other European Criminal Codes. Teitel (2000: 6) points out that:

> Law is caught between the past and the future, between backward-looking and forward-looking, between retrospective and prospective, between the individual and the collective. Accordingly, transitional justice is that justice associated with this context and political circumstances. Transitions imply paradigm shifts in the conception of justice; thus law's function is deeply and inherently paradoxical.

The often *ad hoc* amendments to legislation that can occur leave criminal justice open to political influence and direction. Politicians may come and go and often attract public support by responding to public views and concerns; the judiciary, as a rule, are more static. In Russia, as Solomon notes, increased criminalisation (between 1996 and 2010) did not appear to be part of a 'grand strategy', but rather the *ad hoc* work of, among others, the state Duma and criminal justice agencies, in an attempt to offset the perceived liberalisation of crime and justice policy. Underlying this were the attempts by Duma representatives to please the public and their constituencies. At the same time, however, the most contested aspect of post-Soviet Russian criminal law is that of regulating business. Short-term reforms are often presented by politicians wishing to retain favour with the general public: although, as Juska and Woolfson illustrate, the public as a group can also be on the receiving end of legislative reform that can offset protest against the state.

In terms of wider processes of criminalisation, as Juska and Woolfson show, the differential application of administrative law is experienced through the particular focus of policing and criminal justice practices, which result in the enforcement of the law at the level of society: relations between the entrepreneurial class and political elite are frequently ignored, if not unchallenged.

Fundamental to these developments is the conceptual representation of the law, and its impact, as largely 'symbolic', linked to the legal system as 'social concept'. Criminalisation has a role in maintaining an ideological 'grip' in societies undergoing transition and beyond, evident also in liberal democracies. In part, this can be noted in relation to the diverse impact of constitutional change (i.e. as experienced by different social groups). In this regard, particular groups may be presented as less worthy of certain rights; hence, the support for certain laws to be enforced more fully.

The relationship between criminal justice procedure and rights protection has been complex in the states discussed in this book, as elsewhere (Teitel 2000). There is evidence of some distrust in the court process and the application of the law, in terms of both formal and informal processes; for example, criminalisation through the 'back door' (i.e. the application of civil violations, breach of which can result in criminal charges) as outlined by Peršak. This is situated alongside an ever-growing expectation of what criminal law can be extended to and its expansion into spheres that have previously been unregulated (for instance, environmental crime).

Although there has been a shift to regulate and protect individual rights under the law and through the criminal justice process (illustrated in relation to policing practices by Chistyakova and Robertson), the upholding of these rights in policy is not always the same in practice. For example, although President Medvedev has called for the 'humanisation' of Russia's system of crime and punishment (extending alternatives to imprisonment, lowering the range of punishment for certain offences, decriminalisation of some petty offences), this has been watered down in the bureaucratic process of implementation, as is also evident in the case of Finland, outlined by Nuotio. The form of the state, therefore, can result in liberalising tendencies being overridden by extensive criminalisation (where state and its officials take centre stage). In this sense, criminalisation can be linked to deep-seated structural conflict.

This highlights the challenging impact of attempts to decriminalise in line with social and political liberalisation and the application of the law in attempts to regulate a capitalist or market economy (and the emerging new 'crimes' that result). As a number of chapters note, changes – in practice – often reflect political and special interests, including those of law enforcement agencies. Despite liberal democratic ideas as the basis for police reform, responses to transitions and the social disruption that has sometimes characterised it has, in places, presented a challenge for police reform. Chistyakova argues that effective political accountability is required to achieve change. She charts the instigation of change following Ukraine signing up to the European Convention for the Protection of Human Rights and Fundamental Freedoms – but also notes the role of human rights groups and academics working for the Ministry of Internal Affairs in taking forward reform through the exposition of police criminality and campaigns for greater transparency. Nonetheless, initiatives aimed at ensuring the enactment of reforms, for example the evaluation of police practice through clear-up rates, can themselves create the potential for corrupt practice.

The book has highlighted the developments taking place in legal systems and their impact on processes of criminalisation and, importantly, the wider social and economic transitions that have occurred and the impact that internal change has had on state legal systems, challenging the notion that change has resulted simply from legislative influence from Western 'democratic' states. The growing interdependence of criminal law may indicate a move beyond domestic law, but it is important to avoid confusing convergence with influence from above.

What has been gained and learned from East and Central European studies of democracy and the criminal law?

From the outset, this project endeavoured to seek out what could be gained from a cross-disciplinary approach. What can we learn about criminal justice and rights protection by contrasting the experiences of these societies in and after transition? The main achievement, we believe, has been in bringing together three key analyses. The first is the substantive study of the enactment of criminal law and its initiation. The second is the social and historical study of criminalisation. The third accompanies these with the precision lent by philosophical reflection.

Each is essential. It is has been made clear here, sometimes brutally clear, that lessons for criminal justice procedure and the protection of human rights are specific to each state. The 'failing' society of Lithuania cannot, at a time of crisis such as this, adopt the gentle and pragmatic approach that amended Finnish criminal justice. Russia's battle with endemic corruption in the police and criminal justice procedure has clear and well-documented political origins. Its experiments with criminalisation in other fields have, however, come from quite a different place: they are dogged by a war among special interests. Slovenia's relative success in moving beyond the harms of its past has much to do with the trust in black-letter criminal law that has come with a less awful history of oppression than that endured by some of its neighbours. And the role of the Council of Europe in bringing about a human rights culture in the post-Soviet states has sometimes been exaggerated by observers, to the detriment of an understanding of domestic history in states that had rights traditions of their own.

Some states' experiences resemble those of others, but the contributions to this volume show the inappropriateness of relying upon any ill-thought-out paradigm. Without the insights of criminal law scholars, social and political scientists and philosophers, it would be difficult to give fair recognition to these individual histories – and all the harder to find common directions for new research, instead of simply accepting this diversity and tearing the scholarly field into a wilderness of particulars. Our final section lays out where that research could go next.

New directions (some ideas for future research)

Where next for regional comparisons?

What we have learned about Russia's experience of criminalisation and decriminalisation might now be contrasted with the early entrants to the European Union – the Visegrád group and the Baltic States – says Solomon. It would be useful too, he thinks, to compare Russia's development with the states whose experiences have remained close: Ukraine, Belarus and Kazakhstan. In particular, the factors underlying the process of decriminalisation are worthy of examination.

The work of the Arts and Humanities Research Council (AHRC) Criminalisation project led by Antony Duff et al. has posed, and striven to answer, a normative question regarding the proper scope of criminal law. Peršak suggests that we should bring the insights of such work to the states emerging from transition.

The AHRC project has asked: just how much criminal law we want to have? Whose human rights should we protect, and what is the role of criminal law in declaring the value of each citizen's personhood by criminalising harms caused to them? The next step is to ask these questions as part of an analysis of social formations and as part of a critique of the presumption that those states were empty of traditions of principled justice, that they were simply waiting to be filled with the light of the Western human rights ideals.

Research should ask, too, when criminalisation might be the better way to engrain constitutional values when these have in fact been absent. There can be no *a priori* prescription for the legislator: criminalisation may legitimately take on a role that protects against the discretion exercised under authoritarian powers; yet equally, it may promote despotism by redirecting attention from the state and major actors engaged in oppression and corruption. Likewise, it may be exploited to repress the freedom of the person. Philosophy clarifies the questions; it is the task of social and political analysts to set the context for each state, the better to answer them.

Beyond that work, there must be a bridge to a substantive study of how to reform criminal justice procedure in each state – and an acceptance that, for now, the failure of the West and the implosion of some vulnerable states may mean that this reform may not be possible. However, an examination of the consequences of the strengthening of civil society (in particular through local communities and NGOs) and the influence of democratic institutions on lawmaking and enforcement is worthy of reflection. As outlined in earlier chapters, the impact of new requirements on law enforcers to ensure citizens' rights are protected, and the limitations placed on police powers, have yet to be measured.

Research is necessary to interrogate the claims made by entrenched interests. Critiques of zero tolerance policing and antisocial behaviour legislation are well established in US and European criminology. But it is easy for Western-trained scholars and policy-makers to be more impressionable when confronted with the symptoms of the problems of post-transition states, rather than the causes. It can be counter-intuitive to look beyond these (not least when we face, for instance, terrible human rights abuse by citizens themselves against vulnerable others, such as endemic and violent racism). But Juska and Woolfson remind us that we should be sceptical of purported crises of public order, and remain alert to identify the meta-narratives that define some forms of state and group criminality outwith the frame of what is, or should be, unlawful.

Thus, unquestioned distinctions between historically 'stable' states and post-transition states should be avoided. Greater Europeanisation and internationalisation of criminal law and criminal procedure, for instance, may be a practical answer to problems of stability (even now, in the heart of the European crisis). But research must first learn from the critical findings of Western criminological research, asking about the struggles over authoritarianism in the West.

The concept of transition is fluid, reflecting changes in form that are not static. Attempting to examine forms of 'justice' within this fluid framework is challenging: the ongoing dialectic process leaves the observer watching shifting sands. The notion of 'post-transition' states is a misnomer when the continuing challenges and developments outlined throughout this volume are taken into consideration. Transition is ongoing: current developments in Western liberal-democratic states and across the 'Arab' world powerfully illustrate the dynamic context of fragile economies and democracies. For the future, there is much to be done in making sense of fluctuating state control, throughout the world: yesterday, today and tomorrow.

References

Arato, A. (2000) *Civil Society, Constitution and Legitimacy*, Oxford: Rowman & Littlefield.

Held, D. (1993) 'Liberalism, Marxism and Democracy', *Theory and Society*, 22(2): 249–81.

Stan, L. (ed.) (2008) *Transitional Justice in Eastern Europe and the Former Soviet Union: Reckoning with the Communist Past*, London: Taylor and Francis.

Teitel, R. (2000) *Transitional Justice*, New York: Oxford University Press.

Weber, M. (1978) *Economy and Society: An Outline of Interpretive Sociology*, Vol. II, Los Angeles: University of California Press.

Index

Note: page numbers in bold type refer to tables; those followed by n and another number refer to the numbered note on that page.

For Product Safety Concerns and Information please contact our EU representative GPSR@taylorandfrancis.com
Taylor & Francis Verlag GmbH, Kaufingerstraße 24, 80331 München, Germany

www.ingramcontent.com/pod-product-compliance
Ingram Content Group UK Ltd.
Pitfield, Milton Keynes, MK11 3LW, UK
UKHW022127190926
475702UK00013B/1682
9780415622400